Interpreting Long-term Trends in the Transition to Farming

Reconsidering the Nodwell Site, Ontario, Canada

Lisa Rankin

BAR International Series 830
2000

Published in 2019 by
BAR Publishing, Oxford

BAR International Series 830

Interpreting Long-term Trends in the Transition to Farming

ISBN 9781841711249 paperback
ISBN 9781407351643 e-book

DOI https://doi.org/10.30861/9781841711249

A catalogue record for this book is available from the British Library

This book is available at www.barpublishing.com

BAR Publishing is the trading name of British Archaeological Reports (Oxford) Ltd.
British Archaeological Reports was first incorporated in 1974 to publish the BAR
Series, International and British. In 1992 Hadrian Books Ltd became part of the BAR
group. This volume was originally published by John and Erica Hedges in conjunction
with British Archaeological Reports (Oxford) Ltd / Hadrian Books Ltd, the Series
principal publisher, in 2000. This present volume is published by BAR Publishing,
2019.

BAR
PUBLISHING

BAR titles are available from:

BAR Publishing
122 Banbury Rd, Oxford, OX2 7BP, UK
EMAIL   info@barpublishing.com
PHONE   +44 (0)1865 310431
FAX   +44 (0)1865 316916
www.barpublishing.com

Abstract

This study examines the socio-economic transition from foraging to farming in Bruce County, Ontario which culminates with the appearance of the Nodwell village. The near complete excavation of this site determined that the Nodwell village had both the form (settlement pattern) and contents (material culture and subsistence remains) representative of a small-scale farming community, and was therefore distinct from the earlier forager habitations in the region. As recently as AD 1000 this region was occupied by mobile hunter-gatherers who followed an annual cycle, inhabiting numerous small sites, in nuclear family units. This strategy allowed the foragers of Bruce county to exploit various natural resources throughout the region during the course of the year. In contrast, the Nodwell village was occupied by a much more sedentary community of people, living in extended family groups, and producing domesticated crops. This transition occurred in a maximum of 350 years.

Until recently, this transition was explained using a migration model which suggested that an intact horticultural community had migrated into Bruce county in the mid-fourteenth century and replaced the indigenous foragers. However, this model has become increasingly controversial. Primarily, the migration model over-simplifies the process of culture change by suggesting that culture change is short-term process, initiated from the outside. As a result, this model fails to explore adequately the complex historical, cultural, regional and ecological context in which this event occurred. Furthermore, by failing to situate the appearance of the Nodwell village into historical context this model was unable to negate the possibility that the transition from foraging to farming was initiated locally.

In contrast, this study re-evaluates the transition within a much broader historical and regional framework and demonstrates that the socio-economic transition from foraging to farming in Bruce county was a long-term process influenced by events occurring internally, at the local level, and externally, through inter-cultural interaction.

The process of change from foraging to farming will no doubt vary in other regions, but the historical approach used here provides a valuable explanatory framework which can be applied in other regions and will help to highlight the diversity of cultural behaviour in prehistory.

Acknowledgements

Obviously, this publication began as a dissertation. And there are a variety of people who need to be thanked for their assistance, direction, and encouragement at that stage. First, I would like to thank my supervisor and friend Peter Ramsden. Without his guidance this would have been a far different project and one which I would not have enjoyed nearly as much. I would also like to thank the other members of my thesis committee: Dr. Aubrey Cannon and Dr. Trudy Nicks. Their patience, expertise and assistance was greatly appreciated.

The completion of this work benefited from the support of many other individuals. Dr. Richard Morlan and Rachael Perkins of the Archaeological Survey of Canada helped me locate and access numerous collections of material buried in the depths of storage facilities. Likewise, Benoit Theriault of the Canadian Museum of Civilization, provided access to the many documents I required. JV and Joyce Wright, also from the CMC, generously provided their own data to assist in my research. Other documents and data sources were provided by Barbara Ribey of the Bruce County Museum and Archives, Dr. Chris White and Linda Howie-Lang from the University of Western Ontario, Dr. Bob Pearce of the London Museum of Archaeology, William Fox of the Canadian Parks Service, Penny Young of the Ministry of Citizenship, Culture and Recreation, and the staff of the MacGregor Point Provincial Park.

Paul Prince, Heather Pratt and Jim C. McAlpine were commendable field assistants. Thanks also to the farmers of Bruce county who allowed us access to their property during the autumn of 1995. Since then, Rita Granda, Clare McVeigh, and Greig Parker have provided much needed technical support. Thanks for all your help Clare. Janis Weir, Isabelle Brymer and Rosita Jordan have also provided assistance.

I would also like to thank my family and friends who provided all form of unsolicited support and encouragement throughout this endeavour. Special thanks go to Laura Barnes, Shannon Coyston, Gordon Dibb, Helen Evans, Bruce Jamieson, Marion Maar, Maribeth Murray, Harry Nielsen, Heather Pratt, Jim Pendergast, Lois Prince, Peter Rankin, Phil Rankin and Shiela Whiteside.

Finally, as always, the last word goes to Paul.

L.R. November, 1999

Table of Contents

CHAPTER 3. MATERIAL CULTURE AND SUBSISTENCE

CHAPTER 4. CONCLUSIONS

List of Tables

List of Figures

Chapter 1
Introduction and Theoretical Context

Introduction

Understanding the expansion of farming and the process of regional culture change which occurs with the economic shift from food collection to food production has been a primary focus of archaeological inquiry for many years. This study investigates the process of socio-economic change from foraging to farming by focussing on a specific situation in Bruce county, Ontario, Canada. In this region, the transformation from foraging to farming culminated with the appearance of the Nodwell village site during the 14th century (Figure 1).

The Nodwell village is a Late Woodland village located on a strandline above Lake Huron in southern Bruce county. The near complete excavation and excellent preservation of this village revealed a settlement pattern distinct from that observed at any of Bruce county's earlier Middle Woodland period habitations. The most recent of the absolute dates taken from Middle Woodland sites in this region dates that occupation to the 10th century (Finlayson 1977:228). Relative dating of the Nodwell village places the occupation of this village in the mid 14th century (Wright 1974).

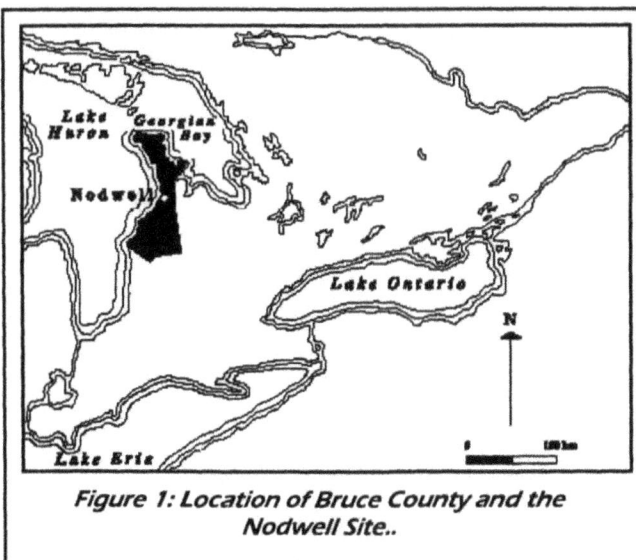

Figure 1: Location of Bruce County and the Nodwell Site..

Details of the internal settlement pattern from the Nodwell site suggest this village was occupied by a sedentary farming community and thus represents a dramatic shift in regional socio-economic organization away from the mobile foraging strategy practised by earlier populations. This dramatic change occurred over a maximum of 350 years.

The current explanation of how this transformation took place assumes that a horticultural population from the east migrated into Bruce county in the 14th century and settled at the Nodwell village site with an intact socio-economic system based on small-scale village farming which was distinctly different from that employed by the indigenous population (Wright 1974). While this model accounts for the obvious changes in settlement and subsistence behaviour reflected in the archaeological record, the migration theory on which this explanation is based over-simplifies the process of culture change. Primarily, this model intimates that culture change is a rapid, short-term process, initiated from the outside. As a result, the migration model does not adequately explore the complex historical, cultural, regional or ecological context in which this event occurred, nor does it address the role of the indigenous foraging population in structuring either the migration or the subsequent adaptation of these immigrants. Furthermore, by failing to situate the appearance of the Nodwell village into the local historical context, this model lacks the sophistication to negate the possibility that the socio-economic transition represented by the Nodwell village may have been initiated locally.

In contrast, the historical framework employed in this study situates the Nodwell village within a much broader historical and regional context and demonstrates how the process of socio-economic change developed diachronically.

1

By situating the transition from foraging to farming in Bruce county into a regional framework I demonstrate that the socio-economic transition in Bruce county represented by the Nodwell village was part of a long-term process influenced by events occurring both internally, within the local region, and externally, through inter-cultural interaction. Therefore, the historical approach utilized in this research allows for a comprehensive re-evaluation of the transition from foraging to farming in this region which incorporates an active role for the indigenous foraging population into the explanation. The introduction of a new socio-economic system in Bruce county is shown to be part of a larger system of social change and one which is structured by both external and local populations.

The Expansion of Food Production: Colonization Models

The simple model of 'neolithic' (small-scale horticulturalist) colonization of southern Bruce county offered by Wright (1974) is not unlike the colonization models which have dominated attempts to explain the transition to farming and the expansion of this socio-economic strategy in other parts of the world (Ammerman and Cavalli-Sforza 1971; Berry and Berry 1986). Colonization models give little credence to the in-situ transition from foraging to farming and instead attempt to link rapid changes in regional subsistence patterns, and the socio-cultural factors associated with food production, with regionally specific farming cultures which migrated out from their homelands to colonize new areas (Matson 1991).

The identification of farming settlements is central to any discussion of 'neolithic' colonization. These settlements are most often distinguished by a set of socio-cultural and economic traits which occur with cross-cultural regularity in simple, non-hierarchical farming communities (Fried 1968; Sahlins and Service 1960; Steward 1955; White 1959). Material correlates of these traits are then sought in the archaeological record.

Cross-cultural ethnographic research suggests that non-hierarchical food producers exhibit

particular socio-cultural behaviours which are strongly linked to decreased group mobility brought about by a need to care for and control predictable resources such as domestic crops and animals (Eder 1984; Gregg 1988:27; Kelly 1992). Associated with this process of sedentarization is a set of behavioural characteristics including the accumulation of property, the storage of surplus resources, greater face-to-face group contact, defined group boundaries and territories, unilineal kin reckoning, and greater internal organizational mechanisms to resolve conflict without group fissioning (Bender 1978; Gregg 1988; Sahlins 1972; Spielmann 1991a).

Archaeologically, it is difficult to correlate these aspects of socio-cultural behaviour with sparse material remains. However, Rafferty (1985:128-136) argues that settlement pattern is the most important and decisive indicator of sedentism, usually associated with resource domestication, that is visible to archaeologists. Archaeological evidence for sedentism includes site aggregation, durable dwelling structures capable of providing housing and private space to several families, the non-random placement of structures, storage features, middens, as well as consumer durables and personal items inside houses (Chapdelaine 1993:184-187; Cribb 1991; Gilman 1987; Hitchcock 1987; Kelly 1992; Kent 1989a:134; Rafferty 1985:128-132). Occasionally, these items may be associated with sedentary hunter-gatherer societies. Therefore, archaeological indicators of small-scale village farming also include access to appropriate soils, tool technology necessary for the production and processing of domesticates, and botanical or faunal evidence of domestic crops and animals (Chapdelaine 1993; Vencl 1986:48).

Colonization models must be able to demonstrate not only that farming settlements existed but also determine why and how 'neolithic' populations expand into new territories. It is believed that simple 'neolithic' societies were forced into a pattern of continuous expansion because early farming technology rapidly depleted soil fertility. Furthermore, population growth in both new and old communities exhausted locally occurring natural resources (Ammerman and Cavalli-Sforza 1971; Clark 1980; Gregg 1991:205; Heidenreich 1971; Sutton

1996; Vencl 1986:46-47). The homogeneity of material culture, architectural style and village organization throughout huge regions, combined with absolute dates from individual sites demonstrates the colonization of new territory by a basal population or culture, in what is referred to as a wave of expansion (Ammerman and Cavalli-Sforza 1971; Clark 1980; Dennell 1983; Gregg 1988; Vencl 1986).

Colonization Models and Interaction

Waves of expansion are thought to occur in small, regular movements which, examined cumulatively, demonstrate large scale colonizations (Ammerman and Cavalli-Sforza 1971; Ammerman and Cavalli-Sforza 1979). Few colonization models attempt to factor in the social, economic or ecological effects of contact between expanding food producers and indigenous foraging societies. Instead, colonization is envisioned as occurring on an open, empty landscape (Ammerman and Cavalli-Sforza 1979:276; Tringham 1971). However, archaeological evidence suggests that many regions colonized by farmers were previously occupied by hunter-gatherers. Thus, the wave model of 'neolithic' expansion implies that there was a constantly shifting frontier between intrusive village farmers and indigenous foragers already utilizing naturally occurring resources in pre-'neolithic' territory (Ammerman and Cavalli-Sforza 1971; Gregg 1988:3).

Cross-cultural ethnographic research suggests that small-scale, non-hierarchical groups of foragers have socio-cultural and economic traits which vary considerably from food producers. Non-hierarchical foragers are generally defined in terms of the degree of group mobility which may range from moderate to highly mobile (Kelly 1992). Patterns of mobility are thought to be dictated by group subsistence strategy, which varies according to the relative abundance of natural resources available in the landscape (Foley 1981a; 1981b; Rossignol 1992). Mobility, in turn, affects other socio-cultural phenomena and is strongly correlated with low forager population density over large territories, lack of attachment to one particular territory, lack of group ownership of naturally occurring resources and fluid membership with groups coming

together and dispersing annually or in times of resource depletion or abundance (Lee and Devore 1968:11-12; Smiley 1980:164). Further, mobile foraging societies tend to lack accumulated property and storage technology (Kelly 1992).

Traditionally, the colonization of new regions by 'neolithic' societies is thought to have exposed foraging societies to the following direct and indirect negative stresses: 1) the sedentary settlement pattern of farming communities places new territorial constraints on small, mobile foraging populations; 2) the migration of farmers and the subsequent growth of these communities increases regional populations and may rapidly exhaust natural resources, making the territory less attractive to hunter-gatherers; 3) food production, which buffers the negative effects of natural resource depletion within farming communities, radically alters the natural ecosystem utilized by foragers; and 4) differences in cultural systems make it difficult for indigenous foraging communities to share or depend on farming communities for assistance in times of resource stress (Clark 1980; Gregg 1988:4; Vencl 1986:46).

Thus, colonization models consider the cultural and economic differences between foragers and farmers to be inherently incompatible and suggest contact between the two communities was either sporadic or short term, occurring only during the initial stages of colonization (Dennell 1985:117; Gregg 1988:3; Vencl 1986:47). When attempting to account for the social and economic ramifications of interaction between societies, proponents of colonization models have suggested three possible outcomes of contact between indigenous foragers and migrant farmers: expulsion and avoidance, elimination, and acculturation.

Expulsion of foragers from newly colonized territories is seen as the simplest and most immediate reaction by colonizers to initial contact with foraging populations. The forager expulsion theory suggests that population growth, resource depletion and alteration of the environment by farmers drove foraging populations out of the colonized region to marginal environments where soils and climatic conditions were not suitable for food production. Once settled in these circumscribed territories, foragers simply avoided further contact with the colonizers (Ammerman and Cavalli-Sforza 1973; Gregg 1991:204; Green 1991:222; Vencl 1986:47).

Forager elimination is suggested as another potential result of contact between the two groups. This theory assumes that foragers desired to maintain access to resources in newly-founded farming territories. Competition for natural resources between the two groups then led to violence and warfare. Farmers, with their larger populations and complex technologies were then able to eradicate their foraging neighbours within a generation (Gregg 1991:205; Vencl 1986:49).

Acculturation or assimilation arguments assume that foragers "adopt the technology, lifestyle and social patterns of their farming neighbours" (Gregg 1988:4). This argument proposes that both foragers and farmers were eager to maintain amicable relationships, and more importantly, that hunter-gatherers were attracted to the new forms of technology brought by the farmers and to the reliability of food production (Dennell 1985:124-125; Gregg 1988 4-5; 1991:204; Vencl 1986:48). Through intermarriage and fictive kin ties, foragers would be rapidly assimilated into farming communities within two or three generations (Dennell 1985:124-125).

Criticisms of the Colonization Models

Recently, colonization models have been criticized for over-simplifying the social and economic processes involved in the transformation of regional culture and economy from foraging to farming (Green 1991; Gregg 1988). Opponents of "wave of advance" models object to the emphasis placed on 'neolithic' societies as the sole agents of change and suggest it is unrealistic to assume hunter-gatherer societies were merely passive participants or victims (Dennell 1985; Gregg 1988; Green 1991). Criticisms frequently address three interrelated themes: 1) that the normative and somewhat evolutionary approach of these models towards socio-economic change and forager/farmer interaction is inherently anti-historical and

therefore, unable to address the complexities of individual situations, 2) that the structure of the colonization models inherently segments the study of prehistoric societies along economic lines, and 3) that the models ignore or misinterpret both ethnographic and archaeological data.

The use of cross-cultural regularities are at the core of most colonization models. Uncritical use of normative concepts such as foraging, farming, sedentism and mobility are detrimental to comprehending the processes these models seek to explain. Recent studies by Kent (1989b), Kelly (1992), Eder (1984), Gregg (1988) and others have demonstrated that there is a far greater diversity and sophistication in the way behavioural categories are expressed than once believed. For example, foraging and farming may not be two ends of a single continuum but rather act as independent variables where one strategy does not preclude the existence of another (Kent 1989b). Further, patterns of residential mobility and sedentism may co-exist within a single society and may not be key criteria for identifying different societies (Stark 1981:352; Kelly 1992).

The sophisticated patterns of socio-economic behaviour suggested reflect the long-term developmental histories and adaptations by societies. Generalizations, like those utilized in colonization models, are anti-historical and over-simplify the processes of socio-economic change by minimizing the significance of unique cultural adaptations and the contingent structure of change (Dennell 1983; 1985; Green 1991). Critical consideration of behavioural categories requires archaeological analysis of regional networks as well as site-specific studies (Clarke 1977). It also requires that socio-economic changes be examined as part of a process of change which may take place in stages over long temporal periods. Studies which focus on the long-term histories of regional and site-specific social and subsistence behaviour are better equipped to identify both rapid and gradual behavioural changes, to identify the types of internal and external forces governing change, and to give both foragers and farmers an active role in contributing to or preventing change.

A second criticism of colonization points out that these models inherently separate the study of farming from the study of foraging along social and economic lines (Dennell 1985:114; Gregg 1988:1; Green 1991:218; Thomas 1988:59). Again, the use of normative concepts distinguishing foraging and farming as discrete, mutually exclusive, socio-economic behaviours has led to this unnecessary segmentation (Green 1991:218). It has resulted in archaeological specialization in the studies of one group or the other and generated models of socio-economic change which are vastly different for each type of society. Changing socio-economic behaviour among forager societies is generally limited to environmental stresses while change in food producing society is interpreted via socio-political models. This segmentation has prevented even the most insightful colonization models from examining the active role which foragers played in preventing, assisting or encouraging the spread of farming into their territories (Dennell 1983).

Realistically, if archaeologists are to explain how foragers can become farmers, or how foragers both participate in and structure interactive relationships with farming communities, then both types of societies must be studied within a single framework. This requires archaeologists to forego the concept of the pristine, autonomous culture group and develop models which are cognizant of the influence and interaction between groups (Kent 1989a:133).

The third criticism directed at colonization models concerns the selective use of extant ethnographic and archaeological data. An abundant literature, produced over the past twenty-five years, demonstrates that foraging and farming communities, both contemporary and prehistoric, may directly or indirectly influence one another's cultural behaviour in a number of ways (Denbow 1980; Gregg 1988; Lintz 1991; Peterson 1978; Spielmann 1991a; Smiley 1980). This literature, largely overlooked in colonization models, suggests that foragers and farmers are capable of sharing information, products and overlapping territories with results other than expulsion, elimination and direct assimilation of foraging societies.

The integration of an historical framework with ethnographic analyses since the 1980's has necessitated that anthropologists evaluate contemporary situations as products of their historical development (Roseberry 1989:14; Wolf:1982). As a consequence, the role of intersocietal interaction and influence has assumed an elevated position in current ethnographic studies. This research suggests that many hunter-gatherer societies exist today largely because of their ongoing relationships with neighbouring farming communities (Peterson 1978; Smiley 1980; Gregg 1980; 1988; Speth 1991). Spielmann (1986) demonstrates that foragers in Africa, India, South America and Southeast Asia have entered into co-operative relationships with farmers which are mutually beneficial for the survival of both groups and help to maintain distinct group identities. The operation of these interactive systems is largely dependent upon the acquisition and trade of specialty resources and foodstuffs between groups with differing economies (Spielmann 1986; Gregg 1988). Generally, natural resources collected by foragers are exchanged with farmers for produce. The benefit of this exchange network not only increases the variety of food and specialty items available to each group, but helps to maintain amicable relationships between groups (Spielmann 1986).

The maintenance of this "mutualistic" economy, thought to benefit both groups, perpetuates the existence of two distinct socio-economic traditions within a given territory (Gregg 1988; Speth 1991; Spielmann 1986:286). Recently, Spielmann (1991b), Lintz (1991) and others have used ethnohistoric evidence to demonstrate that a similar system of interaction existed during the protohistoric and early contact era between Plains hunters and Puebloan farmers in the southwestern United States and that this relationship was essential to the survival of both cultures. Therefore, it is unlikely that mutualistic interaction between foragers and farmers is a product of post-contact circumstances and there is no reason to assume that similar types of interactive relationships did not exist in the prehistoric period.

Ethnographic research has also demonstrated that people frequently mix economic strategies acting as both foragers and farmers. Examples from Kent's (1989c) volume studying farmers who hunt demonstrate that communities have found a number of ways to combine the two economic strategies. In some communities a particular segment is responsible for providing natural resources while another segment remains sedentary to tend domestic produce (Kensinger 1989). A differing situation would have a single community engaged in food production for a given length of time and foraging and hunting during alternate periods (Sponsel 1989; Vickers 1989). That foraging and farming need not be mutually exclusive endeavours in contemporary situations should suggest to archaeologists that models of prehistoric colonization and the subsequent assimilation, elimination or expulsion of foragers from these territories may be oversimplified. Mutual relationships between or even within newly founded communities, as well as the direct and indirect flow of information and commodities between communities may also account for socio-economic transitions.

Recent archaeological research has also challenged the position of colonization as the principal explanation of the transition from foraging to farming. In particular, critical analyses of archaeological data from central and northern Europe suggest that the transition to 'neolithic' farming was strongly influenced by indigenous populations (Ashbee 1982; Clark 1980; Clarke 1976; Dennell 1983; Gregg 1988; Price 1983:771; 1987:283). Demographic studies now suggest that the rate of 'neolithic' population growth was low for at least the millennium following the initial appearance of these settlements (Gregg 1988:4; Hammond 1981). Palaeo-anthropological evidence obtained from skeletal populations in northern Europe shows no distinct changes in palaeo-Europoid traits following the introduction of farming to this region (Vencl 1986:45). Changes in regional settlement pattern and in lithic industries exhibit as many continuities as changes with the introduction of domesticates (Clarke 1976). As well, palynological data have been used to demonstrate intensified resource utilization and changing environmental circumstances during

the Late Mesolithic (Clarke 1976:460; Gregg 1988:8-9; Price 1983:771). It has therefore been suggested that central and northern European foragers were already adapting their cultural behaviour to counter environmental fluctuations and that the transition to a 'neolithic' system may have been a natural outgrowth of this change (Clarke 1976; Dennell 1983:186-187). An awareness of the farming practices employed by neighbours to the south may have made the addition of farming to the adaptive strategy of northern European foragers possible during this unstable period (Dennell 1985).

Other archaeological investigations in regions as diverse as Scandinavia and South America indicate that foragers and farmers can live in proximity for centuries without adopting one another's socio-economic systems (Zvelebil and Rowley-Conwy 1986; Anders 1990). The maintenance of separate traditions in prehistory has been explained in two ways: 1) that foragers with access to a stable and abundant aquatic resource base were able to maintain a viable economy unaffected by landscape changes precipitated by food producers (Vencl 1986), and 2) that foragers who inhabited marginal environments with limited potential for the development of farming were neither affected by farmers nor able to incorporate this strategy into their own socio-economic pattern (Vencl 1986).

A consideration of the above archaeological situations indicates, on one hand, that 'neolithic' expansions may occur without colonizing populations, and on the other, that foraging groups may be able to delay or prevent 'neolithic' expansion into their territory. These examples challenge the underlying assumptions of colonization models which suggest that rapid population growth, and soil and resource depletion make it essential for incipient farmers to colonize all available spaces even at the expense of local foraging societies.

Both ethnographic and archaeological evidence suggest that displacement, elimination and assimilation are not the only possible outcomes of interaction between foragers and farmers. Other circumstances such as mutual economies, the in situ adoption of farming (which can be incorporated in any number of creative ways), and the prevention of 'neolithic' expansion are equally viable outcomes. Each of these scenarios represents the culmination of contact, either direct or indirect, between groups with different socio-economic systems. To explain regional transitions in cultural systems it is essential to go beyond simple colonization models and grant equal consideration and agency to both the 'mesolithic' and 'neolithic' elements in directing the process of change. The uniqueness and complexity of regional transitions can only be understood by introducing an historical perspective to the critical examination of archaeological data. Research which focuses on long-term regional adaptations should have the ability to demonstrate how change is incorporated within the cultural context of the groups involved.

The Alternative: Regional Archaeology and the Dynamics of Change

Having reviewed theoretical models of colonization and the limits of these models in explaining socio-economic change, it must be pointed out that the challenge is not to the fact of colonization itself. Migratory events are definitely recognizable prehistorically and examples of colonization are abundant. For example, both short and long distance migration resulting in the colonization of new territories by farmers are recognizable in Europe where Bandkeramik populations gradually colonized corridors of arable loess country (Thomas 1988:62), and certainly in southern Ontario where groups of Iroquoian farmers expanded to populate new territories in both short, cumulative waves (Warrick 1990:360) and rapid, long-distance migrations into new regions (Sutton 1995:231).

However, the manner in which colonization occurred and the effects of colonization on regional socio-economic organization appear much more sophisticated than these models allow. Critics of these models are therefore not suggesting a revisionist history whereby colonizations are not possible, nor do they anticipate a partisan approach which presents colonization solely from the indigenous foragers' perspective, but instead argue for a more complex, sophisticated analysis of socio-economic change that demonstrates how this structural change is initiated and incorporated by both groups when migrating food producers approach or enter the territories of indigenous foragers.

A more productive approach to comprehending the dynamics of change precipitated by interaction would utilize a broader spatial, temporal and ecological framework than the site-based focus common to colonization models. Only by utilizing a broader analytical framework can archaeologists hope to observe how change is internally structured and incorporated by indigenous populations. The traditional unit of archaeological analysis in colonization models appears to be the archaeological site. From individual sites, artifacts, ecofacts and features are utilized to make inferences about socio-cultural and economic behaviour during a defined period of time. In contrast, regional approaches advocate the use of multiple units of analysis in order to elucidate both synchronically and diachronically the social and economic structures of a society (Clarke 1977; Flannery 1976; Kowalewski 1989; 1990; Trigger 1967; 1968).

By using scaled units of analysis the archaeologist can view the organizational structures of a population as an integrated system and examine the roles played by individuals, communities and the environment in initiating, changing, and/or maintaining the system. Within this framework it has been suggested that the role of the individual is best observed at the household level; the cultural, political and economic activities of a community are localized to the site or settlement system; and the social and economic relationships between communities, or links between communities and environment are expressed within the region (Clarke 1977; Trigger 1967; 1968). However, an understanding of the complexity of the regional system requires that all levels of analysis be interwoven (Crumley and Marquardt 1990).

Regional boundaries are always somewhat arbitrary but the region is generally considered a spatial unit with a high degree of internal integrity which reflects all aspects of human life; ecological, economic, social and historical (Crumley and Marquardt 1990:78; Zvelebil, Green and Macklin 1992:197). Furthermore, the multi-scalar approach allows the archaeologist to discuss and explain the dynamic flow of people, resources, commodities, information and energy within a defined territory, a dynamic rarely accessible from single site analysis (Blanton et al. 1981:20; Clarke 1977:8; Rossignol 1992:8).

Regional approaches also examine cultural processes diachronically, relating changes and continuities within cultural structures to the process of regional development over time (Hammond 1981:211; Hodges 1987:132). In this manner, the social, economic and ecological structures which have developed within a given region mediate the ways in which a population is capable of responding to the stimulus of change and demonstrate that new elements can only be incorporated into the system in a manner which is contingent upon the pre-existing social order (Hodder 1990). In this way, regional archaeology is able to transcend the use of normative cultural concepts and offer instead a more sophisticated picture of human behaviour.

Foraging, Farming and the Regional Perspective

The transition from foraging to farming can occur in three basic ways: 1) through independent invention foragers can initiate the transition in isolation; 2) foragers can initiate the transition in response to external stimuli provided by neighbouring farmers; and 3) farmers may colonize the traditional territories of foragers and directly initiate changes (Green 1991). When foragers and farmers live in proximity to one another, change generally results from direct demographic migrations or external stimuli. In order to explain the process of socio-economic change resulting from either direct or indirect influences, archaeologists must integrate the study of two divergent cultural patterns into a single explanatory framework and thereby shift the emphasis from describing synchronic patterns to explaining the social process of change (Green 1991:218).

When expanding food producers settle near or within a territory with a long-term history of forager occupation, an inter-cultural frontier is formed. The frontier acts as a unifying concept, linking the two groups in an interactive framework across a new socio-economic border (Dennell 1985). The structure of this forager/farmer frontier must be negotiated by both groups in keeping with their traditional organizational systems. However, the direct and indirect interactions which occur across this frontier result in modifications to the cultural behaviour of both groups and in turn alters the structure of the frontier itself.

Direct and indirect interactions along this frontier place new social and ecological constraints on the systems of both culture groups, and therefore have the ability to influence change (Dennell 1985; Green 1991:223; Moore 1985). Indirect interaction resulting from the establishment of a frontier may alter the culture pattern of both societies by changing "the cultural rules for exploiting the landscape" (Green 1991:223). For example, each group must face territorial constraints that restrict their movement and their utilization of naturally occurring resources. Furthermore, newly established farming settlements alter the natural landscape, changing both animal and plant ecology, which may affect indigenous resource procurement strategies (Dennell 1985; Green 1991:223; Gregg 1988). As well, the increased sedentism related to food production reduces the mobility of a farming population and thereby limits its access to resources and information located outside its constrained territory (Dennell 1985). Direct interactions may also influence behavioural change. When two groups live in proximity it can be expected that people, information and commodities will cross the frontier in both directions and initiate new cultural behaviours (Dennell 1985; Gregg 1988; Spielmann 1986).

The complexity of the newly-founded system suggests that a variety of dynamic responses are possible on the part of both foragers and farmers to the new social and economic influences operating on the frontier. At times interaction might encourage the spread of farming. While this may proceed through forager elimination or expulsion, other patterns such as acculturation, and mutual or mixed economies that are structured by both foragers and farmers, may result. Interaction may also discourage the spread of farmers, resulting in their expulsion or acculturation. Further, a complex relationship based on mutual economies, where commodities and information are regularly exchanged may promote the co-existence of both groups (Gregg 1988).

Within an interactive system, migrations of small or large populations of foragers or farmers may occur in either direction across the frontier for purposes other than colonization (Dennell 1985; Gregg 1988; Spielmann 1986). These migrations would bring the two societies together for either short or lengthy periods of time to exchange information, commodities or even labour, and to strengthen the relationship between the two societies (Gregg 1988; Spielmann 1988). Gregg (1988:235-236) draws on the ethnographic record to suggest that marriage and kin relationships are likely to develop between interacting groups of foragers and farmers. Such a situation would result in the permanent migration of a portion of one or both societies across the frontier to the other group's territory.

But interactive relationships develop gradually and involve a sequence of both events and responses so it is unlikely that such migrations would result during the initial contact period (Dennell 1985). Dennell (1985) suggests a period of "curiosity" would preclude the intensive interactions brought about through population migrations. In this initial stage commodities and information are more likely to be exchanged across the frontier than populations. Such interaction is likely to alter the internal dynamics of both groups and should be reflected archaeologically in various classes of data including settlement patterns, subsistence remains, and material culture (Gregg 1988). By using longer temporal periods to examine the ongoing development of the forager/farmer frontier archaeologists should be able to trace the process of socio-economic change brought about through interactive relations from its initial stages toward an increasingly complex system.

Furthermore, in interactive systems both societies are able to structure the interactive process and create the cultural rules for negotiating the frontier in a manner that is contextualized by, and contingent upon, the pre-existing structure of both communities. Therefore, the application of a broad spatial, temporal and ecological framework is necessary in order to decipher the complex process of culture change in an historical context. By utilizing a regional approach, cultural re-organization precipitated by the development of an interactive frontier, can be viewed as a gradual process which is strongly influenced by the indigenous population.

The initial stage of a regional investigation should define the largest unit of analysis as the territory of the indigenous foraging population, in order to identify the primary social and economic structures that define that foraging society prior to the development of an interactive frontier. Within this framework, the territory of the indigenous population becomes a cultural frontier only when food producers settle nearby or inside this region. Depending on the type of frontier formed, it should be possible to identify the types of social and ecological constraints placed on the indigenous society and to trace the sequence of responses to these constraints. By proceeding historically from the pre-contact stage through the foundation of an interactive frontier, the dynamic role of the foragers in structuring the frontier is not only illuminated, but the responses of foragers to interaction are contextualized by their preceding pattern of organization.

Thus, regional approaches to culture change explain rather than describe the socio-economic transitions, and elucidate the responses from stable foraging systems to new stimuli. Interactive models allow for the possibility that foragers encouraged or discouraged farming within their territory and define the ways that foragers may have influenced the organizational systems of both the farming culture and the new frontier. Whether the expansion of food production involved population migration into forager territory or indirect stimulus from outside the territory, regional approaches are able to account for changes to ecological, economic, and social structures in an historical manner (Green 1991).

The Bruce County Example: A New Approach to an Old Problem

The archaeological record indicates that southern Bruce county, located along the eastern shores of Lake Huron in Ontario, has had a lengthy history of human occupation. For millennia this region had been inhabited by mobile populations which occupied seasonal campsites and employed an economic strategy based on hunting, fishing and foraging. During the 14th century an abrupt change to this settlement pattern occurred which is marked by the appearance of a single, large palisaded village known today as the Nodwell village (Figure 2).

This type of community settlement pattern is not common among mobile foragers. The social organization represented by the Nodwell village is generally indicative of a sedentary community pursuing a horticultural economy, and marks a significant deviation from the previous cultural system in this region. Furthermore, the duration of the Nodwell occupation appears to be brief, with abandonment within a century. Then the original foragers return (Wright 1974). In order to interpret the process of socio-economic change within Bruce county, this study employs a broad temporal spatial and ecological context.

Temporal Context

The research undertaken in this study has a great temporal depth, focusing on the period between 200 BC and AD 1400. Earlier research into the culture-history of prehistoric southern Ontario has resulted in a detailed chronology, outlining a variety of periods, traditions and horizons (Figure 3).

The culture-historic sequence is defined by changes in material culture, subsistence strategy and settlement patterns (Wright 1966). Within this established framework, the periods relevant to this research include the Middle and Late Woodland (see Figure 3).

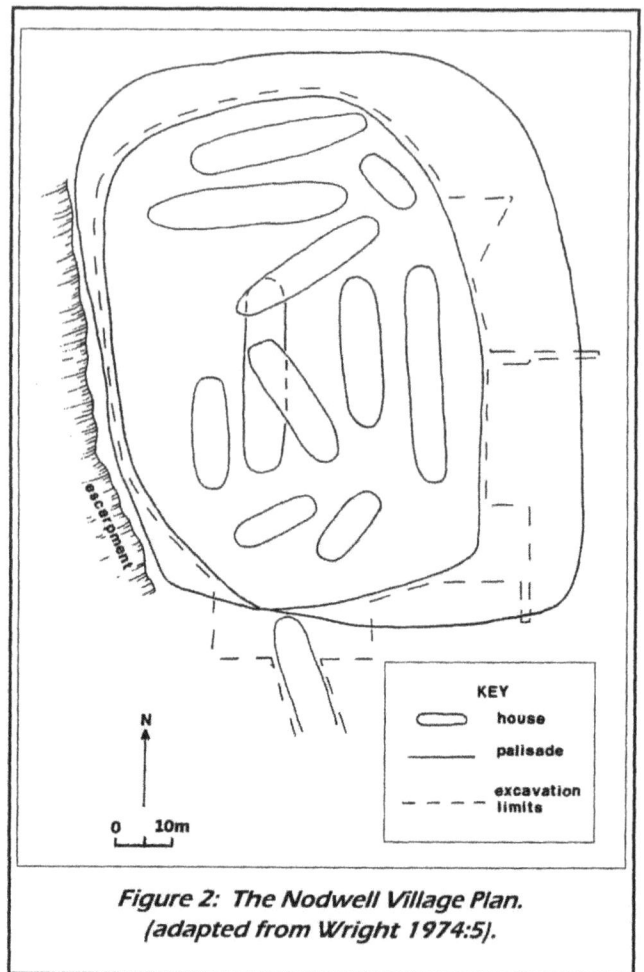

Figure 2: The Nodwell Village Plan.
(adapted from Wright 1974:5).

The Middle Woodland populations of southern Ontario employed an economic strategy based on hunting, fishing and foraging. The settlement data from this period suggest that mobile populations pursued an annual round, exploiting riverine fish resources from multi-family campsites in the spring and dispersing to smaller, nuclear family based special purpose sites during the rest of the year (Spence et al. 1990). Towards the later stages of this period there is evidence for increasing population density, resulting in territorial constraints, increasingly stabilized settlement cycles and greater sedentism (Spence et al. 1990). At this time, populations were likely to return to the same sites annually and occupy these sites for greater periods of time (Cleland 1982; Finlayson 1977; Spence et al. 1990:167-168).

Material culture, including the emergence of a ceramic tradition with a pseudo-scallop-shell impression, is most often used to identify Middle Woodland sites. This ceramic tradition begins to appear at approximately 200 B.C. (Spence et al. 1990:142). However, this period exhibits strong regional diversity which is assumed to be representative of differential access to resources by the inhabitants of Ontario at this time. This diversity, identified by an array of regionally-focused archaeological complexes, is manifest primarily in the lithic and bone tool assemblages, but is also associated with regional variations in the technical production of ceramics (Spence et al. 1990:143).

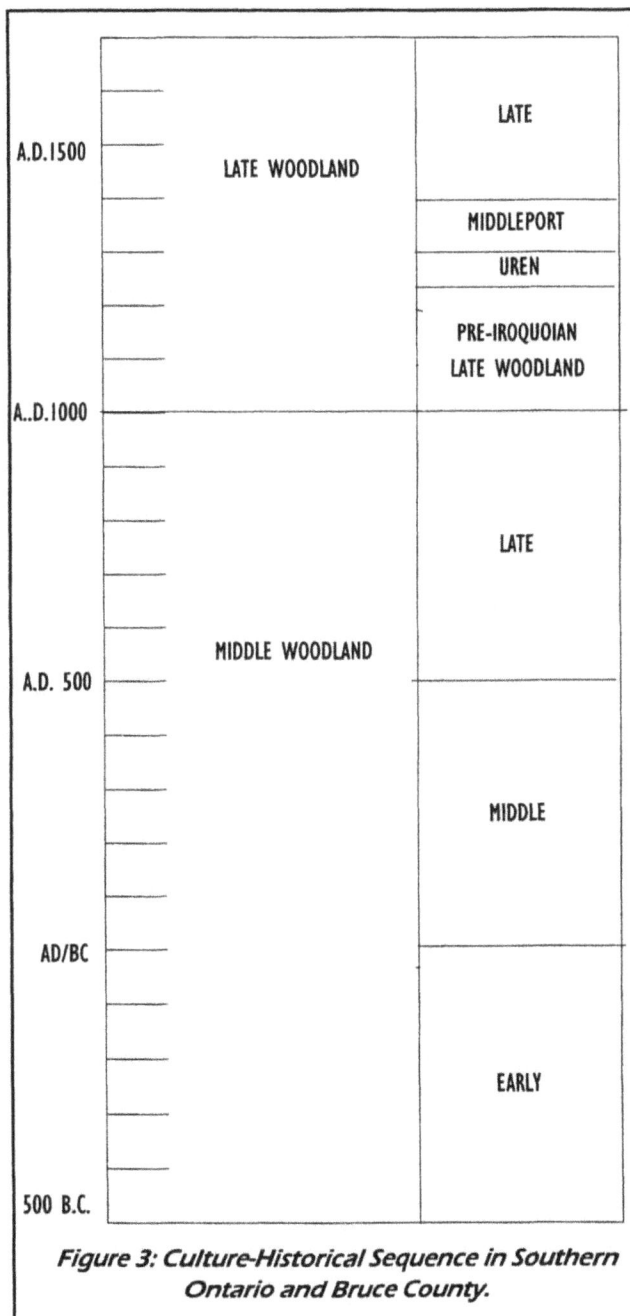

Figure 3: Culture-Historical Sequence in Southern Ontario and Bruce County.

The transition from the Middle to Late Woodland period occurred by approximately AD 1000 in much of southern Ontario, although it is not uncommon for sites associated with this period to have earlier dates (see Crawford et al. 1998;Fox 1990a; Smith 1990; Smith and Crawford 1997). In general, the Late Woodland period was a time of socio-economic change throughout the Great Lakes and is closely associated with the introduction of maize horticulture and the appearance of large relatively sedentary settlements. In much of southern Ontario the Late Woodland period is associated with the stages of Iroquoian development, ultimately culminating with the appearance of historically identifiable ethnic groups. However, foraging populations continued to occupy territories in the western and northern peripheries of the region (Murphy and Ferris 1990).

The Late Woodland period is commonly divided into three temporal stages each associated with increasing experimentation and utilization of maize horticulture and the appearance of larger, more permanent settlements (Dodd et al. 1990:358). The early and middle stages of the Late Woodland period are most significant to this research. The early Late Woodland is a regionally distinct tradition which has a duration of approximately 300 years (AD 1000 - AD 1300). This stage is identified by the appearance of village settlements and changes in mortuary traditions, as well as changes in the manufacturing techniques of ceramics and other types of material culture (Williamson 1990). While there is evidence to suggest that experimentation with maize horticulture may have begun at this time, it is believed that early Late Woodland populations were still largely dependant on naturally-occurring resources (Williamson 1990:306). The primary significance of this stage may lie in the fundamental changes to group social organization which are suggested by the appearance of village settlements (Chapdelaine 1993).

The Middleport horizon is a 100 year substage of the middle Late Woodland period lasting from AD 1300 to AD 1400. It is believed to have been brought about by the fusion of two regionally distinct branches of the earlier Late Woodland populations that inhabited southcentral and southwestern Ontario (Wright 1966:54). Traditionally, the Middleport horizon is defined by the proliferation of a new settlement strategy in southern Ontario which has been characterized by the foundation of large villages, often located in defensible positions, the increasing integration of corn and bean horticulture into the subsistence strategy, and the use of a new ossuary style of burial (Dodd et al. 1990). Material culture, including a distinct ceramic style and an elaborate smoking pipe complex are frequently used to assign sites to the Middleport horizon (Kapches 1981:6).

Evidence from a number of Middleport sites suggests that groups who had previously experimented with cultigens as one of a variety of economic pursuits became far more dependent on food production during this stage (Dodd et al. 1990). Furthermore, the structure of village communities, and the types and distributions of material culture recovered from Middleport villages, closely resembled those associated with the historic period Iroquoian tribes of southern Ontario (MacNeish 1954; Emerson 1954; Wright 1960). By the Middleport sub-stage, the culture-historic sequence developed for southern Ontario strongly distinguishes between Iroquoian farming societies and Algonkian hunter-gatherers, a division which is not fully supported during earlier periods. Finally, the abrupt appearance of a large number of Middleport period sites throughout southern Ontario suggests that this culture region was, by the Middleport substage, largely inhabited by farming populations which underwent rapid population growth and expansion (Wright 1972a:78; Noble 1975:40).

Unfortunately, this culture-historic scheme does not account for the fate of the hunter-gatherers that had been occupying southern Ontario for previous millennia. By the historic era, these foraging societies inhabited the margins of Iroquoian territories beyond the northern limits of food production. What is suggested through omission is that the traditional hunter-gatherer societies of southern Ontario either evolved or assimilated into horticulturalist communities or were pushed out to the marginal lands bordering Iroquoian territory. The descriptive nature of the culture-historic sequence is unable to explain this process.

Regional Context

Southern Bruce county may be considered a distinct region in terms of geography and culture. It is bound to the west by Lake Huron, to the north by the Bruce peninsula, to the east by a series of drumlin fields which slope east into a distinctly different ecological zone and to the south by a several-kilometre-wide zone of wetland which gives way to sandy dune formations along the coast line and arable sandy soils inland. Culturally, southern Bruce county appears to have been settled by a stable foraging population for at least 1000 years prior to the Nodwell intrusion (Finlayson 1977).

During the Middle Woodland period, southern Bruce county was occupied by a Saugeen complex population, a regionally specific Middle Woodland population with a distinct ceramic and lithic tradition. The organization of this population is best known from the Donaldson, Thede and Inverhuron sites, excavated in the early 1970s by Finlayson (1977) (Figure 4). A reconstruction of the seasonal round followed by the inhabitants of these sites suggests that several families gathered to exploit riverine fish

During the late Middle Woodland there is evidence in this region for increasing population in the form of a predominance of macroband occupation sites. It is believed that the exploitation of abundant fish resources, predominantly of riverine origin, allowed more people to reside together for longer periods of time (Cleland 1982; Finlayson 1977).

While no early Iroquoian sites have been located in this region, dates and material culture from several sites in the territory suggest that foragers continued to occupy southern Bruce county in much the same way as before (Finlayson 1977; Fox 1977; Knechtel 1955; Lee 1951; Wright and Anderson 1963:30). Hunting, gathering and fishing remained the dominant economic pursuits even though ceramics stylistically linked to the transitional Late Woodland have been recovered from a minimum of five sites in this region (Finlayson 1977; Fox

resources in the spring, and then dispersed during the late-summer or fall to exploit other resources, moving inland to nuclear family campsites by winter (Finlayson 1977).

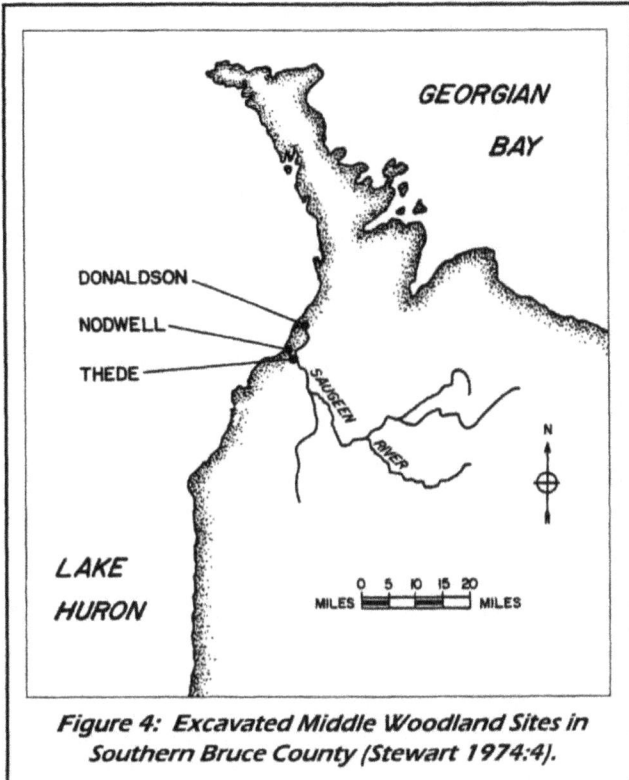

Figure 4: Excavated Middle Woodland Sites in Southern Bruce County (Stewart 1974:4).

1989; Fox 1990a). During the Middleport stage of the Late Woodland period, the Nodwell village abruptly appeared in the midst of this forager territory, then within a century was abandoned. Following the abandonment of the Nodwell village, small groups of foragers continued to occupy a minimal number of sites in the region (Finlayson 1977; Fox 1987a; 1989; Wright and Anderson 1963).

While the body of data utilized in this study is drawn from southern Bruce county the analysis must also be integrated within the body of extant literature which exists for the Great Lakes lowlands, and in particular, other regions of southern Ontario. As a result, this research is situated not only within Bruce county but also within the context of prehistoric events in southern Ontario.

During the Middle Woodland period much of the population of southern Ontario was engaged in a pattern of life similar to that noted for Bruce county. Bands of hunter-gatherers occupied the

southern portion of the province, and even though there was regional differentiation in artifact styles, all groups pursued a similar annual round of fishing, gathering and hunting. Towards the end of this period population growth occurred throughout the province, resulting in more intensive resource extraction from constricted band territories (Spence et al. 1990). This event is witnessed through the proliferation of macroband occupation sites throughout southern Ontario at this time (Finlayson 1977; Spence et al. 1984; 1990; Stothers 1978).

The Late Woodland period is thought to begin circa AD 1000 in southern Ontario, but as Fox (1990a) has recently noted the origin of this culture period varies depending on the criteria used to define the transition. Depending on whether mortuary practice, artifact style, or settlement and subsistence strategy are considered, the dating of Late Woodland origins range throughout southern Ontario from AD 500 through AD 1000 (Crawford et al. 1998; Fox 1990a; Smith and Crawford 1997). This range of dates suggests that culture change in southern Ontario was not only occurring at different rates throughout the province but was also being exhibited in different ways. The sites in southern Ontario which were occupied during the transitional phase from Middle to Late Woodland periods were certainly occupied by populations who continued to hunt, fish and gather as their primary economic pursuit even though small quantities of carbonised cultigens have been recovered from six sites (Fox 1990a; Smith and Crawford 1997).

By the 13th century however, there were dramatic changes to the culture pattern of southern Ontario. Populations began occupying large, permanent villages located in strategic and defensible locations. Both artifacts and botanical remains suggest that horticulture had been well integrated into the economic system, and social organization at the community level appears to have centred around the multi-family longhouse and the longhouse village (Chapdelaine 1993).

In a maximum period of three hundred years the landscape of southern Ontario, previously occupied by hunter-gatherers, became dominated by farmers. Inherent, if not always explicit, in the dominant culture-historic model of change, is the belief that the hunter-gatherers of southern Ontario became horticulturalists in a period of accelerated change (Chapdelaine 1993). Furthermore, during this period of radical change many new sites are established and another population increase is thought to have occurred (Wright 1972a:78), suggesting that a rapidly expanding population of farmers from the southernmost regions of the province migrated north into new territories as populations burgeoned and soils were depleted.

However, throughout this period of horticulturalist expansion the population of Bruce county is believed to have maintained a traditional hunter-gatherer lifeway. Thus, the appearance of the Nodwell village in southern Bruce county must be observed not only as part of the historical development of the small region, but also within the context of prehistoric events elsewhere in southern Ontario, and any explanation of change in this region must take into account the history of culture change occurring elsewhere in the province.

Revisiting the Nodwell Site: What More can be Learned?

The appearance of the Nodwell village in Bruce county has generally been interpreted as the migration of an intact horticultural community which occurred during the Middleport sub-stage. Evidence cited for this interpretation includes 1) the similarity of the village settlement pattern to farming villages historically documented in southern Ontario; 2) the lack of any other similar settlements in southern Bruce county; 3) the uniqueness of the village subsistence pattern in Bruce county as suggested by the appearance of cultigens; and 4) the unique sedentary nature of village life as suggested by large stable dwellings, accumulated middens, accumulation of consumer durables and personal items inside houses, the utilization of pit storage structures and the presence of indirect seasonal indicators representing a complete annual cycle (Stewart 1974; Wright 1974:305).

While the combined evidence suggests a migration of horticulturalists into Bruce county, this model of horticultural colonization may be subject to the same criticisms as other similar colonization models. These criticisms include an over-reliance on normative concepts; selective use of the archaeological data; and the failure to situate the colonization in historical and regional context.

The presence of a longhouse village is generally the basic criterion used when inferring a sedentary, horticultural community in southern Ontario. In fact, the absence of the basic longhouse village structure is considered to indicate the absence of farming. The longhouse village is thought to represent a largely sedentary, internally coherent, horticultural population. Yet, archaeological data from the Nodwell site challenge this normative view. For example, archaeological evidence of a horticultural economy at the Nodwell village is slim. Only minimal quantities of cultigens were recovered from the village excavation and Wright (1974) himself states that the ash middens normally associated with farming villages are conspicuously absent. Ramsden (pers. comm.) has suggested that caches of celts or axes used in field clearing which are frequently recovered outside horticultural villages are also missing from the Nodwell assemblage. In contrast, enormous quantities of fish remains were recovered from pits and middens (Wright 1974), which suggests a dependence on local fish resources for subsistence. Furthermore, the diversity of ceramic styles represented at the Nodwell village suggests considerable cultural and temporal diversity between households and may indicate less socio-cultural coherence among the occupying population than might be expected from a single colonizing population or a greater period of occupation.

The colonization explanation of the Nodwell village also ignores key archaeological evidence. According to current interpretations (Wright 1974), the Nodwell village was established rapidly during the 14th century and occupied for a period of approximately twenty-five years. Wright (1985) bases his interpretation of the temporal occupation of the village on only one radiocarbon date which corresponds to his ceramic seriation, indicating a date of AD 1350. However, eleven other radiocarbon dates, based on large samples excavated from undisturbed contexts throughout the site, indicate a greater temporal occupation beginning several hundred years earlier (Wright 1985). If the other dates are accepted, then the Nodwell village may have been occupied over several centuries. The diversity of ceramic styles represented at the Nodwell village may also suggest a greater temporal occupation of the village than Wright (1974) infers. The temporal data recovered from the Nodwell site do not support the current explanation. Furthermore, these data represent a temporal occupation much lengthier than other Middleport sub-stage occupations in southern Ontario which may have been occupied no longer than one hundred years (Dodd et al. 1990:326-327).

Perhaps the most significant oversight of the migration model is its inability to situate the Nodwell village site into long-term regional or historical context. By failing to accomplish this the Nodwell village is isolated from earlier events in Bruce county. Furthermore, it is the economic practice of the village's inhabitants which is used to justify this isolation. This is unrealistic not only because there is a poor understanding of the Nodwell economy as described above, but because it is known that Bruce county has a long history of occupation. When the temporal range is extended it is observed that socio-economic change was already underway in this region as early as the Middle Woodland period. Throughout the late Middle Woodland period the local settlement pattern strategy was shifting as the indigenous population increased and the duration of settlement occupation was extended (Spence et al. 1990). Concomitant with these changes in population and settlement pattern are significant changes in social organization (Chapdelaine 1993). Provided with these details one might suggest that the Nodwell occupation developed locally as a natural outgrowth of the indigenous restructuring already under way in an earlier era.

These criticisms of the current explanation of the Nodwell village suggest that very little is really understood about the people who built and inhabited the village, and that there is much to learn from re-evaluating the current interpretation.

Approach

This study uses a multi-scalar temporal and spatial framework to develop a regional and historical context in which to situate the socio-economic change in Bruce county represented by the Nodwell village. The archaeological analysis will focus on two distinct spatial scales: 1) a site-based analysis of the Nodwell village, and 2) a regional analysis of archaeological sites from southern Bruce county. A third scale of analysis provides the extra-regional context in which to situate events in Bruce county.

The investigation of the Nodwell site aims to reconstruct the culture pattern of the site's inhabitants, something the current literature does not adequately address. Settlement plans, radiocarbon dates, artifacts and ecofacts are used to provide a comprehensive interpretation of this pattern, and to resolve contentious questions concerning the length of the village occupation, the annual duration of occupation (sedentary or seasonal), community subsistence strategy, and relationships between the inhabitants of the Nodwell village.

In addition, a regional analysis spanning two distinct temporal periods (before and during the Nodwell occupation) is undertaken to contextualize the process of change and to demonstrate how the structure of this site was constrained by regional dynamics.

Extant literature provided from geological and environmental reports, as well as archaeological site record forms and reports, are used to establish the physical and cultural boundaries of the research area. Regional culture patterns are identified via the analysis of archaeological settlement pattern, artifact and subsistence data available from extant collections and from a geographically stratified random sample survey which I undertook in southern Bruce county during the autumn of 1995.

The regional culture pattern of the pre-Nodwell period is determined by examining environmental and settlement data, material culture and subsistence remains from a variety of pre-Nodwell sites and by comparing these data between sites. Relevant observations at the regional level include the placement of sites throughout the territory and the size and layout of individual settlements. Artifacts and subsistence remains are examined to identify seasonal and economic practices, as well as connections between sites, and to sites outside of the region. A similar regional analysis is undertaken for the period during which the Nodwell village is occupied. Change and continuity within the region is then observed by comparing settlement data, artifact and subsistence remains from sites dating to the different periods.

At both the local and regional scales, interpretations are also situated within the context of events in other parts of southern Ontario. In this manner, southern Bruce county is demonstrated to be a frontier zone which was occupied by foragers even after the abutting territory was occupied by horticulturalists. The relationship between the inhabitants of Bruce county and the farmers to the south is explored temporally and the role of this relationship in the socio-economic change in Bruce county is used in the evaluation of both the in-situ and migration hypotheses.

For example, if the Nodwell village was a local development, changes to regional and local site settlement patterns should reflect changing social relations and economic practices over time through a network of increasingly larger, more organized and more sedentary community settlements. Shifts in both organizational and economic behaviour, including experimentation with cultigens introduced through interaction may also be reflected at these sites via artifact and subsistence data. Furthermore, if the Nodwell village had local origins, many of the traditional connections between sites should remain and there should be greater continuity in material culture traditions and economic land use. In this manner, the addition of new organizational elements reflected in settlement

pattern, artifacts and ecofacts would be expected but these new components would not preclude the continuity of some traditional structures.

In contrast, if the Nodwell village was the result of a migration, settlement pattern, artifact and subsistence data should reflect intensive interaction between the indigenous population and outsiders just prior to the appearance of Nodwell when farmers had expanded into abutting territories. Furthermore, if the Nodwell village is the result of a migration, rapid change to the settlement pattern and economic strategy of the indigenous population after Nodwell was occupied are to be expected as this population re-organized in the face of new territorial and social constraints. Finally, if the inhabitants of the Nodwell village migrated into Bruce county the technological, economic and settlement patterns represented at the Nodwell village should be closely aligned with those found on sites outside of the region and have no historical precursors in southern Bruce county.

By utilizing a broad diachronic framework this study situates the Nodwell site in its historical context and explains the construction of a multi-family, longhouse village in the territory of a mobile foraging population. Unlike the current explanation of the Nodwell village, this research gives agency to the indigenous population in the structuring of a new regional system, and establishes a more dynamic regional prehistory.

Organization of Chapters

Chapter 2 presents the analysis and interpretation of both the regional and Nodwell site settlement pattern data. At the regional scale, this chapter outlines the relevant aspects of southern Bruce county geography and environment, and provides a detailed definition of the significant spatial, temporal and cultural boundaries of the research. It provides a discussion of how regional data were generated and the methods and rationale behind my field survey in southern Bruce county. Discussion then uses settlement data to explain the relationships between sites, and sites and the local environment through time in order to demonstrate continuity and changes in indigenous behaviour before and after the appearance of the Nodwell village.

Chapter 2 also introduces the excavations of the Nodwell site and presents the analysis and interpretation of village settlement pattern data. The settlement data from the Nodwell village is critically re-evaluated, and intersite variability is used to define distinct temporal and cultural components. Interpretation then focuses on the relationship between the Nodwell village and the indigenous population of southern Bruce county by comparing the results of settlement pattern analyses through time.

Chapter 3 presents the analysis and interpretation of both the regional and Nodwell site artifact and subsistence data. At the regional scale, artifact and subsistence data are examined in order to demonstrate the relationships between sites in southern Bruce county, and to examine changing socio-economic strategies through time.

My investigations of the material from the Nodwell site focus on defining the cultural pattern of the village inhabitants by answering questions about site sedentism, function and subsistence strategy, as well as the temporal duration of the village occupation. Discussion focuses again on relations between site occupants, and between the inhabitants of the Nodwell site and other occupants of Bruce county.

Furthermore, artifact and subsistence data are used to demonstrate the historical connections between the inhabitants of Bruce county with populations residing in surrounding regions.

Chapter 4 synthesizes the results of the settlement pattern, artifact and subsistence analysis, bringing all categories of data together to provide a coherent explanation of socio-economic change in southern Bruce county. This chapter situates the Nodwell site within the context of regional development in Bruce county and defines the relationship between Nodwell villagers and the indigenous population. The results of this research are examined within the wider context of socio-cultural change taking place in the lower Great Lakes during the Early and Middle Iroquoian stages of the Late Woodland period, making it possible to situate conclusions within the broader issue of forager/ farmer interaction.

Chapter 2
Settlement Patterns

Introduction

Chapter two outlines the collection and analysis of settlement pattern data from southern Bruce county. This chapter begins by situating the research within the environment and culture history of the region. Discussion then focuses on the strategy of data collection, followed by the presentation and analysis of settlement pattern data from both southern Bruce county and the Nodwell site. The application of a chronological format to present the settlement data will help to demonstrate changes and continuities in settlement strategy from the Middle Woodland, pre-Nodwell occupation of the region through post-Nodwell, Late Woodland utilization.

Description of the Region

The complex physiography in southern Bruce county results from numerous geological processes. The bedrock geology of this region is mixed, with three sedimentary formations (the Ordovician, Silurian and Devonian), laid down overtop of a Precambrian stratum of mixed sedimentary, igneous and metamorphic rock (Clark et al. 1980:10-13).

The three sedimentary formations are not necessarily present in distinct layers but are variable and exposed in different locations in the region. The Silurian and Ordovician formations dominate the northeastern portion of the region and the Devonian formation is more evident in the southwest. This variability is further enhanced by differential rates of erosion among the three formations, with Devonian formation limestone more susceptible to wind and water erosion than the dolomites of the Silurian and Ordovician (Clark et al. 1980:12). As a result, the bedrock topography of southern Bruce county has a distinctly southwestern slope (Clark et al. 1980:13).

The retreat of the Wisconsin ice sheet approximately at 10,000 years B.P. deposited unconsolidated glacial till on the surface of the bedrock. This till has mixed with the sand and clays laid down by glacial lakes Warren, Algonquin and Nipissing, eroding bedrock, and decaying organics in water-riddled floodplains to create a variable soil profile in southern Bruce county (Clark et al. 1980:17-24; Hoffman and Richards 1954:16). Present day soils consist of heavy clays and clay loams with smaller amounts of organic peats, and sandy loams and sand (Hoffman and Richards 1954) (Figure 5).

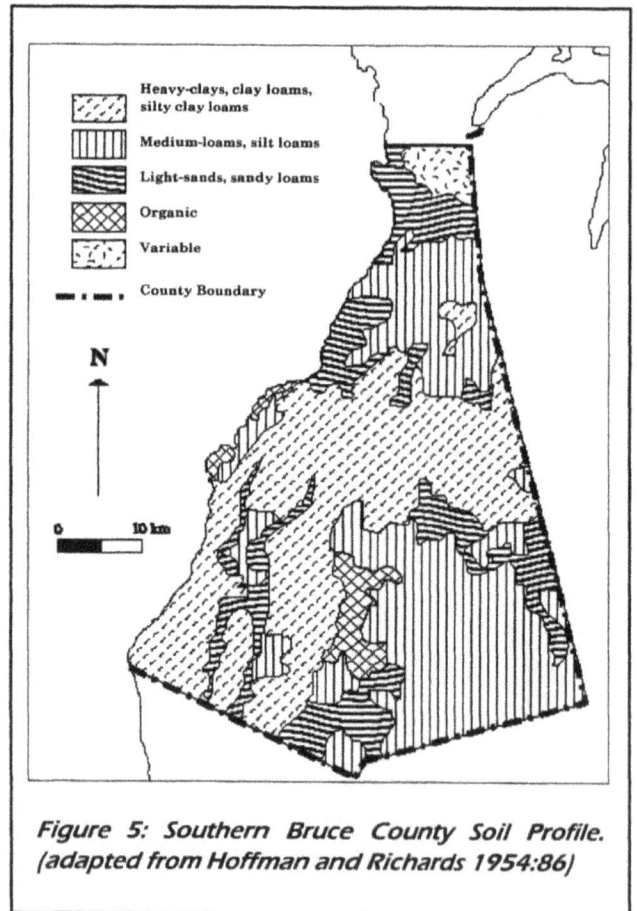

Figure 5: Southern Bruce County Soil Profile. (adapted from Hoffman and Richards 1954:86)

The advance and retreat of the Wisconsin ice sheet also created the pattern of moraines, abandoned spillways, drumlins and shorelines present in the county today. Chapman and Putnam (1966:62) subdivided the physiography of southern Bruce county into seven minor regions based predominantly on these glacial features (Figure 6). Four of these regions are evident within the defined study area described below and include the Huron Fringe, Huron Slope, Arran Drumlin Field and Saugeen Clay Plain.

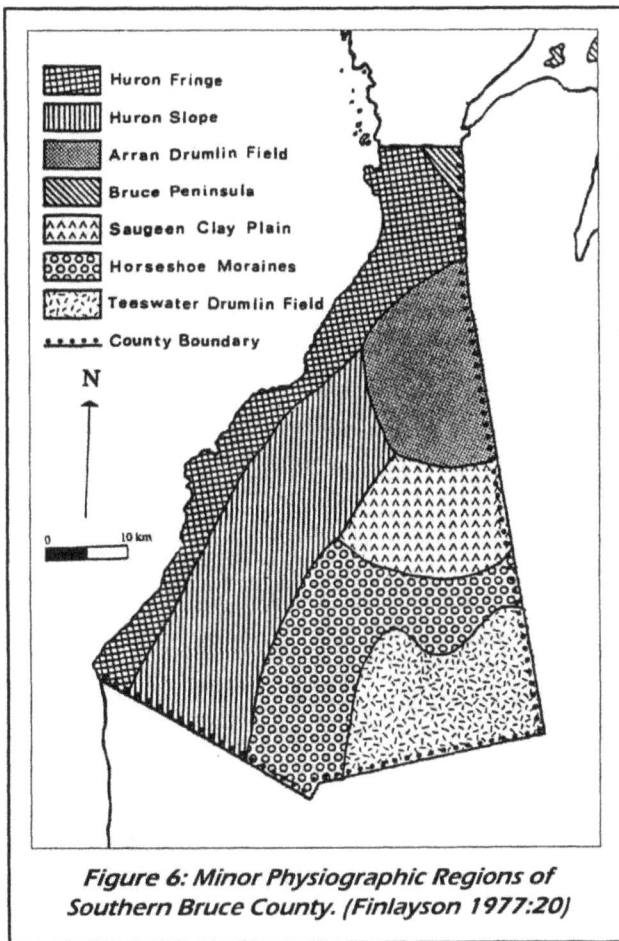

Figure 6: Minor Physiographic Regions of Southern Bruce County. (Finlayson 1977:20)

The Huron Fringe is a narrow strip of land along the Lake Huron shoreline (Chapman and Putnam 1966:264). In this zone, two glacial lakes, Lake Algonquin and Lake Nipissing, have directly affected the physiography. The abandoned shorelines of these lakes have created a series of high bluffs running parallel to the present Lake Huron shoreline. Gravel strands, boulders and sand dunes are terraced below these bluffs and meet the present shoreline of Lake Huron (Clark et al. 1980:14).

The Huron slope is located to the east of the glacial strand lines and is described as a "clay plain modified by a narrow strip of sand" (Chapman and Putnam 1966:263). The Saugeen Clay Plain, located further east, is dominated by heavy clay soils deposited by glacial Lake Warren (Clark et al. 1980:15). Finally, the Arran Drumlin Fields to the north of the Clay Plain are notable for their elevation and variable soil profile. As the Wisconsin ice sheet receded, a portion of this drumlin field remained underwater creating stony surfaces and stratified clay deposits in the inter-drumlin hollows (Clark et al. 1980:15).

The entire study region is dissected and dominated by the Saugeen River valley. Other river systems, such as the Sauble and Little Sauble, also contribute to the southern Bruce county drainage system, especially since these smaller rivers frequently connect with small inland lakes. However, the Saugeen, a pre-glacial river, has the majority of tributaries and is therefore the primary drainage within the research area (Figure 7).

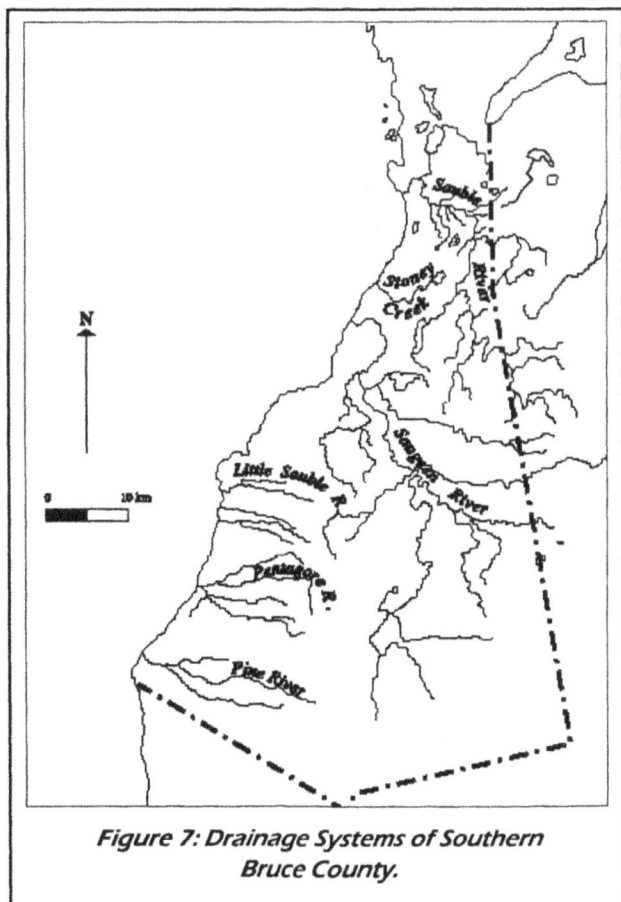

Figure 7: Drainage Systems of Southern Bruce County.

The climate of southern Bruce county today is modified in terms of both temperature and precipitation by Lake Huron. Furthermore, southern Bruce county is located within a polar frontal zone in which polar and tropical air masses meet (Clark et al. 1980:25). As a result, seasonal contrasts are high. Figures recorded at the Southampton weather station report an average summer temperature of 18 degrees celsius and winter temperatures average -5 degrees celsius (Clark et al. 1980:25). The annual number of frost-free days varies from 130-145 and the annual precipitation is approximately 87 cm. (Clark et al. 1980:25). Unfortunately, these climatic data can only reflect the trends of the last century and therefore are merely suggestive of earlier climatic conditions. Periodic fluctuations in temperature and precipitation are to be expected.

Various sources of data can be used to interpret periodic climate changes which occurred prehistorically in the Great Lakes lowlands which probably influenced the prehistoric environment of southern Bruce county, Ontario. Perhaps the best evidence stems from a series of pollen cores taken across a 75 km transect of lower Michigan state (Bernabo 1981). Pollen counts from these cores indicate considerable fluctuations in plant species abundance over the past 2000 years. Climatic change is considered to be the primary cause of variation in species abundance, because climate reorders the competitive advantages of different species and therefore affects the relative success of species reproduction and growth (Bernabo 1981:150). Furthermore, the synchronicity of these changes across various local landscapes suggests that change was not restricted to local environments but was widespread. Because there is no evidence supporting other types of forest alteration, such as large magnitude forest fires, climate change assumes a significant role.

The pollen data indicate that the period from 2000 BP through 1100 BP was dominated by cool average temperatures and frequent precipitation. Between 1100 BP and 700 BP temperatures increased during an era known as the Medieval Mild phase. However, at approximately 700 BP temperatures declined

and a very cold trend known as the Little Ice Age began which continued through the early historic period (Bernabo 1981:153).

Other sources of climate data such as tree rings and ice cores taken from other sites in the Northern hemisphere support these conclusions. Lamb (1974) utilized both historic records and tree ring growth to suggest the same periods for the Medieval Mild phase and the Little Ice Age in Britain. Dansgaard et al. (1971) also noted the same trends in their study of melt periods in ice cores taken from Devon Island in Greenland.

Changes in temperature would likely have affected human behaviour directly and indirectly as climate change would have altered the forest structure in the Bruce county region and may have contributed to periods of drought and flooding. The climate data indicate that the occupants of the Great Lakes lowlands, including those of Bruce county, were probably exposed to a variety of climate induced environmental changes in the prehistoric period, experiencing unusually mild climates during the Middle Woodland occupations, and then a trend towards a cooler climate by the Late Woodland occupation of the Nodwell village.

However, the moderating effect of Lake Huron contributes to the natural environment of Bruce county today, and it is possible that prehistoric temperature fluctuations in Bruce county may have been reduced because of the proximity to Lake Huron. Nevertheless, the predominance of clay soils combined with the cooler climate of the Little Ice Age suggest southern Bruce county would have been a marginal region in which to pursue a horticultural economy, but naturally occurring resources would have been abundant.

Today Bruce county lies within the Canadian biotic province with sugar maple-beech forest predominant in areas of well drained soils, and cedar-white pine-hemlock forest dominating poorly drained soils. A large variety of animal life inhabits the Canadian biotic province and has been well defined by Cleland (1966:9). It should also be noted that the Saugeen River has been described as one of the richest fishing locations in southern Ontario and agriculture, even with modern farming techniques, is still extremely restricted (Chapman and Putnam 1966:133).

History of Investigation

The archaeological investigation of Bruce county began during the 1940s when avocational archaeologists Fritz Knechtel and Donald Shutt collected and mapped a series of archaeological sites. Their collections came to the attention of Walter Kenyon and Kenneth Kidd of the Royal Ontario Museum, and Tom Lee of the National Museum. Lee then launched a series of excavations in the region. The aim of this early research was to get a better understanding of the culture history of southern Ontario and thus "fill in the gaps in the projected sequence of cultural development in Ontario" (Lee 1951a:70).

To that end, the collections produced by these researchers provided evidence suggesting a lengthy history of human occupation in southern Bruce county. Among the earliest occupations were archaic campsites up to 5000 years old, frequently located along the shorelines of glacial Lakes Nipissing and Algonquin (Kenyon 1958; Lee 1951a; Wright 1956:196). Early and Middle Woodland sites dating from 2500 BC through AD 500 were located along the sandy dunes of the Lake Huron shoreline and along the banks of the Saugeen River (Kenyon 1958; Lee 1951a:72). Late Woodland sites with large and variable collections of ceramics as well as small quantities of corn were also located in the region and thought to date to the protohistoric era (Lee 1951a; Kenyon 1958; Wright 1956).

Throughout the 1960s and early 1970s J.V. Wright and W. Finlayson conducted more thorough investigations on some of the sites originally located by Knechtel and Shutt. While the focus of these investigations was once again on the interpretation of the local culture history of Bruce county, another goal was to examine individual sites in order to describe in detail the various aspects of life during specific prehistoric periods (Finlayson 1977:11). The excavation of the Donaldson, Thede and Nodwell sites during this era reflects this trend as researchers described the variety of material culture, burial practices, settlement and subsistence patterns for these Middle and Late Woodland period sites

(Finlayson 1977; Stewart 1974; Wright and Anderson 1963; Wright 1974).

Since the early 1970s only sporadic archaeological work has been undertaken in Bruce county, reflecting attempts to salvage sites uncovered by local developers and farmers. This endeavour has led to the production of a series of government reports on Bruce county sites from several distinct chronological periods (Fox 1977, 1987a, 1988, 1989; Molnar 1989, 1991; Thomas and Zurba 1973). This work has never been fully synthesized but has been cited recently by Fox (1990b) to support his suggestion that the prehistoric population of Bruce county were the antecedents to the historic Odawa who continue to occupy the surrounding territory.

The excavation of the Nodwell site in 1969 and 1971, undertaken by J.V. Wright of the National Museum, was also originally designed as a salvage project to save what was believed to be the only example of a Middleport substage Iroquoian village in the region from destruction during the construction of a housing subdivision (Wright 1974:viii). Even though the excavation of the Nodwell site was in essence a salvage project the work undertaken here was unique because of its scope (Wright 1974:ix). The Nodwell site was almost completely excavated and the ensuing site reports were therefore extremely detailed in their description of settlement, subsistence and artifact data (Stewart 1974; Wright 1974). Wright's (1974) descriptive report offered only a brief interpretation of the village's presence, suggesting that the Nodwell village was the result of an Iroquoian migration from the east by a population eager to access new lands and enter into a trade relationship with nearby Algonkian foragers (Wright 1974:303-304). It further suggests that this migration ultimately failed because the incoming Iroquoian population forced the indigenous Algonkian foragers out of their traditional territory and hostilities between the groups ensued (Wright 1974:305).

Perhaps because of the scope of the project, and the clarity of the report, the Nodwell village has since assumed a prominent role in the archaeological literature of Ontario as an example of Iroquoian expansionism during the

14th century (Dodd et al. 1990). As outlined in the preceding chapter, this interpretation of the Nodwell village relies on similarities between village layout and artifact styles to suggest a relationship between its inhabitants and populations with similar lifestyles in other parts of Ontario.

Unfortunately, the basic assumptions made by Wright (1974) about the occupation and abandonment of the Nodwell village have never been appropriately tested or supported within the context of the local prehistoric record and therefore the possibility that the Nodwell village reflects an in situ development rather than a population migration still exists. Furthermore, contemporary archaeological theory now suggests that the process of prehistoric migration and intersocietal interaction is a far more lengthy and complex procedure than once believed, and takes place incrementally (Anthony 1990; Dennell 1985; Gregg 1988; Green 1991; Kent 1989c).

I believed that a regional archaeological investigation of Bruce county which spanned several centuries of local occupation would help to situate the appearance of the Nodwell village into a local historical context, and thereby test both the migration and in situ hypotheses for the appearance of the Nodwell village. Furthermore, this procedure would help to explain the process of intersocietal interaction between foragers and farmers required by both hypotheses, and in so doing, expand the role of the indigenous foragers in any explanation of local culture change.

Data Collection Strategy

The collection of data for the settlement pattern study proceeded in two distinct stages. The first stage of the investigation used site inventory files obtained from the Ontario Ministry of Citizenship, Culture and Recreation. Because these files are organized and sorted by county and township, they were first used to identify and situate all the recorded archaeological sites of southern Bruce county on a 1:50 000 scale map.

Information was then required to create a typology of these sites focusing on the temporal period of occupation and type of settlement. As this information was not always recorded in the site records files, a search for the original archaeological site reports was undertaken. This proved difficult as many reports were missing from the ministry library and public access is limited to those written by government agencies. Reports submitted by academic researchers, heritage consultants and avocational archaeologists are released only upon the permission of the author. Difficulties in obtaining permission were compounded by deaths and relocations. In the end approximately 90% of the site reports were made available.

Information included within the reports was highly variable. Where possible, the reports were used to develop a typology of archaeological sites. Significant details such as the location of a site, period of site occupation, size of site, number of features, duration of occupation, types of material remains recovered from site and location of archaeological collection were tabulated. These sites were then assigned one of five site type designations including burial, cemetery, campsite, habitation site or village.

Burial is used to define a single isolated interment; cemetery is applied to those sites with multiple interments. Distinctions between campsites, habitation sites and villages are more subjective given that each of these site types reflects a prehistoric living space (Potter 1993:59). Nevertheless, there are real distinctions between the three terms. Village is used to designate a permanent settlement with a high degree of internal coherence. Villages therefore, have a structured and observable internal settlement plan, many cultural features and large quantities of material debris. These sites are therefore thought to have housed a large population at one time. Habitation sites are also large primary dwelling locations with large numbers of cultural features including hearths, middens, storage pits and houses and include large amounts of material debris. Habitation sites, however lack the internal coherence of the village. Instead, the random placement of features suggests the repeated seasonal use of the site by large groups of people over a long period of time. The designation of campsite was used to define small dwelling locations which had minimal numbers of randomly placed cultural features and small quantities of material culture. Some of these sites contain no features at all and were therefore identified on the basis of small clusters of artifacts. Furthermore, campsites are unlikely to reflect the activities of a large population given their small size and limited cultural debris. Instead, it is assumed that these sites are the remnants of single family or special group activities. It should also be noted that site functions may fluctuate, reflecting changes in land use strategy by the prehistoric population over time.

The tables and detailed maps produced from this stage of the investigation were then used to develop a methodology for the second stage of the settlement pattern study; the archaeological field investigation. During the initial stages of the library research it became apparent that Middle Woodland forager habitation and campsites were the predominate site types in the region. Furthermore, these sites appeared to cluster along the Saugeen River valley and along the shore of Lake Huron. However, it was obvious that no previous systematic regional archaeological investigation had been undertaken in Bruce county pertaining to either the Middle or Late Woodland periods and thus the recorded sites tended to reflect only random encounters with archaeological sites.

Therefore, during the spring and summer of 1995 a geographically stratified random sample field survey project was designed to build on what was already known about the prehistoric settlement and land-use strategy in Bruce county. The survey was geared to: 1) locate a representative sample of archaeological sites dating from the Middle Woodland through Late Woodland period in southern Bruce county, 2) compensate for biases in previous archaeological research that concentrated on prehistoric settlement along the Saugeen River valley by searching other important geographical areas identified via library research, 3) ensure that no sites similar to Nodwell existed, and 4) establish a coherent framework from which to evaluate

the reliability of previous work and determine whether the results of this work could be used to address my research problems.

Because the Nodwell village site was the only recorded Middleport village in southern Bruce county, it was used as a starting point from which to define a significant geographical region of investigation. Based on a search of geological and geographic literature and maps it was determined that all significant geographical zones in southern Bruce county were represented within a 20 km radius from this village (Figure 8). In fact, the majority of distinct geographical sub-regions were located within a 10 km radius from the village. Further survey beyond this 20 km range was not considered because the changes to the geography outside this point were extreme. To the north of this radius one enters the unique geographical setting of the Bruce Peninsula. The area to the south is separated from Bruce county by a several-kilometre-zone of wetland which gives way to sandy dune formations and arable, sandy soils. Furthermore, these wetlands were the subject of intense archaeological survey in the early 1970s when the Government of Ontario had developed a provincial campground at MacGregor Point, and no sites dating to the

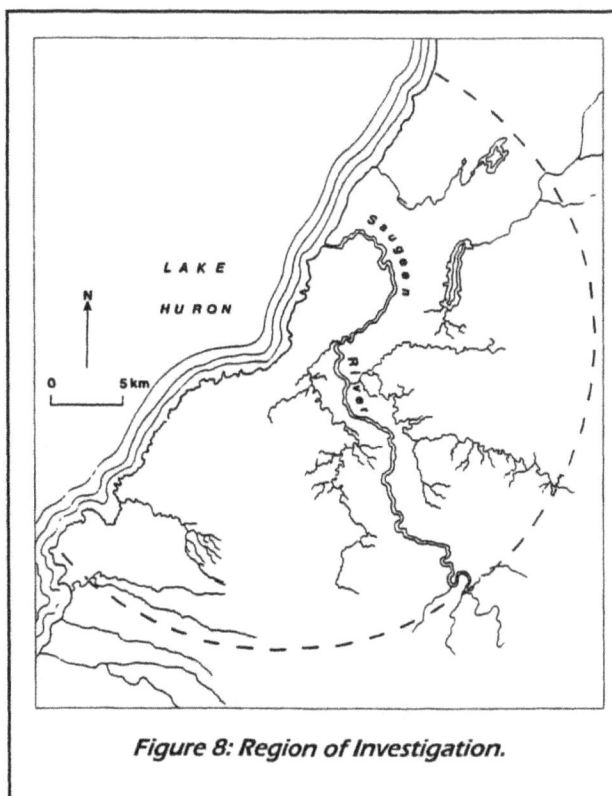

Figure 8: Region of Investigation.

Middle or Late Woodland periods had been located (Thomas and Zurba 1973). At the eastern edge of this radius a large drumlin field separates southern Bruce county from a flat ecozone of arable, sandy soil with a distinctly different environment. Because Lake Huron is located on the western edge of the study region, the total land mass within the study region was approximately 206 square kilometres.

Within this defined area, several distinct geographical settings are encountered including; Lake Huron beach or shoreline; the elevated glacial lake strandlines of Lake Nipissing and Lake Algonquin; a high clay plain, known as the Huron fringe; the Saugeen bluffs and river valley; the Arran Drumlin field; a series of small inland lakes drained by small creeks; and a large wetland which was not examined (Figure 9). A decision was made not to pursue further investigation of the wetlands due to the amount of work which had been conducted there earlier (Thomas and Zurba 1973).

Over a ten week period in the autumn of 1995 approximately 3.4 square kilometres of area were randomly surveyed from each of the remaining six geographical zones. Approximately 10% of the total land mass of the region was observed. The survey strategy involved a crew of three people walking ploughed fields at 10 metre transects. Ten metre transects were also used in woodlots where it was necessary to employ a series of shovel test pits at 10 metre intervals to locate sites.

The settlement pattern data accumulated from both the site inventories and the field survey were then utilized to situate the Nodwell site into both a regional and temporal context. By establishing both a chronological and regional framework to analyse settlement data it was possible to distinguish not only the types and locations of sites utilized in southern Bruce county prior to the establishment of the Nodwell village, but also to examine any changes to this pattern coincident with the appearance and abandonment of the Nodwell village.

Regional Settlement Pattern Data for the Middle Woodland Period

In all, twelve sites occupied during the Middle Woodland period have been located through field and document investigation (Figure 10, Table 1). Table 1 demonstrates that a variety of sites dating to the Middle Woodland period were found in each geographical setting observed. The archaeological literature refers to four more sites located along the Saugeen Bluffs and inland Lake Arran, but these are not discussed because the references did not detail the period of occupation and the information could not be confirmed due to the absence of collections and other primary source material.

The regional settlement pattern reflected by the twelve Middle Woodland sites includes a series of small campsites and larger habitation sites located primarily along the banks of the Saugeen River, the shores of Lake Huron and other inland water-ways. Distinguishing between

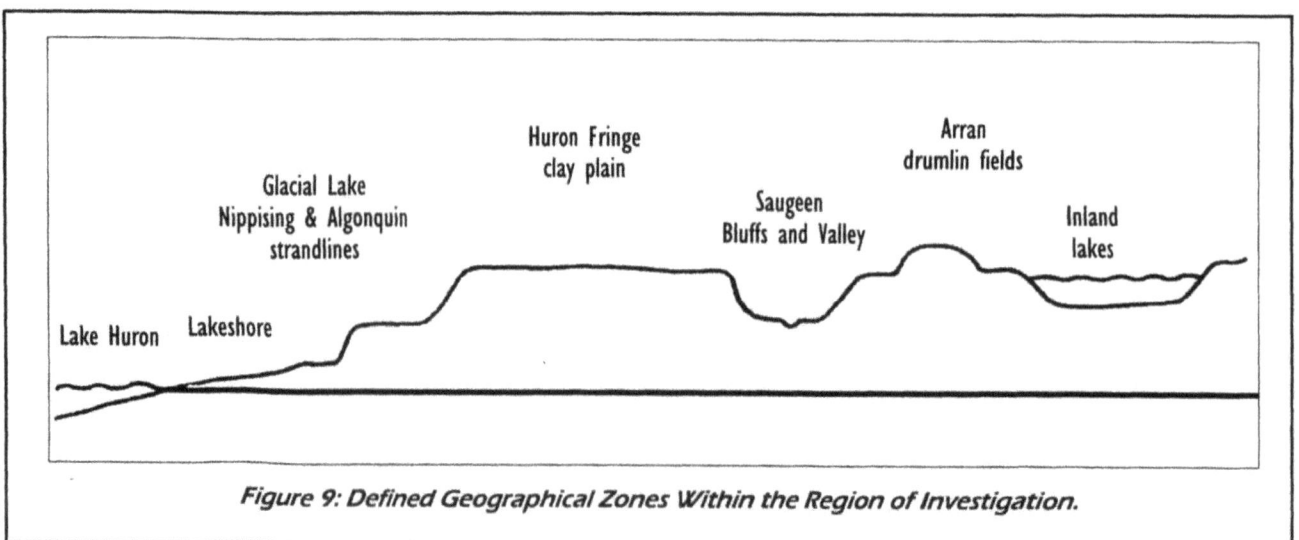

Figure 9: Defined Geographical Zones Within the Region of Investigation.

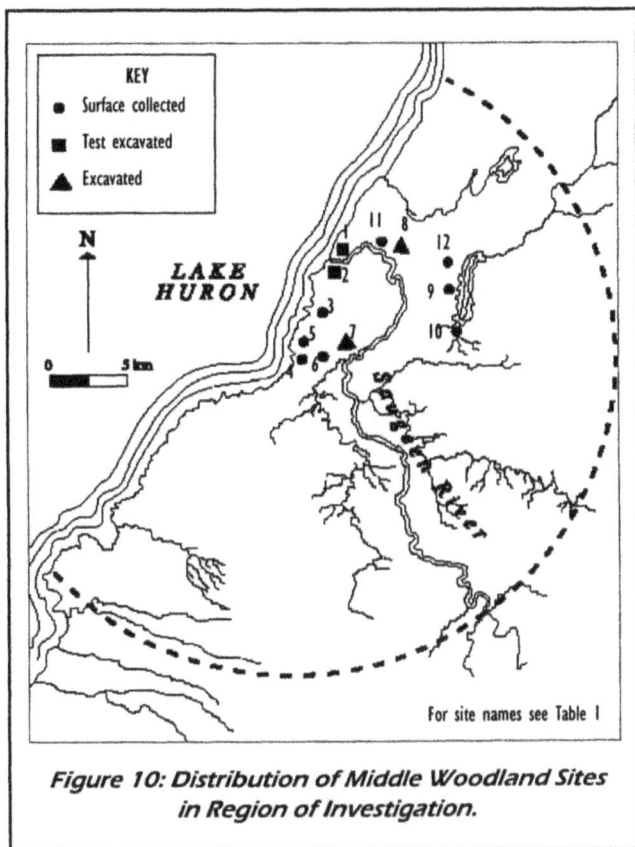

Figure 10: Distribution of Middle Woodland Sites in Region of Investigation.

campsites and habitation sites was difficult given that some of the sites had been excavated, and others subjected only to surface survey. Distinction between the two site types was therefore based on estimated site size, number and types of features, as well as the diversity of the artifact assemblage which is detailed in Chapter 3.

In 1977, Finlayson suggested that this pattern of small campsites and larger habitation sites reflected a series of annually scheduled movements by the occupants of southern Bruce county. Finlayson (1977:572) surmised that large macroband habitation sites located along the banks of the Saugeen River were occupied during the spring months in order to access large runs of spring-spawning fish. Smaller lakefront microband campsites were thought to be occupied during the summer and fall when the occupants would harvest large quantities of nuts and berries and exploit fish from Lake Huron (Finlayson 1977:576). Finlayson also speculated that the small inland sites were hunting-based nuclear family campsites that were occupied during the winter months (Finlayson 1977:578).

The Middle Woodland settlement pattern in southern Bruce county may be considered typical of the land use strategy during this era in other parts of southern Ontario and the Great Lakes lowlands (Spence et al.1990). For example, when the boundaries of the search area are doubled to a 40 km radius and the sites dating to the Middle Woodland period in the site inventory files are plotted, a similar distribution of hunter-gatherer settlements concentrated on the shores of Lake Huron and the banks of major river valleys emerges (Figure 11).

Even beyond the 40km zone, Middle Woodland settlement patterns along the Lake Huron shoreline appear to be similar. Kenyon and Fox (1983) recovered an abundance of spring-spawning fish remains from a Middle Woodland occupation known as the Wyoming Rapids site which is located along the banks of the Ausable River valley in the southwest corner of Ontario. They further suggest that smaller campsites located within 10 km from the Wyoming Rapids sites along the shores of Lake Huron, such as the Burley site, were the autumn components of this settlement system (Kenyon and Fox 1983:9).

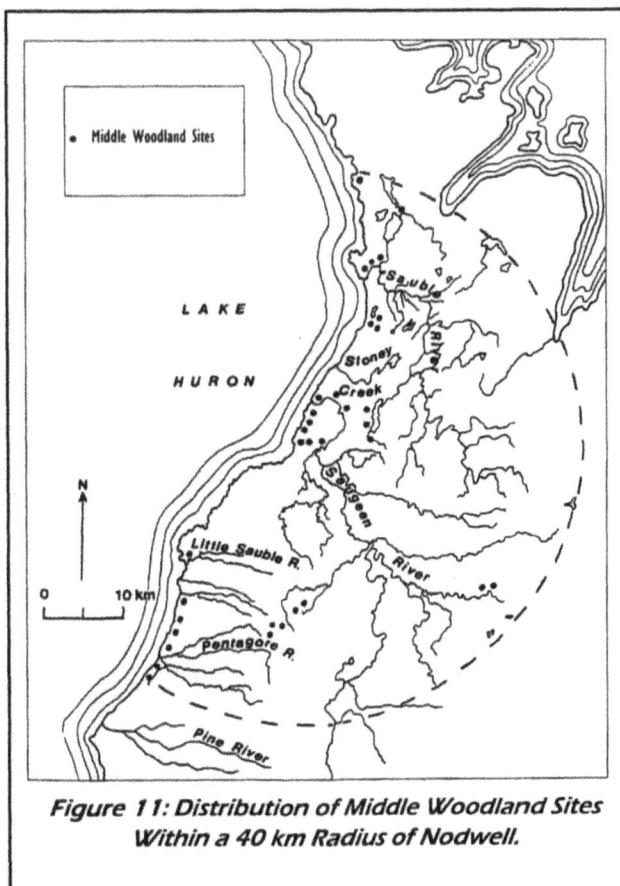

Figure 11: Distribution of Middle Woodland Sites Within a 40 km Radius of Nodwell.

Site Name,	Location	Site Size	Features	Site Type	Dating Method
1. North Shore (BdHi-2)	mouth of Saugeen River	Uncertain "small"	1 artifact cluster	campsite	diagnostics
2. Shutt (BcHi-6)	mouth of Saugeen River	Uncertain "large"	Hearths artifact clusters	habitation site	diagnostics
3. Mirimachi Bay (BcHi-4)	Lake Huron Shoreline	Uncertain "small"	Hearths artifact clusters	campsite	diagnostics
4. Port Elgin Cemetery (BcHi-2)	Huron Fringe, Port Elgin	Uncertain "small"	1 artifact cluster	campsite	diagnostics
5. North Elgin	Lake Algonquin Strandline, Port Elgin	Uncertain "small"	1 artifact cluster	campsite	diagnostics
6. Boiled Baby (BcHi-16)	Huron Fringe, east of Port Elgin	uncertain	artifact clusters	campsite	diagnostics
7. Thede (BcHi-7)	Saugeen Bluffs	1 hectare	Hearth living floor middens storage pits posts activity areas	habitation site	radiocarbon diagnostics
8. Donaldson (BdHi-1)	Saugeen Bluffs	1.2 hectares	cemetery houses hearths living floors middens storage pits posts activity areas	habitation site cemetery	radiocarbon diagnostics
9. Busch (BcHh-6)	Arran Drumlin Field, Arran Lake	1.5 hectares (300x50m)	hearths artifact clusters	habitation site	diagnostics
10. Krug (BcHh-5)	Arran Drumlin Field, Arran Lake	0.5 hectares	hearths pits artifact clusters	habitation site	diagnostics
11. Indian Church	Saugeen Bluffs	0.01 hectares (2x5m)	1 artifact cluster	campsite	diagnostics
12. Kirkland Farm	Arran Drumlin Field	uncertain "limited"	artifact clusters	campsite	diagnostics

Table 1: Middle Woodland Settlement Pattern Data for Bruce County.

(Finlayson 1977; Fox 1986:1; 1987a; Knechtel:1955; Lee 1951a; 1951b; Shutt:1951; 1952; Wright 1953a; 1953b; Wright and Anderson 1963).

Other researchers have observed a similar settlement strategy during the Middle Woodland era in other parts of southern Ontario. Spence et al. (1984) suggest that the Middle Woodland occupants of the Trent River-Rice Lake district of south-central Ontario employed a similar settlement/subsistence strategy. Here, a seasonal pattern of spring riverside settlement, summer-fall lake front sites and inland winter settlements is also observed (Spence et al. 1984:20). Spence et al. (1990:146-166) describe three other regional Middle Woodland settlement systems throughout southern Ontario which also exhibit this pattern.

Even outside of Ontario, Middle Woodland populations observed a similar pattern of settlement. Stothers (1978:23) claims that the Middle Woodland occupants of Michigan inhabited macroband settlements in areas rich in fish resources from spring to fall. During the winter, smaller nuclear family campsites are found in the interior, away from Lake Erie, and hunting becomes the dominant subsistence task (Stothers 1978:23). Cleland (1982:770-771)) also acknowledges this annually scheduled pattern of settlement in the Middle Woodland occupation of Michigan claiming that the same strategy is utilized along all the major drainages of both Lake Huron and Lake Michigan throughout the state.

Every effort was made to determine if the Middle Woodland sites in southern Bruce county were occupied during the latter half of this period, or the time of the most interest to this research. Unfortunately, radiocarbon dates were only available from the Thede and Donaldson sites. The Thede site had a lengthy period of occupation. Four radiocarbon dates taken from this site place the occupation period between (100 BC±200 through AD 770±100) (Finlayson 1977:228). The maximum calibrated date range is therefore 300 BC to AD 870 using a single standard deviation, and 500 BC to AD 970 using a two sigma deviation (Finlayson 1977:228). Four radiocarbon dates from the Donaldson site indicate an occupation range between (530 BC±60 through AD 550±80) (Finlayson 1977:511). The maximum calibrated date range is therefore 590 BC to AD 630 using a

single standard variation, and 885 BC to AD 710 using two standard deviations (Finlayson 1977:511). These radiocarbon dates combined with detailed areal excavations by Finlayson (1977) suggest that these two sites were definitely occupied extensively during the late Middle Woodland period.

It was difficult to determine when the other sites were occupied. Finlayson (1977:618) determined that the ceramic assemblages dating to the late Middle Woodland occupation of southern Bruce county included higher frequencies of dentate-stamped decoration, replacing an earlier emphasis on pseudo-scalloped-shell applications. While it was difficult to observe this trend on the small assemblages from the surface collected sites which represent the remainder of the Middle Woodland occupations, it is noted that these two styles of ceramics are represented at these sites in relatively equal proportions (see Chapter 3). Because both ceramic styles are present it cannot be determined if these sites were utilized throughout the entire Middle Woodland period, as they may date only to the period when the two techniques were in roughly equal use. However, Finlayson (1977:578-589) suggests that this transition occurred between AD 100 and AD 400, placing this transition in the latter half of the Middle Woodland period.

It would appear that the foraging populations in this region always employed a strategy which necessitated the use of several special-purpose sites throughout the year. The radiocarbon dates from both Thede and Donaldson spanned the early and late phases of the Middle Woodland period, indicating the continued re-occupation of these sites over time (Finlayson 1977). It is probable that the other Middle Woodland sites in this region also have multiple occupations during this period.

Nevertheless, some significant changes to settlement pattern did take place between the early and late phases of the Middle Woodland period. Cleland (1982) and Spence et al. (1990:168) suggest that the most significant change to take place was an increased definition of local band territories, as overall population increase throughout the lower Great Lakes resulted in higher population packing and the constriction of band territories. Evidence for this includes the increased utilization of macroband sites. At sites such as the Donaldson and Thede sites in southern Bruce county the easy access to abundant fish resources appears to have allowed more people to live together for a longer period of time (Cleland 1982; Finlayson 1977; Spence et al. 1990). As a result, late Middle Woodland populations in southern Bruce county continued to occupy a variety of sites during the annual cycle but probably experienced a higher degree of sedentism from spring through autumn than did earlier populations.

While similarities exist between the regional Middle Woodland settlement pattern in southern Bruce county and in other regions of the Great Lakes Lowlands, southern Bruce county may also be considered part of a distinct settlement system with its own particular history. This argument is perhaps strengthened by the unique geographical position of southern Bruce county which is distinct from the peninsula to the north, Lake Huron to the west, a flat sandy plain to the east, and separated from the other Middle Woodland sites to the south by a 10-15 km wide swath of wetland.

During the Middle Woodland period distinctions between regional adaptations have been identified based on the differences between assemblages of both material and faunal remains (see Chapter 3). These differences are thought to reflect differential access to resources by local populations (Spence et al. 1990:143). Because of these variations in the frequency of artifact types, artifact decoration and faunal materials, as well as a movement toward increased sedentism during the late Middle Woodland period, some scholars believe that southern Bruce county may have represented a single band's territory (Finlayson 1977:562; Spence et al 1990).

Spence et al. (1990:168) have suggested that Middle Woodland populations may have used elaborate mortuary rituals, such as mound building to demonstrate their rights to specific territories during this period. While no burial mounds have been irrefutably documented in southern Bruce county, at the Donaldson site the remains of some twenty-one individuals interred with an assortment of grave goods was excavated. Severe bluff erosion has probably destroyed more of this cemetery (Finlayson 1977). Given the importance of this site as the largest macroband habitation site, and its location at the first rapids of a major fishing river, these burials were probably used to establish the rights of the southern Bruce county community to this territory during a period of population increase and territorial constriction.

Comparing the intersite settlement patterns between the Middle Woodland sites in southern Bruce county is again difficult given the diversity of site types and sizes as well as the differential results achieved from survey and excavation. Middle Woodland sites in southern Bruce county range from small artifact clusters, like the Indian Church site which covers no more than 10 square metres; through medium size sites like Mirimachi Bay which includes two hearth features and a series of distinct artifact scatters; to large sites like Donaldson which exceeds 1.2 hectares and contains more than one thousand features (Finlayson 1977:246).

The intrasite settlement pattern of the Middle Woodland should be best known from the two excavated sites: Thede and Donaldson. However, continued re-occupation of these sites over several centuries has made the interior settlement pattern difficult to interpret. For example, the Thede site covers an area of approximately 1 hectare but only one hearth floor and one living floor were located (Finlayson 1977:218-219). Nevertheless, 105 middens and storage pits were located along with 48 scattered post moulds, and a few discreet activity areas, suggesting a significant population occupied the site and undertook a variety of activities (Finlayson 1977:219).

Two excavations at the Donaldson site reveal a little more about internal settlement pattern. The 1960 excavation of the Donaldson site revealed two longhouse structures, as well as a number of fired house floors, middens and a cemetery (Wright and Anderson 1963).

These are the only definitive examples of dwelling structures from the Middle Woodland period in southern Bruce county and the earliest examples of longhouses recovered in southern Ontario (Chapdelaine 1993). The two houses were both approximately 7 metres long and 5 metres wide with interior hearths, midline posts, interior pits, posts and bunklines (Wright and Anderson 1963:11-15). These houses are very similar to later longhouses only shorter (Figure 12). Furthermore, the internal features indicate indoor activity areas and might represent the only settlement evidence for winter occupation along the Saugeen River (see Chapter 3). Finlayson's 1971 excavations at this site uncovered 926 post holes, 56 refuse features, 29 pits, 9 hearth floors, 1 large midden and another cemetery (Finlayson 1977:246). Thus, the large size of the site and intensity of debris are suggestive of a large, lengthy occupation. Unfortunately, the hearth floors were all associated with refuse deposits and it is therefore not clear whether they were associated with living areas. A majority of the posts were probably associated with dwelling structures but the continued re-occupation of the site by large numbers of people made patterns impossible to discern (Finlayson 1977:497).

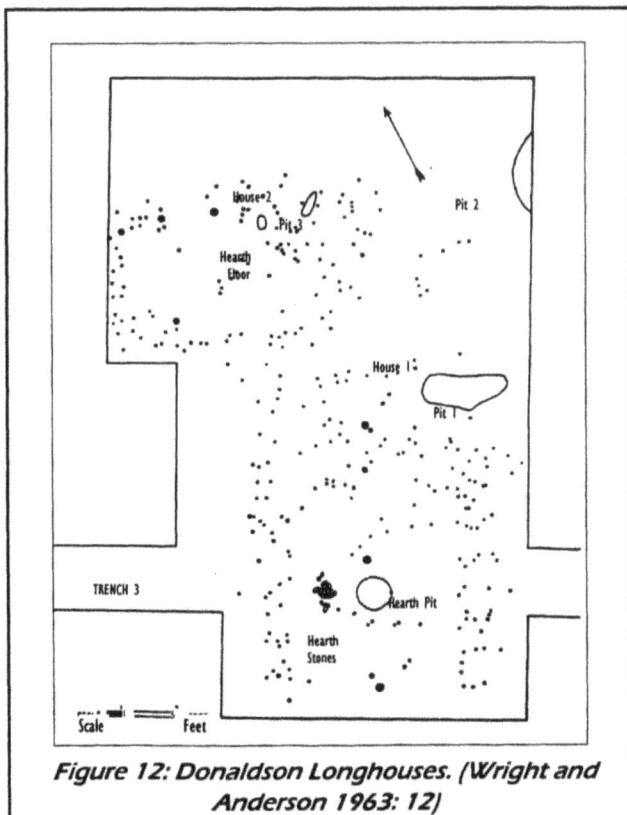

Figure 12: Donaldson Longhouses. (Wright and Anderson 1963: 12)

The community settlement patterns revealed by the excavated Middle Woodland sites of southern Bruce county are in keeping with site plans most frequently identified with hunter-gatherers. Models of hunter-gatherer behaviour suggest that because these groups generally have a highly mobile lifeway, moving for the purpose of accessing different resources at different times of the year, community settlements often lack structured planning as site utilization is short-term (Foley 1981a; Kelly 1992). The internal arrangement of features at hunter-gatherer sites tends to be random, a factor which is intensified by the annual re-occupation of sites and leads to difficulty in interpreting archaeological features (Foley 1981a).

Nevertheless, the regional and site specific settlement pattern data from southern Bruce county allow a basic model of social and economic strategy during the Middle Woodland period which incorporates both general and historical trends in the region. Even though this model is refined in the following chapter to accommodate the analysis of subsistence and material culture remains from these sites, an initial interpretation based solely on settlement data can still be put forth.

At the regional scale, differences in site size, location, and duration of occupation (as noted from the number and types of features observed) suggests that the local population participated in an annually scheduled fishing, foraging and hunting economy during the Middle Woodland period. The nature of the activities, combined with a fluidity of local group membership would have made it possible for groups to merge together at specific locations in times of resource abundance for the purpose of resource extraction. This is demonstrated by a number of large habitation sites located at prime spring through fall resource extraction locations. This was also probably the period during which social and political bonds within the larger population of Bruce county were reinforced (Finlayson 1977). Just as groups merged together during the warmer months when resources were readily available, so too they split apart during the winter season when access to resources declined. During this portion of the annual cycle it was probably the nuclear family that was the primary socio-economic unit (Finlayson 1977). Support for this can be found in the large number of small, ephemeral campsites located throughout southern Bruce county and surrounding areas.

It would appear that southern Ontario experienced a period of population growth during the latter stage of the Middle Woodland period (Spence et al. 1990) and it has been suggested (Finlayson 1977) that southern Bruce county became a tightly bound territory occupied by a single band. Large habitation sites, such as Donaldson and Thede, were probably the focus of settlement between spring through fall, when abundant fish resources could be extracted from the Saugeen River.

Furthermore, surplus fish resources could have been stored to assist with the winter subsistence strategy which may have been more difficult due to territorial constraints. The appearance of longhouses with interior pits and hearths at the Donaldson site may be the first evidence in this region of a winter macroband occupation.

For Chapdelaine (1993:180) the late Middle Woodland is a significant period defined by a rapidly changing social system and a move toward a semi-sedentary settlement strategy. Chapdelaine suggests (1993) that increased group interaction, brought about through extended periods of communal living, helped to redefine intergroup socio-economic relations. It is during this period that the annual economic strategy alters, perhaps in response to population growth and territorial constriction. Nevertheless, the importance of the nuclear family as the basic unit of socio-economic authority appears to decline in favour of larger, perhaps lineage-based, social groups cohabiting at macroband habitation sites for lengthy periods of time. The presence of longhouses at the Donaldson site emphasizes this transition and suggests that larger social groups had assumed an important position in the local socio-economic structure by AD 700. Perhaps as a result of these new socio-economic relations, strong regional identities were forged throughout Ontario at this time (Chapdelaine 1993) (see Chapter 3).

The Nodwell Village Settlement Pattern

The Nodwell village was a Late Woodland settlement located on the Lake Algonquin strandline in southern Bruce county. The near complete excavation and excellent preservation of this site reveals a settlement pattern distinctly different from that observed at any of Bruce county's Middle Woodland period habitations. The most recent of the absolute dates taken from Middle Woodland sites in this region dates that occupation to the late 10th century (Finlayson 1977). Relative dating of the Nodwell village via ceramic typology places the occupation of this site in the mid 14th century (Wright 1974). Details of the internal settlement pattern from the Nodwell village indicate that the social and economic organization of southern Bruce county's population changed dramatically over a maximum of 350 years.

Elsewhere in southern Ontario, Late Woodland village occupations dated to the mid 14th century are associated with the Middleport sub-stage of Iroquoian development. The Middleport sub-stage is recognized throughout much of southern Ontario, and is associated with a shift in settlement to defensible locations remote from rivers in regions of sandy soil (Chapdelaine 1993; Dodd et al. 1990). Furthermore, Middleport villages are organized around a series of large longhouses and are frequently surrounded by palisades. Middleport sites generally have many pit features which contain cultigens, and artifacts associated with the production and processing of plant materials. Middleport villages bear a distinct similarity to the Iroquoian settlements occupied at contact and it is often assumed that the inhabitants of these settlements shared a similar culture pattern. Unfortunately, only four of the sixty known Middleport sub-stage villages have been subjected to intensive investigation and as the sample of material culture, settlement and subsistence data from these sites increases so too does the diversity of prehistoric organization defined by the Middleport sub-stage (Dodd et al. 1990).

The Nodwell site is the best known of all the Middleport villages. The excavation of the Nodwell village revealed a total of twelve longhouses, eleven of which were situated within a double palisade (Figure 13). It is possible that other houses existed outside of the palisade wall, however, earlier construction in this area made further excavation impossible. Large numbers of hearths, pits and middens were located primarily within the longhouse structures. An internal settlement pattern analysis, originally undertaken by Wright (1974) but expanded upon below, demonstrates the development of a socio-economic strategy distinct from that observed in the Middle Woodland occupations of Bruce county.

Determinants of Village Organization

Warrick (1984) and Dodd (1984) have both undertaken analyses of Iroquoian style village and longhouse structures in southern Ontario and both have found that the primary determinants of village organization were socio-political in nature; "related to the composition of

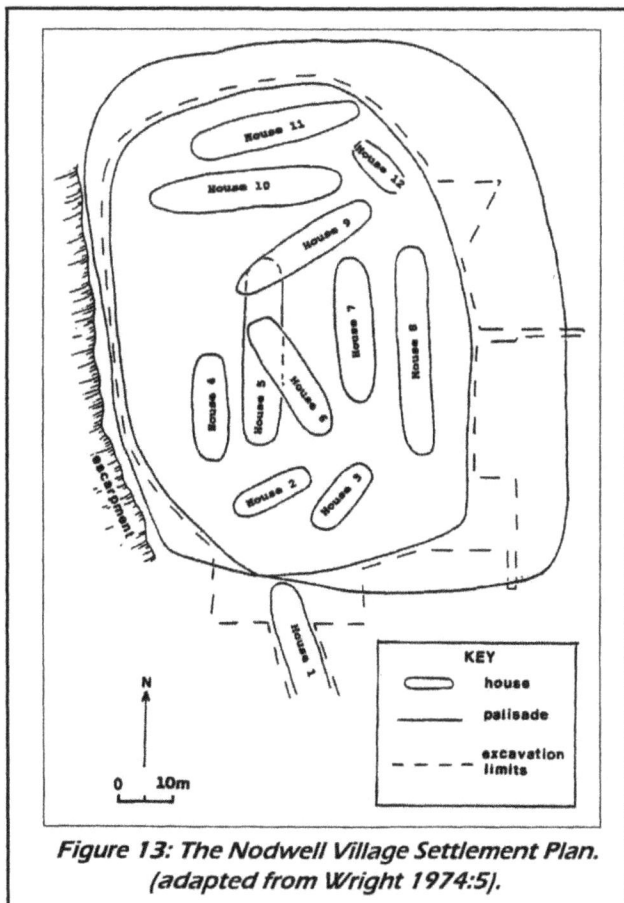

Figure 13: The Nodwell Village Settlement Plan. (adapted from Wright 1974:5).

households, village demography and government" (Warrick 1984:35). Other factors such as cosmology, local geography and environment, sanitation, safety, and space conservation played only a limited role in village settlement plans (Warrick 1984:22-36; Dodd 1984). Dodd (1984) and Warrick (1984) found these factors often had no relationship whatsoever to village organization, or merely imposed technical limitations on the construction of the village. Nevertheless, it is believed that the location, size and alignment of houses, as well as the distribution of hearths, pits, middens and other built features within and surrounding the houses, and episodes of reconstruction can be related very strongly to village social organization (Dodd 1984; Warrick 1984; Chapdelaine 1993; Sutton 1996).

Palisade

The Nodwell village is demarcated by a double palisade that encompasses approximately 6550 square metres, and is thought to be a defensive construction. The two palisades run approximately parallel and in very close proximity to one another along the western portion of the site where the site meets a high banked escarpment. To the north, east and southeast the palisade walls spread apart reaching a maximum range of 9.1 metres. At the southern portion of the site, the palisade walls pinch together for approximately 6 metres. Wright (1974:11) believes that access to the site was provided by a small gap in the palisade wall in the southern end of the site. The post mold diameters of the palisade were recorded during excavation and it was determined from this information that the height of both walls was approximately the same and therefore the walls would have been equal in strength (Wright 1974).

It is impossible to know for certain at what point in the site history the palisade was erected around the Nodwell village, or if both palisades were used at the same time. If it is accepted that the village dates to a culture-historic sub-stage that lasts no more than 50 years, there seems no reason to believe that the double palisade was not constructed immediately. If

No.	House Length	House Width	House Orientation	No. Pits	No. Hearths	No. Entry Ways	End Cubicles	House Extension
1	not known	7.2 m	north-south axis	89	3	1	1	not known
2	16.2 m	5.8 m	east-west axis	21	2	1	2	none
3	16.8 m	7.2 m	east- west axis	79	2	2	2	none
4	22.6 m	7.0 m	north-south axis	89	3	2	1	none
5	39.0 m	8.2 m	north-south axis	27	1	1	2	none
6	26.7 m	7.2 m	north-south axis	258	2	2	2	none
7	30.2 m	7.6 m	north-south axis	165	1	1	2	none
8	42.4 m	7.3 m	north-south axis	237	4	1	2	14.9 m
9	30.5 m	6.9 m	east-west axis	137	3	2	2	none
10	38.7 m	8.2 m	east-west axis	151	6	2	1	none
11	35.7 m	7.0 m	east-west axis	98	3	1	1	none
12	12.2 m	6.1 m	north-south axis	72	2	1	0	none

Table 2: Nodwell Longhouses. (Wright 1974)

the palisade was constructed immediately it may have constrained village settlement plan through the duration of the occupation. Wright (1974) suggests that the palisade was constructed in the early stages of village settlement. He also believes that there is a correlation between the longhouse located outside of the Nodwell village and the palisade (Wright 1974). Because the entrance way to the village is aligned with the entrance to this longhouse, Wright (1974:306) feels that these two structures were erected at the same time. Realistically, the alignment of the two entrance ways may have little bearing on the temporal period in which the palisade surrounding the Nodwell village was erected, but the presence of a palisade may have made it difficult for a new

house to be constructed within the village boundaries. Given the large open area in the west central area of the site, this too seems unlikely.

Nevertheless, it is entirely possible that the construction of this particular longhouse did influence the erection of the palisade feature. It is presumed that palisades were constructed prehistorically for the purpose of defence, but Ramsden (1988) has suggested that the erection of palisade walls may have been used to create a dichotomy between those who lived inside the village and those who lived outside. In this respect, the palisade may not be as much a defensive feature as a physical and symbolic representation of difference. Given that there was room within the Nodwell village for the construction of another house but the longhouse was constructed outside the confines of the palisade, the purposeful separation of those inside from those outside may have prompted palisade construction at any time in the village history.

Intra-site Similarities

Using only settlement data, House 1, while located outside the village and not completely excavated, does not appear to be significantly different from the other houses located within the palisade walls (Figure 14).

All of the houses associated with the Nodwell village were constructed in a similar fashion. Exterior house walls were constructed from posts ranging from 8-13 cm in diameter (Wright 1974). Larger interior posts supported the structure and during the restoration of the village it was discovered that these posts also

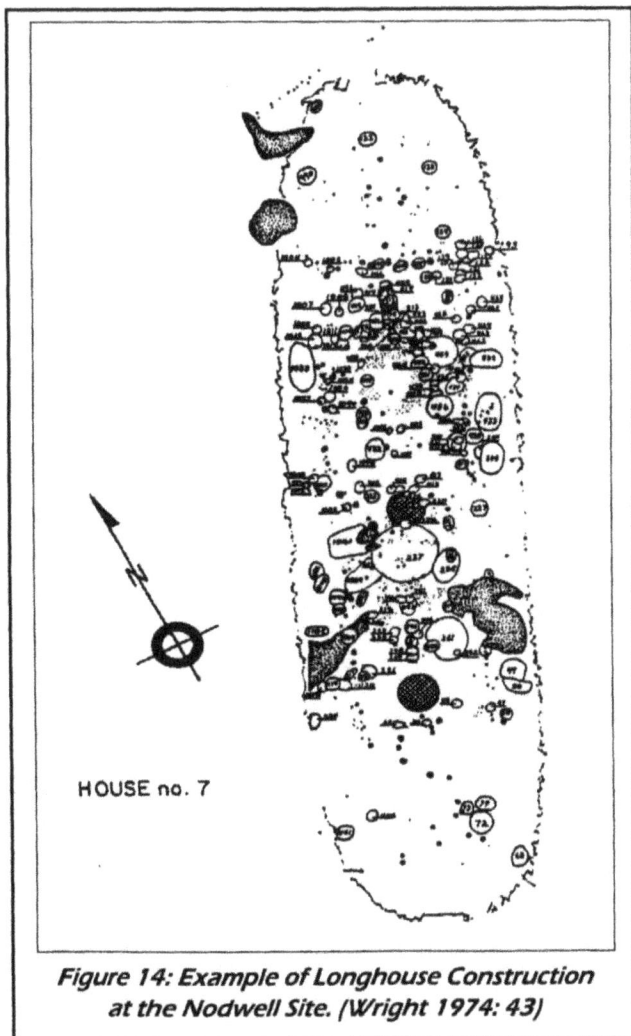

HOUSE no. 7

Figure 14: Example of Longhouse Construction at the Nodwell Site. (Wright 1974: 43)

acted as support posts for the bunklines running along either side of the houses, which were always 1.5 m wide (Wright 1974:15). Central hearth features, and interior pits located predominantly in the central corridor of the house and beneath the bunklines, were found in all houses (Wright 1974).

The uniformity of longhouse construction suggests that the occupants both within and outside the Nodwell village shared a similar residential strategy. Dodd (1984:219) suggested that "similarity of house styles within a village reflects the restrictions imposed by building materials, the communal nature of house building, and group identity and social cohesiveness". Therefore, the similarity of houses at the Nodwell village suggests that household populations shared a similar cultural identity. Another suggestion proposes that village plans may be related directly to the complexity of the economic strategy utilized by the inhabitants (Rafferty 1985). Rafferty (1985) indicates that forager settlements tend to be randomly arranged in keeping with frequent population movements and short term occupations, but agriculturalists, who are generally more sedentary, construct settlements with durable dwelling structures and coherent site plans.

In order to comprehend the cultural significance of village settlement patterns, Dodd (1984) undertook a cross-cultural survey of dwelling structures and found, like Rafferty (1985), that rectilinear houses like those observed at the Nodwell village were most often representative of sedentary, resource-rich communities because these houses are more readily enlarged to accommodate additional people and storage space (Dodd 1984:215). Furthermore, the longhouse symbolizes a communal living strategy, signifying subsistence cooperation, mutual defence and lineage association (Dodd 1984:215-216).

For regions elsewhere in southern Ontario, Chapdelaine (1993), Noble (1969), Trigger (1976:45-46) and others have suggested, via analogy with early historic Iroquoian society, that the appearance of longhouse villages is historically related to the adoption of a socio-political strategy based on matrilineal descent patterns, and the integration of an economic strategy based on food production. In this manner, it is believed that each longhouse is occupied by a matrilineally related household which not only resides under one roof but acts as a co-operative economic unit. Hayden (1977; 1979) challenged this assumption by suggesting that longhouse occupancy need not be restricted to a matrilineally related unit but merely a corporate group whose membership was flexible and related to the economic prosperity of the household. Regardless of the relationship between members, the household group was probably a social, political and economic unit which co-operated economically, lived communally, shared common property, recognized internal leaders, and was responsible for the safety and conduct of members (Warrick 1984:40). Therefore, the settlement pattern at the Nodwell village represents a structured socio-economic behaviour which stands in contrast to the fluid socio-economic strategy represented by settlement patterns at Middle Woodland sites in Bruce county.

Variation

At the Nodwell village the basic form and contents of the longhouse structures are similar, but upon a more vigorous inspection distinct variations between houses are observed. With reference to Table 2 house length, width, and orientation, as well as the number of pits, hearths, entrances and interior storage cubicles shows considerable variation. House lengths range from 12.2 m to 39 m and house widths range from 5.2 m to 8.2 m. The number of hearths per longhouse ranges from 1 to 6 and the number of pit features from 21 to 258. Certain houses have more than one entrance way and some houses include one or two end cubicles while others have none.

Variation due to Population

It has been suggested that longhouse size is related to the number of occupants in each house and that population size can account for much of the variation between houses (Casselberry 1974; Heidenreich 1971:115). Estimating population

in prehistoric longhouse villages in southern Ontario is a difficult procedure which is riddled with assumptions. Population calculations are premised on early historic documentation about Iroquoian villages which claimed that two families, averaging eight persons per family, shared each hearth within a longhouse (Tooker 1967:40; Heidenreich 1971:118). Projecting this type of detailed information into the prehistoric era is somewhat suspect, so Warrick (1990:301) utilized cross-cultural ethnographic references to determine that the average number of family members residing together in small-scale agricultural communities is 5.5.

The use of historical analogy is not the only problem which plagues population estimates at sites in southern Ontario. Many archaeological sites, including the Nodwell village, have been subject to ploughing throughout the 20th century and such activity may eradicate hearth features even in well preserved sites. As a result, many archaeologists will infer a certain number of hearths per longhouse based on house length even if no evidence of those hearths remain. This inference is not entirely logical given that we cannot be certain that these hearths really existed, and hearths inside houses are not always equally spaced (Varley and Cannon 1995).

Therefore, I have re-calculated population figures for the Nodwell village on the basis of eleven people per hearth (two families of 5.5) and multiplied by the number of undisputed hearths in each longhouse. The results of these calculations are presented in Table 3. These figures differ significantly from those reported by Wright (1974) who calculated Nodwell population using a figure of eight persons per family or sixteen people per hearth. Further, Wright increased the total number of hearths at the Nodwell site to account for those hearths he believed had been eradicated by deep ploughing and therefore his population estimate did not reflect the number of hearths actually observed. One final difference concerns the handling of closely spaced hearths within individual longhouses. Wright (1974) did not treat all closely spaced hearths in a uniform manner. In some houses Wright (1974) chose to treat two closely spaced hearths as a single feature, and in other houses as two distinct features. In the first population estimate recorded in Table 3 every excavated hearth is treated as a separate feature and included in the population equation.

Modified population estimates, which further reduce the total population of the Nodwell village, are also presented in Table 3. Wright (1974) observed a bilateral asymmetry in many of the Nodwell houses with regard to the numbers of pits located under bunklines. Since bunklines are believed to represent family dwelling spaces, pits associated with bunklines are generally equated with personal storage areas (Tooker 1967). When the distribution of pits underneath these bunklines is plotted, it is apparent that, in many cases, bunkline pits occur on only one side of the midline hearths (see Wright 1974: Figures 6-19). This suggests that, in some instances, only one family used the central hearth, and in other cases where bunkline pits are on both sides of hearths, two families shared hearths. Furthermore, House 10 was actually constructed with an asymmetrical bunkline which was much longer on one side of the house than on the other (Wright 1974:54). In this situation there was no possibility of family dwelling areas on both sides of three of the six hearths in this house. The modified population estimates therefore reflect the bilateral distribution of bunklines and bunkline pits.

Closely spaced hearths are present in Houses 4, 10 and 11. In each of these houses there are two closely spaced hearths. This may represent the shifting of a single hearth feature through time. Therefore, population estimates must be lowered again, as no more than two families would be associated with these double hearth features. Similarly, the placement of bunkline pits associated with these hearths must also be observed. If the double hearths in Houses 4, 10 and 11 are treated as single features, then population estimates from these houses are 16.5, 44 and 22 consecutively (Table 3).

Table 3 demonstrates that household population did not always dictate the size of the house itself. Some houses with low population densities were

larger than houses with higher population densities. However, if House 5, the biggest house with a population of only eleven, is eliminated then the two houses with the highest population densities (Houses 10 and 8) are also the largest houses. At some point in Nodwell's history House 5 was removed and overlain by Houses 6 and 9 (see Figure 13). If it is assumed that all of the houses in the Nodwell village were occupied simultaneously except House 5, then population estimates per living area do suggest that the houses with the largest populations are the largest.

House Number	Number Hearths	Population	Modified Population Estimate	Total House Area	Total Living Space (- cubicles)
House 1	3	33*	27.5*	unknown	unknown
House 2	2	22	11	94.2 m²	51.6 m²
House 3	2	22	16.5	121.0 m²	72.7 m²
House 4	3	33	22 (or 16.5)	158.2 m²	126.0 m²
House 5	1	11	11	319.8 m²	195.2 m²
House 6	2	22	16.5	192.2 m²	113.0 m²
House 7	1	11	11	229.5 m²	127.7 m²
House 8	4	44	33	309.5 m²	205.1 m²
House 9	3	33	27.5	210.5 m²	118.7 m²
House 10	6	66	49.5 (or 44)	317.3 m²	252.6 m²
House 11	3	33	27.5 (or 22)	249.9 m²	210.7 m²
House 12	2	22	16.5	74.4 m²	74.4 m²
		Total = 352	Total = 269.5 or = 253		

Table 3: Population Estimate for the Nodwell Village.
estimate based on incomplete excavation

Wright (1974) suggests that a more accurate calculation of population per house area should observe total living area but not the area of house end cubicles which are thought to have been used as storage areas. End cubicles include minimal pit features and no hearths, and are therefore not considered part of the living space. If living area (minus end cubicle area) is compared with population density per house then it is observed that houses with the largest populations still have the largest living areas.

Only House 7 and House 11 vary from this format, but House 10, the largest house, with the largest population continues to have the largest living space.

Variation, Population and Social Organization

Population estimates appear to show a strong correlation with house size. Perhaps a more significant question is why such dramatic population variation exists between houses? Hayden (1977; 1979) suggested that large longhouses with high populations may have been associated with high status households that had the ability to attract, direct and maintain larger populations under one roof. In turn, the increase in size of the corporate group occupying the house provides more productive bodies which would sustain or increase that household's wealth and status (Hayden 1977; 1979).

Hayden (1977:4; 1979:24) believes that high status houses are frequently associated with house extensions. Only one house at the Nodwell village provides evidence of a constructed extension. This is House 8 which not only has the second largest population in the village but also has the second largest total area and the third largest living space. Furthermore, Hayden (1977) has suggested that wealthier, larger households will have more storage area, higher pit and post densities, and increased hearth spacing to provide lower density living spaces. Unfortunately, no information regarding interior posts is available, but Hayden's (1977) other criteria have been tabulated in Table 4. Neither House 5, which probably precedes the occupation of the other houses, nor House 1, which was incompletely excavated are included in Table 4.

Table 4 demonstrates that there is only a small correlation between house size and the number of pits, the number of storage cubicles or the total storage area at the Nodwell site. House 8, which is the second largest house in the village does have the largest number of pits and storage space, but in general it is the mid-sized houses which appear to have the largest hearth spacing, storage area and number of pits. Given that House 8 is the only house in the village that was extended, it is possible that this house fits Hayden's high status household model. Nevertheless, this model fails to account for a number of other large houses which have small populations but large numbers of pits and large storage areas.

Total Area	Living Area	Population	Hearth Spacing	No. Cubicles	Storage Area	No. Pits	House
317.3 m²	252.6 m²	49.5 (or 44)	*	1	7.9 m²	151	10
309.5 m²	205.1 m²	33	6.7 m	2	14.3 m²	237	8
249.9 m²	210.7 m²	27.5 (or 22)	*	1	5.6 m²	98	11
229.5 m²	127.7 m²	11	**	2	13.4 m²	165	7
210.5 m²	118.7 m²	27.5	4.9 m	2	13.3 m²	137	9
192.2 m²	113.0 m²	16.5	11.6 m	2	11.0 m²	258	6
158.2 m²	126.0 m²	22 (or 16.5)	*	1	4.6 m²	89	4
121.0 m²	72.7 m²	16.5	4.1 m	2	6.7 m²	79	3
94.2 m²	51.6 m²	11	5.5 m	2	7.3 m²	21	2
74.4 m²	74.4 m²	16.5	1.8 m	none	0	72	12

Table 4: House Variation at the Nodwell Village.

* Hearth spacing too random to calculate distances,
** only 1 hearth in this house

It is possible that the large, empty houses were more recent constructions that were necessary when other houses became overcrowded due to population increase. However, Dodd (1984) has demonstrated that when new houses are added to the village without full village remodelling, the new houses tend to be small and located on the outsides of villages or in open courtyard areas.

Another possibility is that large houses with low populations were prepared for future population expansions such as family growth or immigration (Fogt and Ramsden 1996). Varley and Cannon (1995:94) suggest that these large houses may have been used to induce would-be members to join the household as large, empty houses were both physically capable of accepting new members, and the size of the house itself may have attracted new members by symbolically enhancing the household's prestige.

Warrick (1984) also maintains that there are other reasons for the variation in house size beyond population. He suggests that the largest households were not strictly wealth based because storage areas do not correlate well with household population estimates. Instead, Warrick (1984:42) believes that the longest houses in a village were associated with village leaders who would utilize larger houses not only as residences but to host community village councils, feasts or dances and for diplomatic associations with outside visitors. This situation does not require large residential membership or stores, merely greater space.

While the practice of constructing larger houses for village headmen is recognized in southern Ontario historically, it is difficult to test archaeologically. Warrick (1984:42) suggests that houses occupied by village leaders are likely to be located in different sectors of a village so that different community leaders are afforded the opportunity to host events. At the Nodwell village the two largest houses are located in different sections of the village with House 8 in the east and House 10 in the north.

The criteria which establish House 8 as unique have been outlined above, but there are also some internal features present in House 10 which suggest that it may have served a unique purpose. House 10 is the widest house in the village (if House 5 is eliminated). It has a bunkline which is slightly wider than all of the other houses (1.8 m vs. 1.5 m), and the bunklines running the length of each wall are not symmetrical. Rather, the bunkline on one wall is 9.1 metres longer than that on the other wall.

Furthermore, House 10 has very little storage area, having only one storage cubicle and only 151 pits.

It is therefore possible that some houses grew by incorporating new members, but other large, relatively empty houses may have served several functions including the preparation for future household population growth, the symbolic enhancement or representation of a household's prestige, and as a functional open space in which to hold inter and intra-community events (Fogt and Ramsden 1995; Varley and Cannon 1994; Warrick 1984). A final possibility would be that household variation is linked to temporal factors rather than social organization and that houses may have been constructed during successive re-occupations of the village. This possibility is explored further below.

Relationships Between Village Longhouses

If it is assumed that all of the Nodwell houses except House 5 were occupied simultaneously, then this village was inhabited by a population of approximately 250, living on approximately 1 hectare of land. Cross-cultural analyses of small neolithic communities demonstrate that beyond a threshold of 350 people, village residence patterns will usually breakdown into segregated and distinct residential units (Pearce 1984:208; Warrick 1984:48-50). This process is thought to reduce face to face contact, thereby reducing intra-village conflict and village fissioning (Warrick 1984:48-50). The process of re-organizing village settlement structure can occur with minimal physical disruption and usually involves the segregation of community members into different districts based on socio-political aggregations such as clans or lineages (Warrick 1984:48-50). While the population of the Nodwell site now appears smaller than the threshold number of 350, earlier population estimates by Wright (1974) were much higher than 350. An analysis of residential settlement patterns at the Nodwell site should help determine which of the population estimates is more accurate.

Residentially segregated aggregations of houses have been noted at many Iroquoian villages, both historic and prehistoric. Houses with similar orientations which run parallel to one another, and with entrance ways in close proximity to one another, are thought to represent clusters of affiliated relatives or other socially linked populations (Dodd 1984; Trigger 1973; Warrick 1984). Furthermore, these aggregations may be joined to one another by a series of exterior fences and share mutual middens. Fences are also used to separate aggregations (Warrick 1984:45-46). Each aggregation may contain a large house, thought to be a "chiefly" residence (Warrick 1984:50; Trigger 1981:37).

At the Nodwell village there were two preferred orientations for longhouses. Houses at the north and south ends of the village ran east-west, while houses in the centre of the village were oriented north-south (Table 2, Figure 13). On the basis of this information Pearce (1984:207) has suggested that two, and possibly three, socially distinct groups occupied the Nodwell village. In at least two of these "districts" there were large houses which could have been occupied by village leaders. However, there is no evidence of fences either connecting or separating village segments. Several houses had a series of exterior posts over entrance ways, or connecting houses to palisade walls (Wright 1974) but none of these features was used to connect or separate differing houses. Instead, Wright (1974) suggests that these fences may have been related to internal village defences because of their association with the palisade.

Entrance ways within the three "potential" community aggregations did not open in proximity to one another. Some houses had two doorways which opened to different directions, while others had only one doorway which frequently opened to the opposite direction from the entrance on the house adjacent to it (Table 2). Furthermore, the few middens located at the Nodwell site cannot be correlated with any population aggregations and were just as likely to be located between or outside the village walls as inside (Wright 1974). Interior middens were all located against palisade walls at the edges of the village. Finally, there is little evidence at the Nodwell site of village reconstruction for the purpose of re-aligning houses. Only House 5 was torn down, and while two houses were constructed overtop, this may relate more to the efficient use of village space than to community aggregations (Pearce 1984).

The Nodwell village was not overcrowded, but there appears to have been some concern with maintaining an open area at the western edge of the site, and the distribution of houses within the village may correlate with a requirement for an open, probably communal-use area. There are no houses, hearths or middens in this area and few posts or pits. Yet, entrance-ways for five of the ten interior houses (minus House 5) open onto this space. Furthermore, Houses 2, 3 and 12, the smallest houses in the village are tightly confined at the edges of the village even though they could have been constructed in the larger open western area (see Figure 13).

The placement of houses, entrance ways and middens at the Nodwell village does not support the existence of social aggregations. It is therefore probable that the population was too small to require this type of social organization common at Iroquoian sites. There does, however, seem to be an attempt by the Nodwell villagers to maintain an open area on the western side of the village which may have influenced the placement of houses. Wright (1974) suggests that defence may have played a role in house positioning, but the exterior fences he uses to support this hypothesis probably served other functions as protective entrance ways, porches and outdoor activity areas (Dodd 1984; Warrick 1984; Wright 1974). As a result, the Nodwell village appears to be what Warrick (1984:46-47) would call a "disordered village" that has a haphazard arrangement and no population segmentation.

This type of village organization is much more common among the early Iroquoian villages of the Late Woodland period than Middleport stage villages (Timmins 1997; Warrick 1984). Timmins (1997) and Wright (1986) have suggested that early Iroquoian villages, which lack household alignments and have small or highly variable house sizes, have weakly developed socio-political organization. Following this assumption, the Nodwell village settlement pattern reflects a small population which either had limited socio-political development or lacked the need for an increased level of organization. As a final note, I suggest that the population of the Nodwell site was so small that this group would not need to fission and this may be the reason no other villages similar to Nodwell were constructed prior to the Late Woodland abandonment of this region.

History of Village Occupation

The settlement pattern at the Nodwell site offers little insight into the sequence of village development. There are few superimposed houses (only House 5), and only one house extension (House 8). This reveals that House 5 was constructed prior to Houses 6 and 9 which were erected on top of House 5 (see Figure 13). Similarly, the extension of House 8 occurred sometime after the original construction of the house.

Dodd (1984) has suggested that more recent houses were most likely to be smaller and positioned in patio areas or on the edges of villages. The placement of the smallest houses (2, 3, and 12) is on the extreme edges of the village which might suggest these were the last houses to be constructed at the Nodwell village. As well, House 4 is a small house located in the open courtyard area at the western edge of the village, suggesting that it was also a more recent addition (see Figure 13). This would mean that Houses 6-11, located in the east, centre and north of the village were occupied first, with the smaller houses in the north and south coming sometime later (see Figure 13). However, there are several problems with this analysis. Primarily, there is no significant evidence to indicate that larger houses were constructed earlier. Furthermore, there are no settlement data to indicate if all the houses were even occupied at the same time. Some houses may have been constructed in anticipation of future occupation, and others may have been abandoned throughout the occupational history of this village. Due to the lack of overlapping features such possibilities cannot be determined

from settlement data alone. The addition of faunal and artifact analysis in Chapter 3 sheds more light on this problem.

While it is not possible to determine the developmental sequence of the Nodwell site strictly from settlement data, it may be possible to determine which houses had the longest occupational histories. Wright (1974) and Chapdelaine (1993) have argued that houses with more intensive distributions of pit and post features have greater temporal depth than houses in villages with few pits and posts. Tables 5 and 6 detail pit concentration per house. Figures for interior posts are unavailable.

House Number	No. Pits	No. Pits in Living Area	Living Area	Average Pits/m² of Living Area
2	21	17	51.6 m²	0.3/ m²
3	79	73	72.7 m²	1.0/ m²
4	89	85	126.0 m²	0.7/ m2
6	258	220	113.0 m²	1.9/ m²
7	165	153	127.7 m²	1.2/ m²
8	237	224	205.1 m²	1.1/ m²
9	137	118	118.7 m²	1.0/ m²
10	151	143	252.6 m²	0.6/ m²
11	98	96	210.7 m²	0.5/ m²
12	72	72	74.4 m²	1.0/ m²

Table 5: Pits Concentration Per House.

House Number	Pit Concentration	House Population
House 6	1.9/ m²	16.5
House 7	1.2/ m²	11
House 8	1.1/ m²	33
House 3	1.0/ m²	16.5
House 9	1.0/ m²	27.5
House 12	1.0/ m²	16.5
House 4	0.7/ m²	22 (or 16.5)
House 10	0.6/ m²	49.5 (or 44)
House 11	0.5/ m²	27.5 (or 22)
House 2	0.3/ m²	11

Table 6: Pit Concentration Per House in Descending Order.

Assuming that house pit density per square metre of living space provides a relative indication of the duration of house occupation, then House 6 would have been occupied longer than any other house in the village, and House 2 would have had the shortest occupation. There is almost no difference in pit density between Houses 7, 8, 3, 9 and 12 suggesting that they were occupied for a similar amount of time, while Houses 4, 10 and 11 may have had shorter occupations. Oddly, Houses 4, 10 and 11 are the only houses with grouped hearths, a factor usually associated with lengthy occupational periods.

Table 6 demonstrates that there is little correlation between the density of pit features and house population, suggesting that occupational duration rather than population numbers, may be a better explanation of pit density. Nevertheless, pit density as an indicator of temporal occupation of houses must be balanced against the social variables which may affect the density and distribution of pits within houses described above. For this reason, Houses 8 and 10 particularly, must be observed more closely because these two houses may have been the focus of intra-community socio-political activities and the distribution of features within these houses may reflect something other than duration of occupation (see Table 4).

Warrick (1988; 1990:265-293) has demonstrated that density of house wall-posts per metre of house circumference also reflects the duration of house occupation. Warrick (1990:268-269) assumed that throughout the history of every occupied longhouse, repair posts would need to be added at regular intervals to compensate for wood decay and other structural problems (Warrick 1990:268-269). Following this assumption, houses with higher densities of wall-posts/metre are assumed to have longer occupational histories because a higher incidence of repairs would have been necessary.

The primary step in estimating duration of house occupation using wall-posts density is to establish the original number of house-posts required to construct a longhouse. In order to establish the original number of wall-post density at the Nodwell site I analysed the

number of wall-posts per metre on the extension of House 8. The extension to House 8 was chosen because it is the only feature at the Nodwell village which definitively reflected a shorter period of occupation. The wall extension to House 8 had a 99.4 metre circumference and included 155 posts, giving an average of 3.5 wall-posts per metre. Table 7 presents the density of house wall-posts from the Nodwell village for all houses except House 5 and House 1, and demonstrates that all the Nodwell houses had a higher density of wall posts than the House 8 extension.

The analysis of wall-post density indicates a different set of houses had lengthy occupations from that indicated by the pit density analysis. Nevertheless, wall-post density may be a better indicator of duration of occupation than pit density as pit density may be influenced by other variables. Wall-post density indicates that Houses 11, 8, 9, and 2 had the lengthiest occupations. In terms of comparison between pit and wall-post density, only Houses 8 and 9 had relatively high densities of both features.

House Number	House Posts/Metre	
11	6.3	(540 posts)
8	5.7	(564 posts)
9	5.3	(394 posts)
2	5.2	(227 posts)
3	5	(238 posts)
10	5	(465 posts)
6	4.8	(325 posts)
4	4.7	(275 posts)
12	4.6	(168 posts)
7	4.5	(342 posts)

Table 7: House Wall-Post Density in Descending Order.

Perhaps a more significant result of the wall-post density analysis was that the average numbers of posts per metre at all the Nodwell houses was quite similar, suggesting that the duration of occupation for each house was about the same. The only exception to this was House 1, the only known house which was not completely excavated. Nevertheless, a significant proportion of House 1 was unearthed (a 59 metre circumference), and when the density of house-posts per metre was calculated, an average of 3.3 posts per metre was determined. This number is similar to the number of wall-posts calculated for the House 8 extension (3.5), and suggests that fewer replacement posts were added to this house and therefore the occupation of House 1 was brief.

Warrick (1988:49; 1990:272-295) estimated that Middle and Late Iroquoian longhouses in south-central Ontario had an average of 5.5 wall-posts per metre and that these houses had a lifespan of 20-30 years. This estimation was based on a combination of factors including: post deterioration rates for the most common woods used for longhouse construction (Eastern White Cedar and White Pine), the original numbers of posts per metre in longhouse walls, and the pattern of post replacement after decay. Given that the average number of wall-posts per metre from all houses at the Nodwell village except Houses 1 and 5 is 5.1, and that Eastern White Cedar was probably the wood used to construct houses at this village (Wright 1974), a similar lifespan is probable for these houses.

Annual Duration of Occupation

Middle Iroquoian villages are assumed to represent the year round sedentary settlement of the majority of the village population. Nevertheless, a small representation of Middleport special purpose sites, such as Methodist Point on Georgian Bay, suggests that portions of the village population left to pursue off-site activities such as fishing and hunting during the warmer months (Dodd et al 1990; Smith 1979). Of the 1492 pits excavated at the Nodwell site only 4.6%, or 69 pits, were located outside of the village longhouses. Furthermore, no hearth features were recovered outside of houses. It is unlikely that historic era ploughing would have systematically obliterated external features and left internal features intact. Therefore, there is no reason to suspect that this type of feature distribution is unrealistic.

Similar arrangements of features at other Iroquoian villages have been used to designate winter season occupations - when most of the activity would have occurred indoors (Sutton 1996:194). Wright (1974:292) believes that the Nodwell village achieved its peak occupation during the winter months, when off-site activity was most limited. This suggests that the Nodwell population sustained itself through the winter months on stored resources since naturally occurring resources are not readily available to large populations in the winter, and may further suggest that the palisade surrounding the Nodwell village was used to provide security for those resources. There are no data which clearly demonstrate the annual abandonment of the Nodwell village during the spring through fall period, so it should be assumed that a portion of the village population was always in residence. Without the integration of artifact and faunal data to shed light on the sequence of village development (see Chapter 3) we cannot know if the annual pattern of settlement changed through time.

Burials

The final settlement pattern data left to be examined concern the burial strategy associated with the Nodwell village. Partial remains of no more than three individuals were recovered from the Nodwell village. House 4 contained an articulated human leg and a single toe bone, and House 7 contained five human toe and finger bones along with a single canine (Wright 1974:87-88). No other human remains have been recovered from the Nodwell site.

Middleport stage interment patterns are dominated by ossuary burials which contain the remains of multiple, disarticulated, secondary interments (Dodd et al. 1990). The fragments of human remains recovered at the Nodwell village have therefore been interpreted as disinterred primary burials, disturbed when moving remains to ossuary locations. An ossuary burial has been located several kilometres from the Nodwell village which dates to the Middleport period and is probably related to the Nodwell village because no other cemeteries from this period have been identified in southern Bruce county. Unlike other Middleport ossuaries which contain as many as 512 individuals, BcHi 16 contains the remains of no more than 5 individuals (Dodd et al. 1990:354). This may reflect the small population of this village, although some would suggest it reflects a short occupational history for the entire village (Warrick 1990:252-253).

Dating the Nodwell Village

Wright (1974) has used ceramic seriation to date the Nodwell village to the mid 14th century (see Chapter 3). However, a sample of twelve radiocarbon dates taken from the pit contents of four of the Nodwell houses may also help to shed light on village chronology. These absolute dates, published in 1985, were largely dismissed by Wright (1985) as they represent a temporal occupation far greater than he expected.

Three of the dates recorded in Table 8 represent chronological periods not directly relevant to this research, but do illustrate the sporadic occupation of the Nodwell site by several populations ranging from early Archaic period hunter-gatherers, to the early Middle Woodland occupants, as well as a later historic period population. Furthermore, all the dates taken from the Nodwell site demonstrate the long-term use of the Nodwell site locale, a factor not considered by Wright (1974) in the development of his migration model.

Figure 15 demonstrates that the nine calibrated radiocarbon dates most significant to this research fall into three distinct clusters, deemed early, middle, and late.

House Number	Material Dated	Sample Number	Radiocarbon Years	Calibrated Date
House 3	wood	S-503	610 ± 75	AD 1270 - 1410
House 7	carbonised corn	S-1719	90 ± 45	AD 1420 - 1655
House 7	deer	S-1717	883 ± 120	AD 915 - 1280
House 7	fish	S-1718	910 ± 110	AD 905 - 1265
House 8	immature bear	S-1710	710 ± 40	AD 1230 - 1340
House 8	bear	S-1711	920 ± 65	AD 1015 - 1235
House 8	deer	S-1712	700 ± 40	AD 1235 - 1345
House 8	beaver	S-1714	895 ± 40	AD 1030 - 1250
House 8	fish	S-1713	1460 ± 45	AD 440 - 630
House 8	carbonised mammal	S-1716	2695 ± 70	1030 - 775 BC
House 8	clam shell	S-1715	1850 ± 50	AD 5 - 245
House 10	carbonised corn	S-1720	790 ± 55	AD 885 - 1155

Table 8: Nodwell Village Radiocarbon Dates. (Wright 1985)

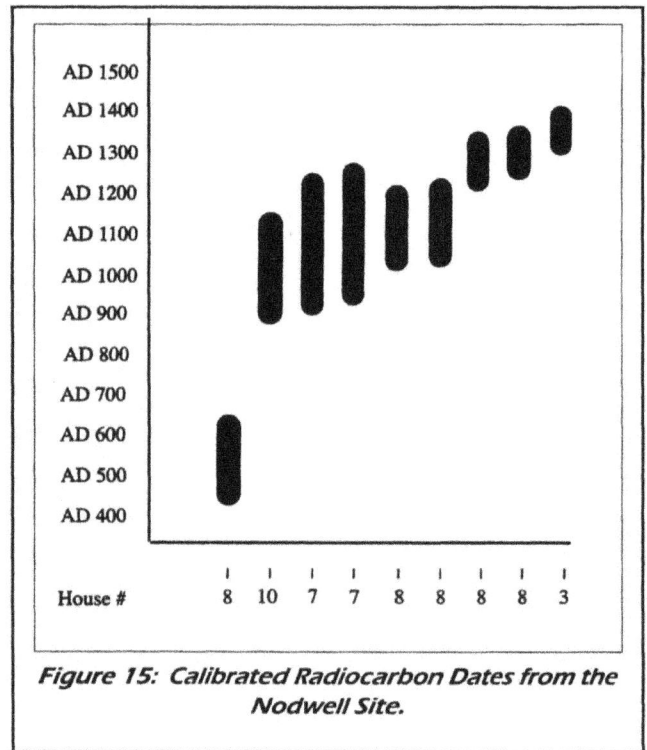

Figure 15: Calibrated Radiocarbon Dates from the Nodwell Site.

Overlapping time frames within the three clusters are highlighted (Figure 16) such that the early cluster is best defined by the period AD 440-630, the middle cluster cross-cuts the period AD 1030-1155, and the late dates cluster between AD 1270 and 1340.

Radiocarbon dates should always be used with a certain degree of caution. Sutton (1996) and Timmins (1985) have emphasized the problems of using radiocarbon dates to interpret the

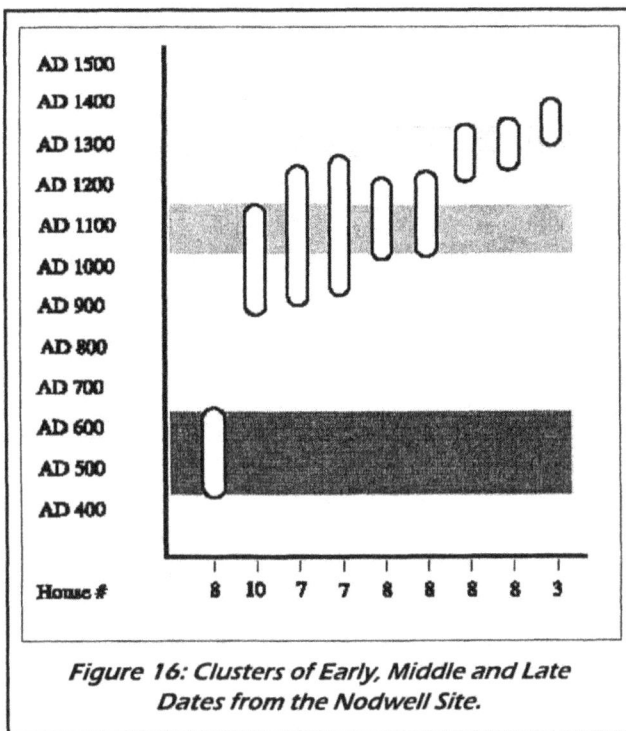

Figure 16: Clusters of Early, Middle and Late Dates from the Nodwell Site.

period of site occupation. Of particular concern is the dating of "old wood". Sutton (1986:83) points out that dating wood, or wood charcoal, does not date the period of site occupation but the period of the tree's death and therefore may lead to dates which are much older than the actual occupation of the site. Wright (1985) attempted to compensate for this problem by utilizing different types of organic remains to date the Nodwell occupation, not simply wood. Furthermore, Wright (1985) increased the sample of dates from one to twelve in order to reduce the significance of erroneous dates.

Sutton (1996:84) points out that radiocarbon dates attained from cultigens may be more closely related to the actual date of site occupation than other remains. Wright (1985) included two portions of carbonised maize in his dating sample. Furthermore, radiocarbon dated material from the period between AD 1280 and 1400, may have been subject to large fluctuations in cosmic ray intensity during this period and therefore a corresponding increase in the calibration curve for this period must be applied which increases the potential for dating error (Sutton 1996:84).

While the radiocarbon dates taken from the Nodwell site are not without problems, the large sample of dates, and the fact that these dates

are closely clustered within three time periods increases confidence. Because there is only one date associated with the early cluster this date should be treated more cautiously than the other clusters which are based on several dates each (see Figure 16).

Each of the radiocarbon dates were taken from pit contents within the longhouse structures at the Nodwell site. However, the early date taken from House 8 reflects the late Middle Woodland period, and villages like Nodwell are not associated with this period, so it is unlikely that this date reflects the temporal period during which House 8 was occupied. I suggest that this date represents an earlier Middle Woodland occupation of the Nodwell site and that the pit from which the dated fish bone was removed was associated with the Middle Woodland period. Given the large number of features in House 8, and the randomness of Middle Woodland settlement features, pits associated with an earlier occupation could have easily been overlooked in this structure. The same argument can be made for the even earlier archaic and early Middle Woodland dates from the Nodwell site. Unfortunately, there was no way to determine the exact pits from which the dated material was removed, or if these pits were associated with any temporally diagnostic remains.

The implications of the two remaining clusters of dates are intriguing. They suggest that a more intensive occupation of the Nodwell site began much earlier than the 14th century and perhaps as early as the 11th century. This time frame is associated with the transition from Middle to Late Woodland periods elsewhere in southern Ontario and suggests that the origin of the Nodwell village could be dated to the preceding Early Iroquoian period when longhouse village settlements are first established in other regions of the province (Fox 1990a; Timmins 1997; Williamson 1990).

If all twelve dates are accepted, then the Nodwell site had its origins centuries before the village itself developed, and was certainly part of the Middle Woodland settlement system. Although the radiocarbon dates indicate that the Nodwell occupation continued throughout the

Middleport sub-stage of the 14th century, they also imply that the Nodwell village could have developed gradually throughout the Late Woodland period rather than appearing abruptly on the cultural landscape of southern Bruce county at this time. Furthermore, the two clusters of Late Woodland dates may be used to suggest that there were two distinct phases of village development. At the very least, the expanded temporal range provided by the radiocarbon dates suggests that the occupation of the Nodwell village was much longer than the 25 year period suggested by Wright (1974) and this lengthy period of occupation may explain the variability of the settlement data outlined above.

Unfortunately, the random sample of radiocarbon dates sheds little light on the sequence of village development given that dates were sampled from only four houses, and multiple dates were taken from only two houses. Furthermore, it is possible that some of the dates may be associated with pits which predate the actual longhouse structures. Nevertheless, an attempt to define the sequence of longhouse occupation based on the radiocarbon dates would suggest that House 3 was a recent house, with Houses 7, 8 and 10 somewhat earlier. Recent dates were also associated with House 8, but continued occupation of this house over time could explain this discrepancy. Given that the life expectancy of this house was assumed to be no greater than thirty years based on house-post density, the possibility that the house itself was occupied or re-occupied over several centuries is highly unlikely. Therefore, it is probable that the dates represent various occupations of the site and the material from which the dates were taken may have mixed with settlement features from later occupations.

The various dates from the Nodwell site suggest repeated occupation over several centuries, and during that time the Nodwell settlement probably took various forms. However, various Late Woodland dates from the site indicate that there was a more intensive occupation of the Nodwell site during this period, and that there may have been a greater duration to the Iroquoian style village settlement of the Nodwell site than previously suspected (Wright 1974).

The possibility that the Nodwell village developed in increments with several periods of house construction and abandonment must now be considered. Timmins (1997) demonstrates this scenario at early Iroquoian villages which were frequently abandoned and re-occupied over lengthy temporal periods. The analysis of material culture in Chapter 3 will be used to further explore this possibility.

Summary

In summary, the Nodwell village is a multi-house, palisaded village with an interior settlement pattern distinct from earlier sites in the region. The location, size and structure of this village combined with cross-cultural ethnographic studies suggest that Nodwell represents a major shift in social, political and economic behaviour amongst the inhabitants of southern Bruce county.

The village includes a double palisade wall probably constructed for the purpose of defence but which probably also functioned to constrain the structure of later village development and separated those who lived inside the village from those who lived outside in both a physical and symbolic manner. Eleven houses were located inside the village and one outside. The similarities in the construction of all of the houses suggest that the occupants of the houses both inside and outside the village shared a similar cultural pattern.

The type of houses observed at Nodwell are most often associated with sedentary, resource rich communities, most frequently agriculturalists, because rectilinear houses are the easiest to expand when populations increase or more storage area is required. Furthermore, the village structure and housing style is thought to represent a communal living pattern in which multiple families inhabit each house and co-operate economically, and politically. Unlike the earlier Middle Woodland macroband settlements in Bruce county which appeared to have been occupied during warm months, the Nodwell village may have had its peak occupation during the winter as it appears that much of the activity at the Nodwell village occurred within houses (Wright 1974). Large winter villages are generally dependent on stored resources. If this is the case, the palisade surrounding the Nodwell village may represent attempts to protect those resources

Although the house forms are essentially the same, variation between these houses exists primarily with regard to the size of house, the location of house within the village plan, and the density and distribution of features associated with the houses. This variation is associated with household population density but may also reflect the standing of the inhabitants in terms of both wealth and political status, as well as the differential utilization of house space throughout the village, and the temporal period and duration of house occupancy.

Relationships between the houses were observed, and it was determined that the Nodwell village had a disordered settlement plan with few indicators of the household aggregations associated with Middle and Late Iroquoian villages. However, care was taken to preserve an open courtyard area in the westernmost portion of the village which served an undetermined use but which lacked hearth, pit or midden features.

Settlement data were utilized to examine the occupational history of the village, but few indicators of occupational sequence were found. There is evidence for only one house relocation as House 5 was torn down and superimposed by Houses 6 and 9. Pit and house wall-post density were examined by house in an attempt to establish differences in the duration of occupation, but it was determined that most houses were probably occupied for approximately thirty years. Further data are needed to established if these houses were occupied simultaneously or if there were periodic house abandonments.

Elsewhere in southern Ontario the type of settlement pattern observed at the Nodwell site is generally associated with the adoption of corn horticulture and the emergence of the Iroquoian culture pattern observed during the contact era. But the Nodwell village, with its disordered and variable settlement pattern is unlike other Middleport stage villages (Dodd et al. 1990). In

contrast to Middleport villages elsewhere in southern Ontario, the Nodwell village had a smaller population (Pearce 1984). The total area of the Nodwell village is also smaller than other known Middleport villages (Pearce 1984). Further, the settlement plan shows no evidence of the aggregated social groupings found at other Middleport villages (Pearce 1984). The small population at the Nodwell site probably made village aggregations unnecessary, and in this respect Nodwell may be similar to villages of the early Iroquoian phase. Like other Middleport villages though, the Nodwell site is located on sandy soil, and its placement and design demonstrates a concern with defence.

The differences which exist between the Nodwell village and other Middleport villages may reflect regional variability, but the differences may be due to the duration of the occupation of the Nodwell village which radiocarbon dates suggest was lengthier than the Middleport substage. If the dates are accepted, then the Nodwell village may have originated during the early Late Woodland period.

Late Woodland Regional Settlement Pattern

Late Woodland Pre-Iroquoian

Although radiocarbon dates indicate that the Nodwell site was occupied from the Middle Woodland period through the middle Late Woodland period, little is known about the regional settlement system of southern Bruce county during this 300 year period. This lack of information has tempted some researchers to suggest that southern Bruce county was abandoned following the Middle Woodland period (Finlayson 1977; Wright 1974). Given that the Nodwell site was occupied during this period it is unlikely that the rest of the region was abandoned. The material culture analysis from each of the known sites in southern Bruce county (see Chapter 3) identified ceramics diagnostic of the pre-Iroquoian early Late Woodland period at five sites (Figure 17 and Table 9). Furthermore, body sherds with cord-impressed designs which were common during the period spanning the very late Middle Woodland through the Uren sub-stage of the

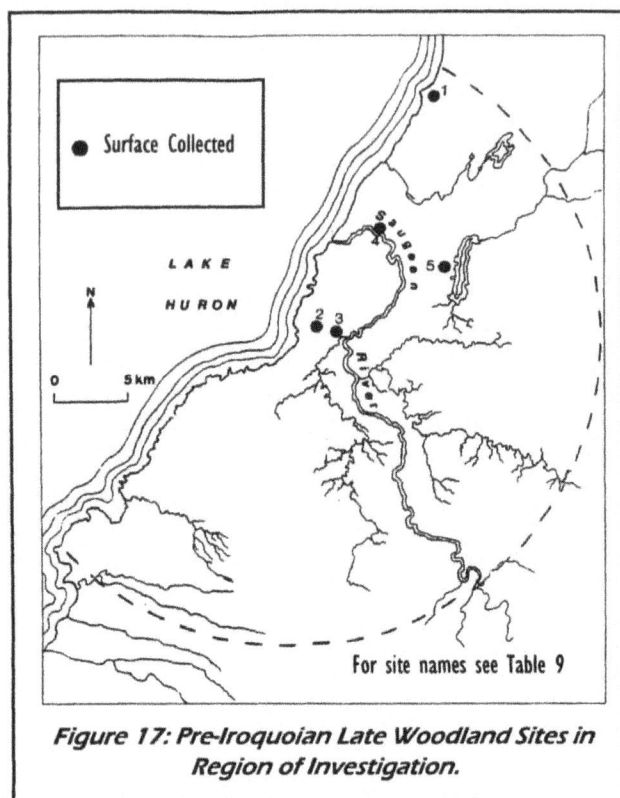

Figure 17: Pre-Iroquoian Late Woodland Sites in Region of Investigation.

Map legend: Surface Collected · LAKE HURON · N · 0 5 km · For site names see Table 9

radiocarbon dated to AD 928 ± 138 when calibrated with a single standard deviation (Ferris 1988).

Unlike the Hunter/Frenchman's Bay site, the remaining four sites containing pre-Iroquoian Late Woodland diagnostic material were all occupied throughout the Middle Woodland period and it is impossible to directly associate specific settlement features from these sites with the early Late Woodland period. However, it is probable that these sites continued to be inhabited for many of the same reasons they were occupied during the Middle Woodland period. Two of these sites are situated in places where fish resources would have been abundant, while BcHi-16 and BcHi-2 are situated inland and were probably hunting campsites. Furthermore, assemblages of ceramic body sherds with cord- impressed designs, associated with the transitional period between the late Middle Woodland through to the Uren sub-stage of the Late Woodland period were identified at an additional five sites in southern Bruce county, all of which had earlier Middle Woodland occupations (see Table 22, Chapter 3). Again, it appears that most of these sites were small campsites during this period.

Late Woodland period, were also present in the collections made at nine sites in southern Bruce county (see Table 22, Chapter 3) (Wright 1966).

Unfortunately, the multi-component nature of most of these sites makes it impossible to associate specific settlement data with this time period, and it is therefore difficult to interpret the nature of the early Late Woodland occupation. The only definite settlement features associated with this period are from the Hunter/ Frenchman's Bay site, a 0.35 hectare site located along the Lake Huron shoreline to the north of present day Southampton, Ontario. This site, which includes a lithic chipping area and a variety of fish and land mammal remains clustered in "activity areas" is not known to be occupied before the early Late Woodland period (Fox 1989:10).

The ephemeral settlement features, and the location of the Hunter/Frenchman's Bay site can be used to suggest that this site was a small campsite which had a similar form to most of the Middle Woodland sites of southern Bruce county. The faunal remains recovered from the site, which are detailed in Chapter 3, indicate that the site was occupied between spring and fall. Carbonised residue from a diagnostic pot was

Site Name	Borden Number	Location	Site Size	Site Type	Dating Method
1. Hunter/ Frenchman's Bay	BdHh - 5	Lake Huron Shoreline	0.35 hectares (70x50 m)	campsite	diagnostics
2. Port Elgin Cemetery	BcHi - 2	Huron Fringe, Port Elgin	unknown	campsite	diagnostics
3. Boiled Baby	BcHi - 16	Huron Fringe, east of Port Elgin	unknown	campsite	diagnostics
4. Donaldson	BdHi- 1	Saugeen Bluffs	unknown	campsite	diagnostic
5. Busch	BcHh - 6	Arran Drumlin Fields, Arran Lake	unknown	campsite	diagnostic

Table 9: Pre-Iroquoian Late Woodland Settlement Pattern Data for Bruce County.

(Finlayson 1977; Fox 1988; 1989; Shutt 1951; 1952).

46

Elsewhere in southern Ontario, early Late Woodland ceramics are associated with the shift to a sedentary settlement pattern and the addition of corn horticulture to the annual pattern of resource extraction, but in southern Bruce county there are no settlement data to indicate that a similar shift in socio-economic behaviour occurred at this time. Given that there are numerous early Late Woodland sites in this region, and that these sites are located in the same places as the earlier Middle Woodland sites, much of the settlement-subsistence system of the early Late Woodland population appears to be a continuation of the Middle Woodland pattern. This may be the reason that previous researchers have not recognized pre-Middleport "Late Woodland" settlement in this region.

However, the paucity of diagnostic remains recovered from these sites indicate that there was some change to the overall settlement system in southern Bruce county. Primarily, the early Late Woodland occupations appear to have been smaller, with no macroband settlements along the Saugeen River valley like the Middle Woodland Thede and Donaldson sites. It is possible that macroband habitation sites dating to the early Late Woodland period have just not been located, but it is probable that the focus of macroband settlement during the early Late Woodland was inland at the Nodwell site. Not only are there numerous radiocarbon dates suggesting this site was occupied at this time, but the Nodwell site had a much higher frequency of cord-impressed sherds than any other site in southern Bruce county (see Table 22, Chapter 3).

Radiocarbon dates demonstrate that as many as three of the Nodwell village houses may have been constructed during this period. However, it may be unwise to base the sequence of longhouse construction simply on radiocarbon dates (see above). It is therefore possible that the Nodwell site was simply a large campsite at this time. However, settlement data from the Nodwell site do not support this hypothesis. Furthermore, the occupants of the earlier Donaldson site were already living in longhouse structures and there is no reason to assume that this practice did not continue into the early Late Woodland period.

An analysis of the material culture from the Nodwell village presented in Chapter 3 indicates that the majority of cord-impressed sherds came from House 5, which settlement data demonstrate to be one of the earliest houses constructed at the site. Unlike the other houses at the Nodwell village, House 5 contained no material diagnostic of the middle Late Woodland period. Furthermore, the rimsherds recovered from House 5 were unlike those recovered from other Nodwell houses because they are not representative of the Iroquoian tradition. The House 5 rimsherds resemble those made by Western Basin foragers at between AD 1100 and 1200 (see Chapter 3) (Murphy and Ferris 1990). While population estimates for House 5 were very small, hearth features used to estimate population may have been destroyed in this house which was torn down and replaced by two later houses, and the population was probably larger than estimated.

I therefore suggest that House 5 at the Nodwell site became the focus of macroband occupation at some point during the early Late Woodland period, representing a shift in the settlement system away from the Middle Woodland macroband habitation sites along the Saugeen River, to an inland location where natural resources were not as abundant. For this move to have been possible the occupants of the Nodwell site would have had to have access to stored fish resources which were not readily available in the area surrounding the Nodwell site. These resources could have been harvested at the same resource extraction locations always used by the indigenous inhabitants of the region, explaining the continued use of these regional campsites. The shift in macroband habitation location during the early Late Woodland period may have been a defensive strategy designed to protect subsistence goods following the period of territorial constriction and population growth experienced in that late Middle Woodland period. By moving the primary settlement away from the major river and canoe route in the region, the population of southern Bruce county could better protect their staples from outside threats.

Another possibility is that the Nodwell site became the focus of a winter macroband habitation during the early Late Woodland period. If this was the case, then the population of southern Bruce county may have gathered at the inland Nodwell site for the winter and dispersed to smaller resource extraction sites from spring through fall. Limited evidence including the distribution of pit features and pit contents (see Chapter 3) can be used to suggest that the earlier Donaldson longhouses were already being occupied during the winter months. It is difficult to determine from settlement features at the Nodwell site, if House 5 represents a winter occupation, but the analysis of subsistence remains and material culture in Chapter 3 explores this possibility in greater detail. Winter settlement aggregations definitely require stored foodstuffs, and the shift to winter habitation at the inland Nodwell site may have therefore been a defensive measure designed to protect these stores which may have been at risk along the major waterway of the Saugeen River.

Middleport Horizon

During the Middleport sub-stage twelve sites were occupied and utilized in southern Bruce county (Figure 18), a reduction from the thirteen (if Nodwell is included) sites known to be occupied during the preceding Middle Woodland period. Only one site remained on the shore of Arran Lake, while one site continued to be utilized in the Arran drumlin fields. Three sites remain in use along the bluffs fronting the Saugeen River, and the two sites which clustered around the mouth of the Saugeen River at the shore of Lake Huron during the Middle Woodland period were still functioning. Two sites were now located atop the glacial Lake Algonquin strandline overlooking Lake Huron, and two sites located at the eastern edge of the sandy Huron fringe within the town limits of present day Port Elgin, Ontario continued to be occupied. Finally, a single site located along the shore of Lake Huron in the sheltered Mirimachi Bay continued to function. No other sites have been located within the study area dating to the Middleport sub-stage. The regional settlement pattern reflected by the twelve sites above

includes a series of small and large campsites, as well as a single village and a cemetery.

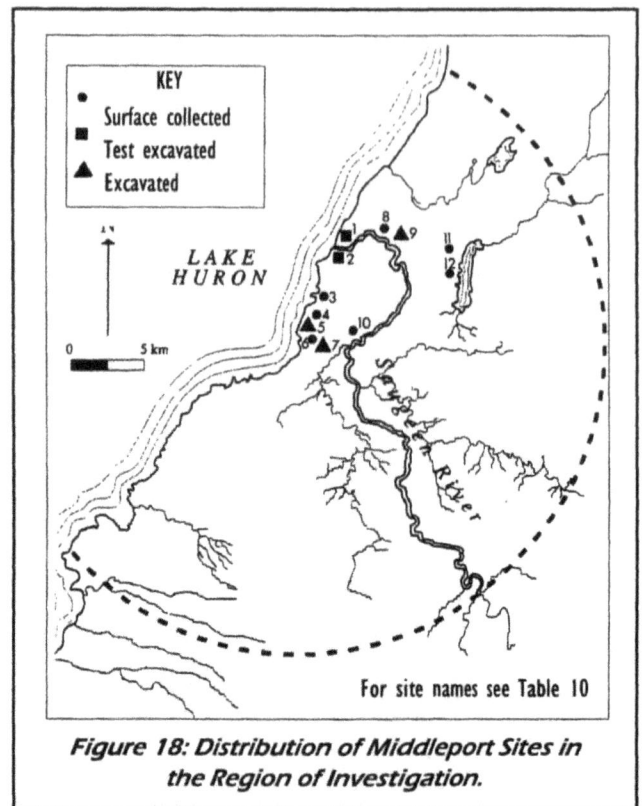

Figure 18: Distribution of Middleport Sites in the Region of Investigation.

To date, Middleport settlement patterns have been well investigated at two levels. Primarily, research has concentrated on interpreting the internal settlement patterns of specific village sites and therefore sheds light on the internal organization of individual communities (Dodd 1984; Pearce 1984; Wright 1974). Secondly, settlement pattern research has focussed on explaining the distribution of Middleport horizon villages across southern Ontario (Dodd et al. 1990; Kapches 1981; Pearce 1984; Warrick 1984). As a result, regional investigations have helped to define local and extralocal village settlement sequences, explored regional variability between village sites and defined chronological and cultural relationships between Middleport villages clustering in different regions. The Middleport sub-stage has thus been identified as the era when horticulture became the dominant economic pursuit, populations grew rapidly, and an Iroquoian-style culture pattern expanded, largely through migration, throughout most of southern Ontario. However, much of the research into Middleport

Site Name, Borden#	Location	Site Size	Features	Site Type	DatingMethod
1. North Shore (BdHi-2)	mouth of Saugeen River	uncertain "small"	artifact clusters	campsite	diagnostics
2. Shutt (BcHi-6)	mouth of Saugeen River	uncertain	hearths artifact clusters	campsite	diagnostics
3. Mirimachi Bay (BcHi-4)	Lake Huron Shoreline	uncertain "small"	hearths artifact clusters	campsite	diagnostics
4. North Elgin	Lake Algonquin Strandline, PortElgin	uncertain "small"	artifact clusters	campsite	diagnostics
5. Nodwell (BcHi-3)	Lake Algonquin Strandline, Port Elgin	1 hectare	houses, middens palisade, pits	village	radiocarbon diagnostics
6. Port Elgin Cemetery (BcHi-2)	Huron Fringe, Port Elgin	uncertain "small"	artifact clusters	campsite	diagnostics
7. Boiled Baby (BcHi-16)	Huron Fringe, east of Port Elgin	uncertain "substantial"	burials hearth floor artifact clusters	campsite, cemetery	diagnostics
8. Indian Church	Saugeen Bluffs	0.01 hectares (2x5m)	1 artifact cluster	campsite	diagnostics
9. Donaldson (BdHi-1)	Saugeen Bluffs	uncertain "small"	artifact clusters	campsite	diagnostics
10. Thede (BcHi-7)	Saugeen Bluffs	uncertain "small"	artifact cluster	campsite	diagnostics
11. Kirkland Farm	Arran DrumlinField	uncertain "limited"	artifact clusters	campsite	diagnostics
12. Busch (BcHh-6)	Arran Drumlinfield, Arran Lake	1.5 hectares (300x50m)	hearths artifact clusters	habitation site	diagnostics

Table 10: The Middleport Horizon Regional Settlement Pattern of Bruce County.

(Fox 1987a; Knechtel 1955; Lee 1951a:70-75; 1951b; Rankin 1997; Shutt 1951; 1952; Wright 1953a; 1953b; 1974; Wright and Anderson 1963:30).

settlement patterns has been initiated within the context of culture-history and has ultimately been used to explore the development of the historical Iroquoian culture pattern by demonstrating the expansion and subsequent regional evolution of the separate ethnic Iroquoian tribes witnessed during the contact period (Kapches 1981; Wright 1966). The focus on explaining contact period culture patterns has overshadowed attempts to explain the process and context of the Middleport expansion. Furthermore, village based settlement studies have dominated research into the Middleport horizon and the role of smaller, special purpose sites has frequently been overlooked. This has resulted in a limited understanding of community socio-economic structure. Given the

reliance on simple culture-historic models, ethnohistoric analogy and the incomplete use of local settlement strategies, Middleport settlement patterns remain poorly understood. The diversity of known Middleport period settlements in southern Bruce county creates an opportunity to move outside of village based settlement pattern studies and examine the settlement system of a Middleport community.

The Middleport occupation of southern Bruce county appears to be based on a series of small and large settlements, not simply a single village community. At the core of this complex occupation is the Nodwell village itself, but other smaller campsites, most often associated with fishing localities, are located throughout the region. Understanding this pattern is difficult given that very few similar settlement patterns have been analysed for this period. However, several other cabins and campsites associated with the Middleport sub-stage have been recorded throughout southern Ontario suggesting that the range of sites present in southern Bruce county is not unusual (Dodd 1990; Smith 1979; Kenyon 1959). The interpretations offered for these miscellaneous sites suggest that they were used for specific purposes such as fishing, gathering or trading (Stewart 1974; Smith 1979). Furthermore, the regular appearance of these sites throughout southern Ontario suggests a high degree of residential mobility occurred in the Middleport substage and that village settlements were only part of a seasonal round. In southern Bruce county the regional settlement system appears to represent a community land use strategy based largely on access to desirable natural resources from a variety of special purpose sites. Settlement data including the location, size and distribution of site features can be used to examine this assumption.

Of the eleven Middleport habitations and campsites in southern Bruce county none are located in defensible positions; no sites are located strategically on hilltops or isolated locations. In fact, five sites are located along the Saugeen River valley at either the river mouth or along small sets of rapids, one site is found along the swampy shores of inland Arran Lake, one site is located in a sheltered bay fronting Lake Huron and four sites are located in forested zones near small creeks. The sites along the Saugeen River are located in ideal positions for fishing river spawning species. Even today these locations remain popular destinations for fishermen. The site located along the shores of Arran Lake may have been inhabited for a number of reasons. The swampy shoreline would have created the ideal environment from which to hunt various avian and mammalian species, and provided access to a large number of plant species for gathering. Arran Lake, which is fed by numerous creeks could also have been used as a fishing location. The function of the four inland sites cannot be determined from site location, but they probably represent small campsites associated with hunting and

gathering activities. Finally, the site located on the sheltered Mirimachi Bay of Lake Huron provides an ideal location for lake fishing.

The locations of these sites alone suggests that these places were desirable for hunting, fishing and collecting but the size of campsites and distribution of features can also be used to define the role of these campsites in the southern Bruce county settlement system. The size of the campsites within the research area can generally be considered small. Unfortunately, the exact size of the campsites was not always recorded by the original investigators, and it is often difficult to determine site size from the surveyed surface scatters and test pits. Furthermore, no full excavation has been undertaken of any of the Middleport components at these sites. However, general estimates of size were recorded for some of the eleven non-village sites. Wright (pers. comm.) claims that the majority of these sites appeared no bigger than a single longhouse and Knechtel (1955) claimed that the Middleport material from the Thede, Donaldson and Indian Church sites was limited to small, discreet components that would not exceed more that a few square metres. Furthermore, the Middleport components of the Shutt and North Shore sites were located in less than ten closely packed test units respectively. Only the Busch site with an approximate size of 300 x 50 metres can be considered substantial and for this reason has assumed the label of habitation site in the region typology (Fox 1987a).

If these sites were used by small populations for the purposes of resource extraction it would follow that most of the sites would be of a limited size, particularly since some of the sites are located at tightly circumscribed resource gathering locations like those beside sets of rapids. The size and locations of the resource extraction areas themselves may therefore have limited the size of the adjacent campsite. Given that five campsites are located along the banks of the Saugeen River during the Middleport substage, it is possible that small groups, or perhaps family units, utilized differing, well spaced and circumscribed locations for fishing activities. The same scenario may exist for the four campsites probably associated with inland hunting and gathering. The small size of these campsites may also reflect their limited annual use.

However, the Busch site on Arran Lake is much bigger than the other Middleport campsites and may represent a different type of site. Unlike the small campsites of southern Bruce county which were probably restricted in terms of both size and population due to both function and geographical constraints, the large open shoreline of Arran Lake and the potential for differing types of resource extraction activities to take place in the vicinity of the Busch site, could have made this location accessible to a larger population for longer periods of time, perhaps even have acted as a small summer village. This assumption finds some support in the number of identifiable surface features, consisting of a number of hearths and dense artifact clusters which were absent from all but one other campsite in southern Bruce county. Most small, seasonally utilized campsites accumulate only minimal amounts of cultural debris so it is not unlikely that a campsite could be re-established annually in approximately the same location (Foley 1981a). This is especially true when the campsite is established to access resources from a specific location. However, when larger groups of people gather together debris accumulates rapidly, even in seasonally occupied sites, and the placement of succeeding occupations may shift position so that it will not necessarily overlay the previous year's refuse. The linear arrangement of hearth features at the Busch site across 300 metres may reflect this strategy and therefore the entire site probably represents the accumulation of several annual occupations of a large population.

The only other site with known cultural features is BcHi-16, located on a small creek on the outskirts of present day Port Elgin. Features, including a single hearth floor and several human interments were located due to surface erosion (Wright 1953b). Numerous clusters of artifacts were also recorded here (Knechtel 1955). Wright (1953b) believed BcHi-16 served two purposes; 1) as a seasonal campsite, and 2) as a Middleport cemetery. This site's importance as a burial ground was suggested because the disarticulated remains of at least

five individuals here are, apart from a scattering of disarticulated human remains recovered at the Nodwell village, the only known Middleport burials in the region. Furthermore, the BcHi-16 cemetery marks the transition in cemetery style from the individual burials of the Middle Woodland Donaldson occupation to an ossuary style interment. The surface scattering of artifacts, and single hearth feature found at the site also identifies BcHi-16 as a campsite.

The Middleport campsites in southern Bruce county are predominantly small, special purpose resource collection sites where small groups went to engage in seasonally significant hunting, fishing and gathering activities. Most of these activities would have been undertaken during the period from spring through fall when spawning fish, migratory birds, and plants were most abundant. Mammal hunting could no doubt occur throughout the winter and certain sites may have been utilized during this season. Nevertheless, the pattern of small campsites, as well as the larger Busch habitation site on Arran Lake which may have acted as a summer village, suggests that the Middleport population used a wide range of sites throughout a considerable territory.

The only known village settlement located in southern Bruce county during the Middleport sub-stage was Nodwell. When observed in isolation, the Nodwell village, with its twelve longhouses and double palisades appears to represent a sedentary Middleport period farming community. However, when the Nodwell village is observed within a regional context, the interpretation of village organization must shift to accommodate the variety of off-site activities and land-use strategies used during this era.

The distribution of pit features at the Nodwell village suggested that this site experienced its primary occupation during the winter months (Wright 1974). While it is unlikely that the Nodwell village was ever completely abandoned between spring and fall much of the community was probably engaged in activities elsewhere. Given the large number of small sites located in places where spring through fall resources were abundant it is probable that the focus of community activity was away from the village during warmer months. The limited size of the majority of these campsites suggests that they were probably occupied by small populations, perhaps work parties or family units from this larger community, for the purpose of acquiring naturally occurring resources. The large size of the Busch site, on Arran Lake, suggests that this site may have become the focus of community settlement during the warmer months. The settlement pattern observed in southern Bruce county suggests that the Nodwell village was only part of the annual settlement system and that the occupants of southern Bruce county engaged in a semi-sedentary residence pattern. As explained above, this settlement system may have its origins in the earlier Late Woodland.

Given the marginal nature of southern Bruce county in terms of agricultural success even today, it may have been necessary for the local Middleport population to acquire the abundant natural resources of this region (see Chapter 3). It should also be pointed out that none of the small sites in southern Bruce county appear to be farming cabins, from which crops were tended during the summer months. This further suggests that farming may not have been a significant economic pursuit in this region.

The settlement strategy suggested has been identified elsewhere in southern Ontario. Ramsden (n.d.) has recently suggested that the 15th and 16th century Iroquoian population of the Upper Trent valley, in central Ontario, employed a semi-sedentary strategy, making seasonally scheduled moves to different sites throughout the year in order to access a variety of resources. Ramsden (n.d.) suggests that this strategy was chosen to allow for long-term sustainable use of the natural resources available in the Upper Trent. While the 15th and 16th century inhabitants of the Upper Trent valley were obviously a distinct population from the 14th century inhabitants of southern Bruce county, similarities exist between the regions of occupation. Both regions face climatic and geographical constraints which make the pursuit of a farming economy difficult.

Chapdelaine (1993:175) has suggested that many of the Iroquoian groups in southern Ontario employed a semi-sedentary strategy.

He believes that villages were only occupied by a fraction of the community at any given time, and that some portion of the community always maintained a high degree of mobility (Chapdelaine 1993). Chapdelaine (1993) further states that mixed farming and foraging economies were vital to the survival of Iroquoian communities, and at times natural resources may have been more important than horticultural produce.

Furthermore, when the parameters of the Bruce county research area are expanded from 20 km radius to a 40 km zone a Middleport sub-stage settlement pattern similar in nature to the one found in the research area is observed (Figure 19). Small campsites situated at the mouths and rapids of large rivers, along the shore of Lake Huron, and along small creeks dominate the regions to the north and south of the research area. The campsites in the southern portion of the expanded zone may be associated with the occupation of the larger Inverhuron site. The Inverhuron site is a Middleport horizon occupation which may not have been a village but which was definitely larger and more permanently occupied than the campsites which surround it (Kenyon 1959).

Unfortunately, the Middleport occupation of the Inverhuron sites is not well understood because the site contains a mixture of material from both earlier and later occupations making the Middleport occupation difficult to discern (Kenyon 1959). It may not be unreasonable to assume however, that a pattern of semi-sedentism like that which existed in southern Bruce county was employed here during the Middleport era. In southern Bruce county, Inverhuron and the Upper Trent valley the climate and geography may have limited the success of a horticultural economy and contributed to the development of a semi-sedentary community settlement system.

If the Nodwell village was not present in southern Bruce county the regional settlement system would resemble that normally associated with mobile foragers, given the small scatter of ephemeral sites located at key resource extraction areas. In fact, the regional settlement system identified in southern Bruce county is

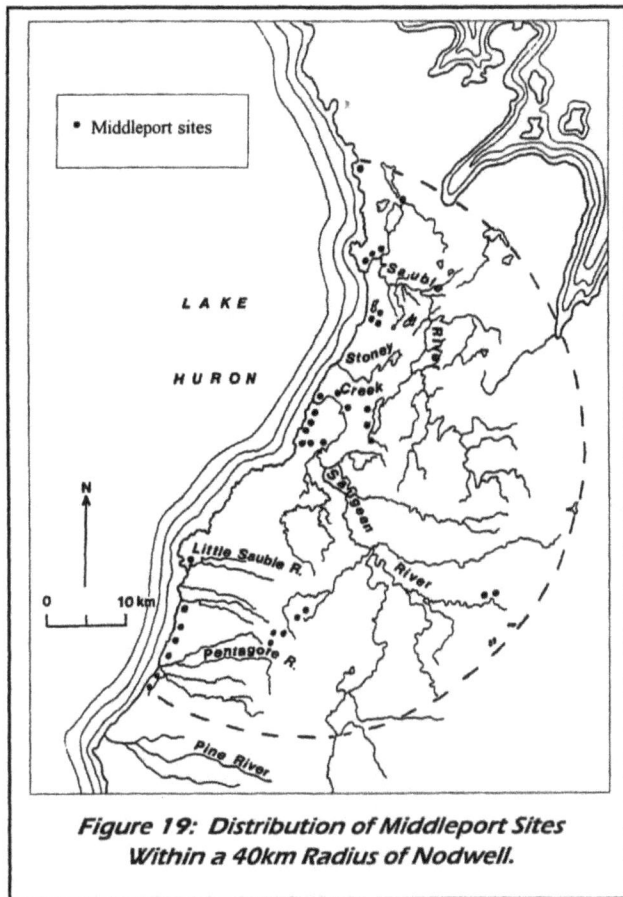

Figure 19: Distribution of Middleport Sites Within a 40km Radius of Nodwell.

almost identical, except for the appearance of the Nodwell village and the discontinuance of the Krug site on Arran Lake, to that observed in the Middle Woodland period, though future excavation of these campsites may shed light on other settlement differences. However, radiocarbon dates from Nodwell increase the occupational span of this site and demonstrate it was part of the earlier Middle Woodland settlement system. If this is the case, there is a great deal of continuity in the regional settlement system of southern Bruce county throughout the Middle and Late Woodland periods and the changes to the socio-economic system may not be as dramatic as was first supposed.

After Nodwell: The Regional Settlement Pattern

Following the abandonment of the Nodwell village there appears to be a drastic change in the regional settlement pattern of southern

Bruce county as only four archaeological sites post-date the Middleport horizon (Table 11, Figure 20). The Donaldson site occupation dates to the early historic era. The Nodwell site, the Port Elgin site and Hunter-Frenchman's Bay were all used during the late prehistoric or early historic period. This suggests that southern Bruce county was more or less abandoned following the Middleport occupation.

The location of the Donaldson and Hunter-Frenchman's Bay sites, combined with the small distribution of features from these sites, suggests that they functioned as fishing camps. Given that no artifacts or features associated with the protohistoric period have been recovered from Nodwell, the site was probably no more than a small campsite. The Port Elgin site contained no more than an isolated burial. The pattern represented by the distribution and size of the sites suggests that southern Bruce county was used only sporadically during this era, perhaps by groups travelling through the area en route to other locations. It is possible that either Algonkian foragers or Iroquoian farmers periodically passed through Bruce county during the protohistoric period and established these sites.

Site Name, Borden #	Location	Site Size	Features	Site Type	Dating Method
1. Donaldson (BdHi-1)	Saugeen Bluffs	0.12 hectares (12x10m)	longhouse hearth artifact cluster	campsite	diagnostics
2. Port Elgin Burial	Huron Fringe, Port Elgin	0.002 hectares (1x2m)	burial	burial	bone condition
3. Hunter/ Frenchman's Bay (BdHh-5)	Lake Huron Shoreline	0.35 hectares (70x50m)	activity areas	campsite	diagnostics
4. Nodwell (BcHi-3)	Lake Algonquin Strandline, Port Elgin	unknown	unknown	campsite	radiocarbon date

Table 11: The Post Nodwell Settlement Pattern Data for Southern Bruce County.

(Clark-Wilson and Spence 1988; Finlayson 1977:498; Fox 1987a:6; Fox 1989:3; Wright 1985).

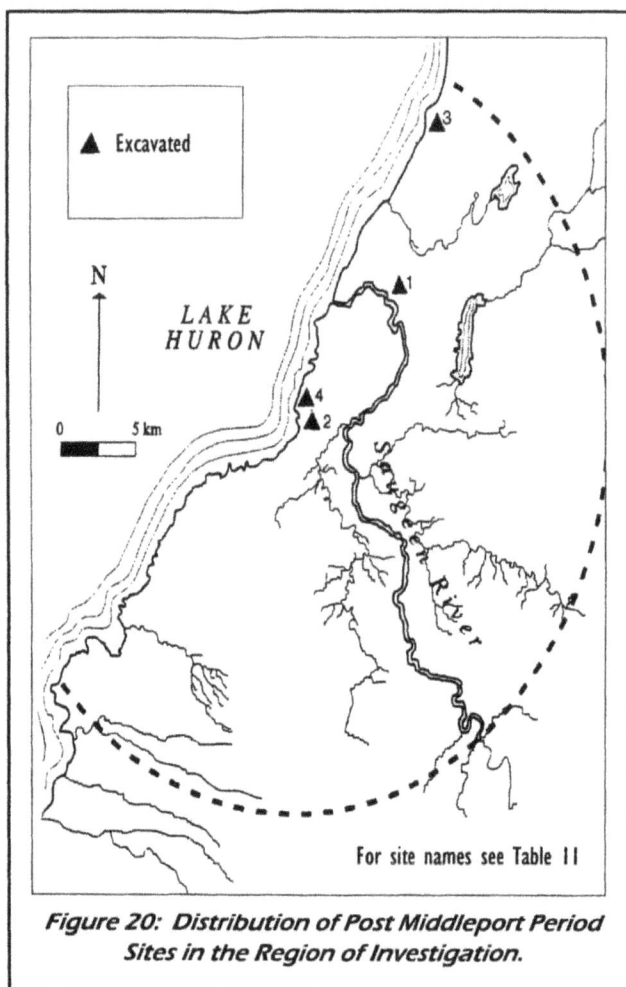

Figure 20: Distribution of Post Middleport Period Sites in the Region of Investigation.

Chapter Summary

This chapter has focussed on the analysis of settlement pattern data from southern Bruce county dating from the Middle and Late Woodland periods. Descriptions and analyses of both regional settlement systems, and where possible, site based settlement strategy have been presented. The application of a chronological format was chosen to present these data so that changes and continuities to the settlement of the region over time could be easily observed. A summary of these data is now presented in order to highlight the major settlement trends observed within Bruce county from the Middle through Late Woodland periods.

Both regional and site based settlement pattern data from the Middle Woodland period indicate that southern Bruce county was occupied as recently as AD 1000 by a foraging population that employed a series of annually scheduled movements to access naturally occurring resources from a variety of small and large campsites (Finlayson 1977). The location, size and number of features observed at the thirteen known Middle Woodland sites in this region suggest that the annual round was based on a spring through fall macroband settlement on the banks of the Saugeen River and the shores of Lake Huron, followed by a winter dispersal to nuclear family hunting campsites further inland. This strategy, which allowed large multiple family units to reside together for lengthy periods of time is common toward the end of the Late Woodland period throughout the Great Lakes lowlands (Cleland 1982; Kenyon and Fox 1983; Spence et al. 1990; Stothers 1978).

The unusually mild climate throughout the Great Lakes lowlands during the Middle Woodland period may have increased the annual abundance of naturally occurring resources and indirectly contributed to a period of population growth that is evidenced throughout southern Ontario at this time (Spence et al. 1990). Population growth restricted local-group territories so that by the end of the Middle Woodland period southern Bruce county was occupied by a single band. Multiple burial cemeteries at the Donaldson site may have been used by the population of southern Bruce county to demonstrate their rights to this territory.

Territorial constriction also reduced overall forager mobility and the large habitation sites along the Saugeen River demonstrate increased sedentism in locations where natural resources were abundant. Chapdelaine (1993) believes that increased communal living during this period also necessitated the realignment of group socio-economic relationships. The appearance of longhouses at the Donaldson site late in the Middle Woodland period emphasizes the social changes brought about through increased sedentism, suggesting that larger social groups were replacing the nuclear family as the primary social and economic units. These houses may also represent a trend toward multi-family winter habitations common to later periods.

Little is known about the early Late Woodland period in southern Bruce county. Elsewhere in southern Ontario this period is represented by a movement toward large multi-family villages and the blending of horticultural practice with the traditional hunting, fishing and foraging economy of the Middle Woodland period (Fox 1990a; Smith and Crawford 1997; Timmins 1997). In southern Bruce county there are no settlement data to indicate that a similar shift in socio-economic behaviour occurred at this time.

However, artifacts diagnostic of the early Late Woodland period have been identified at five sites in the region of investigation, and ceramics indicative of the longer period spanning the late Middle Woodland through the middle Late Woodland are found at nearly all sites cited in this research. Given that most of these early Late Woodland occupations are located in the same places as the earlier Middle Woodland sites, much of the settlement-subsistence system of the early Late Woodland population appears to be a continuation of the Middle Woodland pattern. This may be the reason that previous researchers have not recognized pre-Middleport "Late Woodland" settlement in this region (Finlayson 1977; Wright 1974)..

Nevertheless, the paucity of diagnostic remains recovered from these sites indicate that there was some change to the overall settlement system in southern Bruce county at this time. Primarily, most early Late Woodland occupations appear to have been smaller, with no macroband settlements along the Saugeen River. It is possible that macroband habitation sites dating to the early Late Woodland period have just not been located, but it is probable that the focus of macroband settlement during the early Late Woodland shifted inland to the Nodwell site.

Even though Wright (1974) did not recognize an early Late Woodland occupation of the Nodwell village, five radiocarbon dates from the Nodwell site clearly span the early Late Woodland period. Furthermore, rimsherds diagnostic of the 12th century have been recovered from House 5 (see Chapter 3), the house which settlement data demonstrated to be one of the earliest structures at the Nodwell site . Unlike the other houses at the Nodwell village, House 5 did not contain any material culture diagnostic of later cultural phases.

Because the Nodwell site is located inland from the Saugeen River, natural resources would not have been as abundant here. Therefore, it is probable that the other sites in the region which were occupied during the early Late Woodland period functioned as small campsites for the purpose of extracting natural resources (primarily the harvesting of fish resources) between spring and fall, and that these resources were brought back to the Nodwell site. The shift in macroband habitation location during the early Late Woodland period may have been a defensive strategy designed to protect stores of subsistence goods from outside threats. This may have been a natural outgrowth of territorial constriction and population growth experienced in the late Middle Woodland period.

Settlement data from the Nodwell village indicate that this village was occupied primarily during the winter months (Wright 1974). However, due to later construction on top of House 5, it is difficult to determine if House 5 became the focus of a winter macroband habitation during the early Late Woodland period. The analysis of subsistence remains and material culture in Chapter 3 explores this possibility in greater detail. If this was the case, then the population of southern Bruce county may have gathered at the inland Nodwell site for the winter and dispersed to smaller resource extraction sites from spring through fall.

Limited evidence, including the distribution of pit features and pit contents (see Chapter 3) from the earlier Donaldson longhouses may provide an historical precursor for winter settlement aggregations. At the very least, the Donaldson longhouses provide evidence to suggest that a communal socio-economic strategy was in place by AD 700, providing the opportunity for the population to amass large stores of foodstuffs, a strategy which would not have been as feasible when organizational units centred around the nuclear family. Given that winter macroband settlements generally require large stores of food to sustain the population through the winter months, a shift in settlement location from the Saugeen River to the inland Nodwell site at this time may have been a defensive measure designed to protect surplus foodstuffs from outside threat.

Numerous radiocarbon dates from the Nodwell village demonstrate that this location was the focus of community settlement throughout the middle Late Woodland period and settlement data indicate that the Nodwell village was occupied intensively during the winter months. However, eleven of the fourteen known sites relevant to this study continued to be occupied, apparently as campsites, throughout warm months. By the middle Late Woodland period the regional settlement strategy appears to revolve around the winter-based community habitation at the Nodwell village followed by the spring through fall dispersal of smaller segments of the village population to key resource extraction sites. This pattern continues until the abandonment of southern Bruce county toward the end of the Middleport substage.

The analysis of settlement data from the Nodwell site indicated that this village was somewhat different from other Middleport villages in southern Ontario, and in many respects this village has more settlement similarities with early Late Woodland villages elsewhere in southern Ontario (Timmins 1997). These differences include the size of site, the level of internal settlement organization, and the degree of household variability in the village. The primary reasons for these differences can probably be related to three associated themes including; inter-regional variation, temporal duration of occupation, and population size.

Every local population, even within a larger cultural focus can be expected to exhibit cultural elements in slightly different ways. Local culture history, environment, and resource availability will all enhance variation. Nevertheless, it is more probable that the Nodwell village is distinct from other Middleport villages in southern Ontario because the initial occupation of the Nodwell village preceded this culture-phase (Wright 1985). Radiocarbon dates place the origin of the Nodwell village within the early Late Woodland period and perhaps as early as the late Middle Woodland. Support for this early date, in terms of settlement pattern data, is associated with a distinct change to the regional settlement system during the early Late Woodland period as outlined above.

Given that the average length of longhouse occupation was established to be approximately thirty years, it is unlikely that all of the Nodwell longhouses were inhabited simultaneously, and radiocarbon dates suggest there may have been two distinct phases of village construction. Furthermore, the occupation of House 5 may precede the construction of the larger village altogether. Therefore the Nodwell village probably developed over a lengthy period, perhaps as much as 200-300 years. If this is the case, then it is also probable that the Nodwell village experienced periodic abandonment. Such an abandonment may have occurred sometime after the construction of House 5 and prior to the construction of the larger village. Timmins (1997:236) recognized a similar abandonment at the early Late Woodland Calvert site in southwestern Ontario following the occupation of a single longhouse at this village. This possibility is explored in Chapter 3.

The size of the Nodwell population may have also contributed to the distinct appearance of this village when compared to other Middleport sites in southern Ontario. Most Middleport villages are believed to have populations greater than 350 persons, and village settlement plans which restrict the daily face to face contact of community members (Pearce 1984; Warrick 1984). Nodwell's population would never have surpassed the population threshold of 350 persons generally required before village settlement planning was essential, particularly if the village was constructed incrementally (Pearce 1984; Warrick 1984). In fact, the population of southern Bruce county probably remained relatively constant from the Middle Woodland period through the abandonment of the Nodwell village in the 14th century.

Following the abandonment of the Nodwell village the entire settlement system in southern Bruce county appears to have broken down. Only four sites were used after the 14th century. As one of these sites is an isolated burial, only three small campsites can truly be considered occupations. The outward migration from Bruce county in the mid- 14th century may have been precipitated by the cooler climate of the Little Ice Age, which may have altered the local environment at this time. A number of large settlements along the Bruce peninsula may have become the focus of settlement at this time.

The analysis of settlement pattern data from southern Bruce county suggests that there is little reason to assume the appearance of the Nodwell village was brought about by the migration of a horticultural population from outside the region during the 14th century. Actually, there are many more reasons to suggest that Nodwell was a local development. There does not appear to be any real occupational hiatus in southern Bruce county prior to the appearance of the Nodwell village. In fact, there is clear evidence in the form of Middle Woodland macroband settlements, and the construction of longhouses at the Donaldson site during the late Middle Woodland to suggest that the socio-economic structures associated with village settlements were already developing here. Furthermore, while there is reason to assume that the majority of the sites in Bruce county were utilized in a different manner while the Nodwell village was occupied, it is probable that this change in use strategy began during the early Late Woodland period. Finally, the numbers and locations of sites in southern Bruce county remained relatively constant between the Middle Woodland period and the 14th century abandonment of the Nodwell village.

If immigrants had constructed the Nodwell village during the 14th century, all evidence would point to the rapid establishment of the village at this time. Not only would radiocarbon dates have to be overlooked, but the historical trend in southern Bruce county toward larger more sedentary community settlements would have to be ignored. Furthermore, there were no radical changes to the local settlement system through time as the same sites continued to be used and few sites appear to have been either added or subtracted. If an outside population had suddenly appeared in southern Bruce county there would probably have been dramatic changes to the settlement system very quickly as this new population altered the stability of the local settlement system by changing the local environment through both village construction and exploiting local resources. Nor is there evidence for the abandonment of the region following the establishment of the Nodwell village. Perhaps most significant however, is that the settlement pattern of the Nodwell village is unlike that recorded at other Middleport villages outside of Bruce county.

When viewed historically from within Bruce county the radiocarbon dates and settlement pattern data suggest that the indigenous population of southern Bruce county established the Nodwell village early in the Late Woodland period as a result of internal changes already underway in the region. This is not unlike transitions which occurred elsewhere in the province. However, it is possible that the settlement pattern data alone are not capable of representing a migratory event. Chapter 3 uses both material culture and subsistence data recovered from the Bruce county sites to evaluate further both the migration and in situ hypotheses. Furthermore, Chapter 3 explores the role of external stimuli and interaction in the process of culture change in this region.

Chapter 3
Material Culture and Subsistence

Introduction

This chapter focuses on the material culture and subsistence data recovered from the archaeological sites in southern Bruce county described in the preceding chapter. Artifacts and subsistence remains recovered from these sites are discussed in a similar temporal format and are used both to elaborate and refine the themes outlined in Chapter 2 including: site occupation chronologies, site type/function, settlement systems, culture patterns and interaction. This format allows for an historical analysis and comparison of data within and between sites in order to identify changes and continuities to the social and economic structures of Bruce county's inhabitants through time, and to explain the appearance of the Nodwell village. As a result, particular attention will be paid to the analysis of artifact and faunal remains recovered from the Nodwell village. The data presented in this chapter are drawn from both extant literature and new collections made specifically for this research.

Middle Woodland Material Culture and Subsistence Data

Material Culture

Items of material culture diagnostic of the Middle Woodland period have been recovered from all twelve sites identified to the Middle Woodland period in the preceding chapter (see Table 1). This list now includes the Nodwell site which was radiocarbon dated to this period and which contains a very small sample of Middle Woodland artifacts. The inclusion of the Nodwell site brings the number of identified Middle Woodland sites in southern Bruce county to thirteen.

Ceramic assemblages dominate the collections of material culture from every site in southern Bruce county dating to the Middle Woodland period. Researchers in Ontario have consistently relied upon this artifact class when establishing relative site chronologies for both Middle Woodland and Late Woodland period sites. Specific features including technology of manufacture, combined with attributes of style and design are thought to be both temporally and spatially significant since particular types of ceramics increase and decline in popularity through time in different regions (Emerson 1961; MacNeish 1952; Wright 1974).

Middle Woodland ceramics were constructed using a coiling technique. In southern Bruce county these ceramics are identified using this and a number of other features. These ceramics are characterized by "course paste, thick walls, concoidal bases, weakly defined shoulders, wide necks and vertical to flaring rims with rounded or flat lips" (Spence et al. 1990:148). This pottery is considered highly friable. Decoration including dentate, pseudo-scallop-shell and linear stamping, or rocking, generally covers the vessel surface (Finlayson 1977; Spence et al. 1990:148).

Table 12 demonstrates the presence of this diagnostic artifact at each of the thirteen Middle Woodland sites in southern Bruce county. Because Table 12 draws together information from various types of collections including area excavations, test excavations and surface collections, the size of the samples is variable. Nevertheless, all site assemblages resulted from systematic sampling strategies and are equally relevant. Furthermore, the information analysed for this research was located in written reports, as well as institutional and private holdings. Every effort was made to observe collections directly in order to maintain a consistent level of reporting. As this was not possible in all situations, poorly described material from early collections has not been included below.

Site	Dentate Stamp Sherds	Pseudo Scallop Stamp Sherds	Mixed Dentate / Pseudo Scallop Stamp Sherds	Linear Stamp Sherds
North shore (BdHi-2)	3 rim 16 body	1 rim 11 body		
Shutt (BcHi-6)	2 rim 21 body	1 rim 9 body		
Mirimachi Bay (BcHi-4)	1 rim 3 body	10 body		
Port Elgin Cemetery (BcHi-2)	1 rim 4 body	7 body		
North Elgin	3 body	4 body		
Boiled Baby (BcHi-16)	194 body	3 rims 114 body		
Thede (BcHi-7)	269 rims 3133 body	34 rims 549 body	3 rims 19 body	11 rims 93 body
Donaldson (BdHi-1)	449 rims 4547 body	370 rims 2313 body	1 rim 193 body	63 rims 374 body
Busch (BcHh-6)	1 rim 10 body	3 rims 9 body		
Krug (BcHh-5)	3 rim 20 body	2 rim 15 body		
Indian Church	7 body	4 body		
Kirkland Farm	1 rim 17 body	11 body		
Nodwell (BcHi-3)	3 rim 16 body	4 body		

Table 12: Diagnostic Middle Woodland Ceramics from Bruce County Sites.

the term body is used to denote any non-rim sherd.

(Finlayson 1977:78, 142, 287, 363; Fox 1986:appendix 1-10; Knechtel 1955; Rankin 1997; Shutt 1951; 1952; Wright 1953a; 1956; Wright and Anderson 1963:23-42).

A variety of other artifact classes are commonly associated with the Middle Woodland period in southern Bruce county including a well developed rough and ground stone tool industry, a chipped lithic technology and a smaller bone tool industry (Wright and Anderson 1963; Finlayson 1977). The most prevalent artifacts are side and corner notched projectile points, pitted or faceted hammerstones, anvil-hammers, celts and choppers (Finlayson 1977). However, Spence et al. (1990:148) claim that only very few artifacts can be considered diagnostic of the Middle Woodland Saugeen complex in southern Bruce county. Diagnostic items, other than ceramics, include cobble spall scrapers, end-notched net-sinkers and projectile points with broad shallow side notches and convex bases.

A diagnostic bone technology probably existed, but this class of artifacts is only well represented at the Donaldson site and therefore poorly defined at the regional level (Finlayson 1977; Spence et al. 1990). This may be due, at least in part, to poor preservation resulting from the acidic nature of soils in this region (Wright 1956; Finlayson 1977; Spence et al. 1990:148). Table 13 represents the frequency of the most diagnostic artifacts other than bone tools and ceramics which have been collected from good contexts in southern Bruce county.

No non-ceramic artifacts diagnostic of the Middle Woodland period in southern Bruce county were collected at the North Shore or North Elgin sites. However, Tables 12 and 13 demonstrate that artifacts diagnostic of the Middle Woodland period were found on each of the thirteen sites, so there is no question of their occupation during this time.

The duration of the Middle Woodland period is lengthy in Bruce county, persisting for at least 1000 years (Finlayson 1977; Spence et al. 1990). Finlayson (1977:578-590) attempted to refine the sequence of Middle Woodland site occupation in southern Bruce county through a ceramic

Site	Cobble Spall Scrapers	End-Notched Net Sinkers	Saugeen Points
Shutt (BcHi-6)	2		1
Mirimachi Bay (BcHi-4)	2		1
Port Elgin Cemetery (BcHi-2)	1	1	
Boiled Baby (BcHi-16)	3	2	1
Thede (BcHi-7)			13
Donaldson (BdHi-1)	27	3	25
Busch (BcHh-6)	3	2	7
Krug (BcHh-5)		1	1
Indian Church			1
Kirkland Farm	2		1
Nodwell (BcHi-3)		1	1

Table 13: Other Diagnostic Artifacts from Middle Woodland Sites in Bruce County.

(Finlayson 1977:161-166, 194, 220-221, 377-382, 404, 408; 414-417,503; Fox 1986:appendix 1-10; Knechtel 1955; Lee 1960; Rankin 1997; Shutt 1952; Wright and Anderson 1963:36-41).

seriation analysis based on both the tool of design application and design style produced on the large ceramic assemblages from the Thede and Donaldson sites. These attributes were chosen because they appeared to vary spatially. Finlayson (1977:590) concluded that pseudo-scallop-shell stamping was popular during the early Middle Woodland and was gradually replaced by dentate stamping which peaked in popularity towards the end of the Middle Woodland period. Unfortunately, the ceramic assemblages from other Middle Woodland sites are too small for a similar seriation analysis, and therefore it is difficult to estimate the sequence of their occupation during this period. Nevertheless, Table 12 demonstrates that relatively equal amounts of the two types of pottery have been recovered from other Middle Woodland sites in the region suggesting that these sites were occupied during the mid to latter stages of the Middle Woodland period

when both ceramic decorative techniques would have been common.

The Middle Woodland components at the Thede and Donaldson sites included a full range of non-diagnostic artifacts, made from a variety of materials. As well, the material culture assemblage from the single component Krug site, while more limited than Thede and Donaldson, also includes a selection of non-diagnostic artifacts. Similar classes and types of artifacts have been recovered in smaller quantities from other sites in the region, but cannot be directly associated with the Middle Woodland period given the multi-component nature of these sites and the lack of detailed excavation. Table 14 describes the frequency of different artifact types recovered from Thede, Donaldson and Krug. Only collections made by Finlayson in 1969 and 1970 at the Thede and Donaldson sites are described below because other assemblages were

Site	Ceramics	Ground/Rough Stone	Chipped Stone	Bone/Antler/Shell	Copper
Thede (BcHi-7)	136 smooth body sherds 58 smoothed over body sherds 17 trailed body sherds 7 striated body sherds 4 pieces fired clay	13 celts 1 gorget blank 1 ground shale frag. 1 ground stone blank 5 choppers 1 cobble modified frag. 45 hammerstones 3 anvil-hammers 1 abrader 1 mano 1 rubbing stone 1 chopper blank	3 projectile points 2 cache blades 2 bifacial knives 28 bifacial fragments 2 drills 27 scrapers 85 cores 359 utilized flakes 1183 flakes	1 bone bead 1 modified bone fragment	1 awl 1 bar 2 beads
Donaldson (BdHi-1)	238 smooth body sherd 46 smoothed over body sherds 171 trailed body sherds 63 striated body sherds	15 celts 1 chisel 3 gorget blanks 1 pendant blank 1 earspool 1 bipointed object 15 choppers 50 hammerstones 2 anvil stones 2 anvil hammers 3 abraders 5 rubbing stones 1 metate 1 atlatl hook 3 cut sheet mica 1 rectangular object	5 bifacial knives 30 biface fragments 3 drills 3 unifaces 32 scrapers 76 cores 130 utilized flakes 1623 flakes	1 bone bead 9 bone chisels 7 bone beamers 2 bone harpoons 2 bone pins 1 bone flaker 6 bone awls 3 bone projectile points 3 modified bone 6 modified beaver teeth 5 antler harpoons 2 antler spikes 3 antler handles 1 antler flaker 3 modified antler 3 shell beads	1 awl 1 bar 1 bangle 1 gorge 2 panpipe covers 1 patch 1 scrap
Krug (BcHh-5)		3 hammerstones	1 biface fragments 11 utilized flakes 38 flakes		

Table 14: Non-Diagnostic Middle Woodland Artifacts from Thede and Donaldson.

(Finlayson 1977:142, 220-221, 363, 503-504; Fox 1986: appendix 1-10; Knechtel 1955; Lee 1960; Rankin 1997; Shutt 1952; Wright and Anderson 1963: 36-41).

not collected with the same degree of chronological control. No diagnostic materials are included in Table 14.

The artifact assemblages recovered from these three sites were larger than the assemblages recovered from other Middle Woodland sites in southern Bruce county. There are a number of reasons for this. In general, the overall size of the other sites is much smaller, suggesting that they served different functions within the settlement system (see Table 1). Furthermore, no sites except Thede and Donaldson were subject to areal excavation. Finally, the largest artifact assemblage was amassed at the Donaldson site where most artifacts were extracted from burial contexts, and to date no other Middle Woodland burials have been located in southern Bruce county. Nevertheless, the artifact data from each of the Middle Woodland sites in southern Bruce county presented in Tables 12-14 have the potential to inform us about site chronology, site type/function and settlement systems and are discussed below in detail.

Among the diagnostic and temporally contained Middle Woodland artifact assemblages described above it is possible to identify numerous artifacts and raw materials which originated outside of the southern Bruce county culture region. The presence of a variety of exotic items including native copper, cherts and perhaps some ceramics associated with distant regions suggests that either certain desired materials had to be obtained outside of the territory or that people from outside Bruce county frequented the region. As a result, these items reflect either long-distance travel by the inhabitants of Bruce county or inter-regional interaction. The presence of these exotic items demonstrates that the Middle Woodland inhabitants of southern Bruce county were well connected to regions outside their local territory occupied by other local groups.

Table 15 presents the frequency of exotic items recovered from Middle Woodland contexts in southern Bruce county. Unfortunately, many non-diagnostic exotic items could not be directly associated with the Middle Woodland period. For example, numerous copper artifacts were recovered from the Nodwell site and exotic cherts in both nodular and modified forms have been recovered from almost every identified site. Nevertheless, there is a distinct possibility that many of these items were associated with the Middle Woodland occupation of Bruce county because the frequency of foreign cherts, specifically the abundant Kettle Point chert, and

Site Name	Copper (Artifacts and Scrap)	Chert (Artifacts and Wastage)	Ceramics
Mirimachi Bay (BcHi-4)		- I diagnostic item of Kettle Point chert from Port Franks, Ontario	
Port Elgin Cemetery (BcHi-2)			- I cord wrapped stick sherd with annular punctates
Boiled Baby (BcHi-16)			- 4 cord wrapped stick sherd with annular punctates
Thede (BcHi-7)	- 4 items	- 15 items of Selkirk chert from Port Dover, Ontario - 999 items of Kettle Point chert from Port Franks, Ontario - 15 items of Fossil Hill chert from Collingwood, Ontario - I item of Bayport chert from Saginaw Bay, Michigan	
Donaldson (BdHi-1)	- 8 items	- 55 items of Selkirk chert from Port Dover, Ontario - 1105 items of Kettle Point Chert from Port Franks, Ontario - 47 items of Fossil Hill chert from Collingwood, Ontario - 2 items of Bayport chert from Saginaw Bay, Michigan	- 27 cord wrapped stick sherds with annular punctates
Busch (BcHh-6)		- 2 diagnostic items of Kettle Point chert from Port Franks, Ontario	-I cord wrapped stick sherd with annular punctates
Krug (BcHh-5)		- I item Selkirk chert from Port Dover, Ontario - 33 items of Kettle Point chert from Port Franks, Ontario	
Indian Church		- I diagnostic item of Kettle Point chert from Port Franks, Ontario	

Table 15: Exotic Goods Collected from Middle Woodland Sites.
(Finlayson 1977:153-160, 221, 287, 375-376, 504; Eley and von Bitter 1989; Wright and Anderson 1963:29).

native copper drastically declines at the end of the Middle Woodland period (Janusas 1984:85 and Fox 1990a:172). Only temporally diagnostic artifacts were included in Table 15, with exception of artifacts from the Thede, Donaldson and Krug sites, where the Middle Woodland context of both exotic chert and copper has been firmly established.

The artifacts listed in Table 15 demonstrate that the occupants of southern Bruce county had connections to outside regions radiating in every direction from their territory. Native copper, which was found in significant quantity at the Thede and Donaldson sites probably originated to the north, along the northern shores of Lake Huron and Lake Superior, where up to one ton of native copper was mined annually between 4000 BC and AD 1200 (Finlayson 1977; Patterson 1971:299). However, Turff (1997) notes 257 sources of native copper throughout North America and without chemically sourcing the copper artifacts, it is impossible to know the exact location from which they originated.

Four distinct types of exotic cherts were found at southern Bruce county sites and can be sourced to regions in the east, west and south. The most abundant chert is Kettle Point which can be quarried along the southeast shore of Lake Huron, near the present-day town of Port Franks, Ontario some 160 km to the south of Bruce county. Travel to this area during the Middle Woodland period would have necessitated by-passing several distinct band territories (Spence et al. 1990; see Chapter 2). Given the prominence of this chert in southern Bruce county, it is probable that connections to these other communities were strong. Selkirk chert is found along the north shore of Lake Erie, near Port Dover, Ontario some 225 km southeast of Bruce county. This region was also occupied during the Middle Woodland period (Spence et al. 1990). Fossil Hill chert would have been collected at outcrops near Collingwood, Ontario on the south shore of Georgian Bay approximately 100 km to the east. A series of Middle Woodland sites also existed in this region (Sutton 1996:47). A small collection of items made from Bayport chert have also been recovered in Bruce county. The source for this chert is some 200 km west across Lake

Huron on the southeast shores of Saginaw Bay in Michigan. Whether the inhabitants of southern Bruce county were accessing these cherts through quarrying or trade, the pursuit of these materials would definitely have brought them into contact with surrounding populations.

Further support for this interaction is found in Spence et al. (1990). Spence et al. (1990) assign the occupants of the Middle Woodland site clusters found near each of the three chert quarries in Ontario to the Saugeen culture complex; the cultural complex originally defined in southern Bruce county. This cultural complex incorporates numerous local groups which shared a similar culture pattern exemplified by settlement strategy, economy and artifact assemblages. Theoretically, the similarities between Saugeen complex groups throughout southern Ontario are perpetuated through frequent inter-community interaction. Gaining access to raw materials, either directly from the source or through community exchange is no doubt part of this interactive process.

Table 15 also details the presence of cord-wrapped-stick impressed ceramics with annular punctates and interior bosses. These ceramics are representative of pre-Iroquoian Late Woodland ceramic production elsewhere in southern Ontario, but the origin of this style of ceramic is generally associated with the Princess Point culture complex situated in the lower Grand River valley, Cootes Paradise and Long Point, all in southwestern Ontario (Fox 1990a). The Princess Point complex has been dubbed a "transitional culture" which blended horticultural practice with the traditional Middle Woodland settlement/subsistence strategy (Fox 1990a; Smith and Crawford 1997). Recent research by Smith and Crawford (1997:23) has determined that the Princess Point sites along the Grand River were occupied as early as AD 500 and as late as AD 1100. Furthermore, dates of AD 540 and AD 570 which were derived from maize kernels excavated from the Grand Banks site in the Grand River valley provide the earliest direct evidence of domesticates in southern Ontario (Smith and Crawford 1997:26). These dates not only overlap chronologically with the Middle Woodland occupation of southern Bruce county, but with Middle Woodland Saugeen complex habitations situated near the mouth of the Grand River along the north shore of Lake Erie and close to the Selkirk chert quarries (Smith and Crawford 1997; Spence et al. 1990). This suggest that a forager/farmer frontier between the Grand River valley and other parts of southern Ontario developed before the end of the Middle Woodland period.

The presence of Princess Point-like sherds at the Middle Woodland Donaldson site prior to AD 710 marks the earliest appearance of this style of pottery outside of southwestern Ontario (Fox 1990a) and suggests that this ceramic tradition was introduced to southern Bruce county as a result of interaction between the occupants of this region and the Princess Point population inhabiting the Grand valley. However, the production of this type of ceramic continued in southern Bruce county through the early Late Woodland period (Ferris 1988; Fox 1989), and the appearance of these ceramics on sites other than Donaldson may be related to the later cultural period.

Interaction between the occupants of the Middle Woodland Donaldson site and the Princess Point farmers in southwestern Ontario could have been either direct or indirect. Direct interaction may have occurred when the inhabitants of Bruce county made trips to the Selkirk chert quarries on the north shore of Lake Erie. The most efficient route to the Selkirk chert quarries would have been by canoe via the Saugeen and Grand River valleys to Lake Erie. This trip would have taken people directly past Princess Point sites located on the floodplain of the Grand River. Another hypothesis is that the Saugeen complex groups living near the Selkirk quarries traded with both the neighbouring Princess Point groups and the population of southern Bruce county, thereby transferring pottery from the Grand River region to the Bruce. It is also possible that members of the Princess Point complex communities travelled to Bruce county.

It has not been determined whether the Princess Point ceramics recovered in southern Bruce county were manufactured locally by potters who replicated the design techniques and motifs of the Grand Valley potters, or if these ceramics were transferred intact into southern Bruce county. The only way to establish the region of manufacture for these ceramics with any certainty would be to submit the sherds to a trace element analysis and establish which clay source was used for vessel construction. Unfortunately, this was beyond the scope of this project.

The appearance of this style of pottery in Bruce county is significant whether contact was direct or indirect because it is the first definite evidence that the Middle Woodland occupants of southern Bruce county had knowledge of farmers who lived to the south. As such, the presence of Princess Point ceramics in southern Bruce county establishes both the existence of a forager/farmer frontier between southwestern Ontario and Bruce county and a history of interaction across this frontier.

Interaction between the Bruce foragers and Princess Point farmers may have been both desirable and beneficial to both groups (Gregg 1988; Spielmann 1986). For example, farming populations are likely to be more sedentary than foragers and may find it difficult to access exotic items of material culture or adequate supplies of meat protein without the assistance of foragers to bring these items into farming communities (Spielmann 1986). Likewise, foragers often trade goods desired by farmers for domestic produce which supplements their traditional subsistence strategy (Gregg 1988; Spielmann 1986). Furthermore, trade across forager/farmer frontiers also results in the exchange of ideas and information which may effect long-term changes to the internal structures of both groups (Dennell 1985; Gregg 1988).

Subsistence

In addition to material culture, faunal remains were recovered from six of the thirteen Middle Woodland period occupations and have been fully analysed. However, collection strategy and multiple period occupations at each of these sites once again precludes the direct association of most of the faunal remains with the Middle Woodland period. As such, most faunal material can only provide a general idea of site type, function and site subsistence strategy. However, the Donaldson, Thede and Nodwell sites were subject to intensive excavation and faunal material was firmly associated with the Middle Woodland components at both Donaldson and Thede. Table 16 presents the frequency of the identified faunal remains from these two sites recovered during Finlayson's 1969 and 1970 excavations.

From the faunal remains collected at the Donaldson and Thede sites Finlayson (1977) determined that fish and land mammals were the most important sources of food, although birds, amphibians and reptiles are also represented. Finlayson (1977) suggests that the large quantities of fish bones recovered from Donaldson and Thede indicate that these sites functioned predominantly as fishing stations during the spring through fall period. This hypothesis is also supported by the artifact assemblages from these two sites which include net-sinkers and/or bone harpoons which Finlayson (1977) believes were used for fishing.

All of the fish recovered from the Thede site spawn in the spring or early summer in the Saugeen River. Finlayson (1977:204) believed

Site	Mammalia	Aves	Osteichthyes	Amphibia	Reptilia
Donaldson (BdHi-1)	Woodchuck=19, MNI=2 Eastern Chipmunk=9, MNI=2 Northern Flying Squirrel=2, MNI=2 Beaver =275, MNI=8 Deer Mouse=1, MNI=1 Southern Lemming Mouse=1, MNI=1 Meadow Vole=9, MNI=3 Mouse sp. =9, MNI=3 Muskrat=8, MNI=1 Porcupine =9, MNI=2 Rodentia sp.=2 Timber Wolf=3, MNI=1 Canis sp.=54, MNI=1 Black Bear=54, MNI=5 Racoon =7, MNI=2 Marten=5, MNI=1 Fisher=5, MNI=1 Otter=3, MNI=1 Carnivora sp.=4 Elk =9, MNI=1 Whitetailed Deer=169, MNI=4 Moose=1, MNI=1 Cervidae sp. =11	Common Loon=3, MNI=1 Canada Goose=1, MNI=1 American Merganser=1, MNI=1 Aythyinae sp.=2, MNI=1 Bald Eagle=2, MNI=1 Osprey=1, MNI=1 Snowy Owl=1, MNI=1 Grackle=1, MNI=1	Lake Sturgeon=510 Trout sp.=1 Whitefish sp.=8 Northern Pike=3 Sucker sp.=912 Creek Chub=2 Catfish sp.=250 Bass sp.=1 Small mouth Bass=37 Percidae=465 Perch=1 Freshwater Drum=98	Ranidae sp. =9, MNI=2	Snapping Turtle=41, MNI=2 Spotted Turtle=6, MNI=1 Wood Turtle=5, MNI=1 Blanding's Turtle=17, MNI=3 Map Turtle=3, MNI=1 Painted Turtle=6, MNI=2 Garter Snake=2, MNI=1
Donaldson	Total # Bones=669	Total # Bones=12	Total # Bones=2288	Total # Bones=9	Total # Bones=80
Donaldson	Total MNI=43	Total MNI=8	Total MNI=unknown	Total MNI=2	Total MNI=11
Thede (BcHi-7)	Woodchuck=8, MNI=1 Beaver=50, MNI 3 Meadow Vole=4, MNI 3 Porcupine=1, MNI 1 Canis sp. 4, MNI 1 Black Bear=7, MNI 2 Elk=6, MNI 1 Whitetailed Deer=7, MNI 2	Wild Turkey=2, MNI=1 Passenger Pigeon=1, MNI=1	Lake Sturgeon=70 Percidae=4 Channel Catfish=1 Sucker=1	Ranidae sp.=8, MNI=1	Chelydridae=35
Thede	Total # Bones=87	Total # Bones =3	Total # Bones=76	Total # Bones=8	Total # Bones=35
Thede	Total MNI=14	Total MNI=2	Total MNI=unknown	Total MNI=1	Total MNI=unknown

Table 16: Frequency of Identified Faunal Remains Recovered From Donaldson and Thede.

(Finlayson 1977:201-209, 222,460-479).

that the other vertebrate classes represented could be best exploited during the spring through fall period, given that some species such as bear, woodchuck and turtles hibernate over winter, and others such as the passenger pigeon migrate. This evidence suggests that Thede was occupied from spring through autumn, but this does not preclude the possibility of a winter occupation given that some of the species represented would have been available during winter months and others foodstuffs could have been stored.

At the Donaldson site most of the fish remains are from spring/early summer spawning species. However, whitefish and trout spawn in the Saugeen between October and December. Again, the fish remains combined with the presence of both hibernating mammals and migrating birds suggest a spring through fall occupation of the site. Nevertheless, the period of occupation was probably longer at this site given the presence of whitefish and trout. Other species would have been available year-round and therefore it is possible that the Donaldson site could have been occupied over the winter months. In fact, the presence of a single snowy owl bone does suggest at least a limited winter occupation because these birds only frequent southern Ontario when food becomes scarce in their regular northern habitat (usually between December and March) (Finlayson 1977:483).

While the majority of the faunal remains recovered from these two sites should be considered direct evidence of the inhabitant's subsistence strategy, in at least one situation animal remains may reflect other cultural behaviours. Finlayson (1977:472) indicates that the 36 Canis species bones recovered from a human burial pit at the Donaldson site, represent a single immature dog or wolf burial rather than the remains of a subsistence animal. The presence of dog burials is among the traits used to identify hunter-gatherer sites in southern Ontario and appears to originate in the late Middle Woodland period (Brizinski and Savage 1983; Prevec 1987; Smith 1985). Dog burials are rarely associated with Iroquoian farming sites (Smith 1985). Therefore, the presence of this phenomenon in southern Bruce county during the Middle Woodland period has been used to demonstrate an ethnic connection between this population and the Algonkian foragers who inhabited northern Bruce county during the contact period (Fox 1987b). The presence of similar dog burials at the Nodwell village, during the Middleport sub-stage of the Late Woodland period, may be evidence for in situ development in this region.

Fauna was also recovered from four other sites in Bruce county known to have Middle Woodland occupations. If we discount the Nodwell site, whose primary occupation was somewhat later, some general observations can be made about the faunal assemblages from the remaining three sites. At the Shutt site, the remains of white tailed deer, beaver, duck, sturgeon, and sucker were recovered. At the Mirimachi Bay site, fish remains of both Lake Trout and Northern Pike were identified. Finally, at BcHi-16, white tailed deer, passenger pigeon and sturgeon and sucker bones were present. Based on the spawning habits of the fish species represented at these sites an early spring through fall occupation can be determined. However, other classes of fauna would have been available during the winter season. The mammals could have been hunted during any season, and birds were probably hunted during the spring or fall while migrating through Bruce county.

Flotation techniques were used to accumulate botanical samples during Finlayson's investigation of both the Donaldson and Thede sites. No floral material was recovered from any of the other Middle Woodland occupations. 89 identifiable carbonised seeds were recovered from the Thede site including 46 raspberry seeds, 41 elderberry seeds and two dogwood seeds (Finlayson 1977:212). These fruits would have been available between June and October adding support for the spring through fall occupation of this site. However, it is possible that these fruits were dried and stored for winter use. At the Donaldson site 43 identifiable carbonised seeds were recovered (Finlayson 1977:489). Forty raspberry seeds, two elderberry seeds and a single fire-cherry pit, all available between June and October make up the assemblage. While these specimens help to detail the subsistence practices of the site's inhabitants little more can be said about the annual duration of the occupation.

Further evidence about the subsistence practice at the Donaldson site is documented in Molto's (1979) analysis of the human skeletal material. Molto (1979:39-41) details a variable dental wear pattern for the late Middle Woodland burials at this site. This pattern indicates that there was both heavy attrition to adult dentition resulting from an abrasive diet, and dental caries (of which 78% were pit and fissures lesions) which are a common dental pathology among horticulturalists with softer diets. As a result of this study, Molto (1979:49) suggested that the late Middle Woodland inhabitants of the Donaldson site were probably experimenting with horticulture, even as they continued their primary subsistence strategy of hunting, fishing and gathering. No cultigens were recovered from Finlayson's investigation of the site, but we now know that the Middle Woodland inhabitants of the Donaldson site were familiar with the Princess Point farmers inhabiting the southern margins of the province, who were definitely growing cultigens by the sixth century (Smith and Crawford 1997). Interaction with this Princess Point population may have resulted in either cultigens, or the knowledge and technology of horticulture to have been transferred to the Saugeen River valley.

Before summarizing the material culture and subsistence data from the Middle Woodland period it is necessary to examine collections from the Donaldson longhouses in greater detail. It is not possible to tabulate the material culture and subsistence data from these houses due to the sketchy nature of the report. However, Wright and Anderson (1963:11-20) do report that House 1 contained masses of fire stones, Middle Woodland pottery, chipping detritus, stone artifacts, and bone refuse. Wright and Anderson (1963) claim at least one pit was particularly rich in fish bones. The second house also contained pits filled with refuse but no information was given to suggest the nature of the fill.

In the previous chapter it was suggested that these houses may represent a winter occupation of the Donaldson site. This assumption was based on the presence of hearths and interior pit features inside the house structures. In contrast, summer season longhouse occupations lack internal features and hearth pits (Wright

1972b; Williamson 1983). At summer longhouse sites activity tends to be focussed in the area adjacent to houses (Wright 1972b; Williamson 1983). While the material culture, subsistence remains and settlement data available from the Donaldson houses cannot directly confirm winter occupation, they do suggest that a variety of activities took place inside the houses. Fish bones recovered from the house structures most probably represent species which spawned in the Saugeen River between spring and fall, but this resource can be stored for later use. Furthermore, the presence of chipping detritus suggests that an activity best performed outside was occurring within the house structure and this provides some support for the suggestion that these houses represent winter habitations.

Interpretations

The artifact and subsistence data presented above provide evidence about site chronology, site type and function, economy, settlement systems and regional interaction spheres. Primarily, diagnostic artifacts were used to establish that thirteen sites were occupied in southern Bruce county during this culture period. Both artifact and faunal assemblages were small at most of the Middle Woodland sites, with the exception of Thede and Donaldson. While this no doubt reflects different data collection strategies, it also suggests that the sites served different purposes or functions during this period. Large sites including Thede, Donaldson, Krug, Shutt and Busch, which were located on the Saugeen River or inland Lake Arran, have medium to large assemblages of artifacts and fauna. Other sites are small and have smaller assemblages of artifacts and fauna. Smaller sites tended to be located near the shores of Lake Huron or on small inland creeks.

Therefore, the artifact and faunal data support assumptions made about the local settlement system outlined in Chapter 2; that the inhabitants of Bruce county employed an annual settlement strategy based on macroband occupations located at major waterways during the seasonal peaks in resource availability and dispersed, probably in nuclear family groups, to smaller sites during other parts of the year. Both artifact and faunal material from the larger sites like Thede and Donaldson suggest that macroband habitations were focussed on exploiting the spring through fall fish spawns, though other subsistence activities were also undertaken. Smaller sites were probably nuclear family hunting and gathering locales. As discussed in Chapter 2, this settlement strategy is not limited to southern Bruce county but is employed in a similar format throughout the Great Lakes lowlands.

A variety of large sites, which probably represent macroband habitations exist in southern Bruce county, but the Donaldson site is unique. The Donaldson site is the only Middle Woodland site in southern Bruce county which has both burials and houses. The presence of burials not only suggests this may have been a significant settlement (see Chapter 2), but also provides a much greater assemblage of material culture. The exotic items recovered from burial contexts have demonstrated the importance of group interaction to the occupants of southern Bruce county.

The evidence for inter-regional interaction is perhaps the most significant result of the material culture and subsistence analysis of the Middle Woodland period. The data demonstrate that the inhabitants of Bruce county had connections to Middle Woodland Saugeen complex groups elsewhere in southern Ontario, and that the occupants of southern Bruce county were familiar with early horticulturalists residing in southwestern Ontario, a factor which must be considered in any evaluation of culture change in this region.

The presence of two houses at the Donaldson site emphasizes that changes in group social relations were underway in southern Bruce county during the late Middle Woodland period. Furthermore, the features and materials within these houses suggested that they may have been occupied during the winter. As discussed in Chapter 2, winter occupations generally require stored resources to sustain the population through the winter months. Unfortunately, the only identified fauna from these houses was fish, which is associated with a spring through fall occupation. Nevertheless, these fish could have been dried and stored for winter use (Heidenreich 1971:212). However, indirect evidence from the Donaldson site skeletal analysis suggests that the Middle Woodland residents were consuming horticultural produce, a commodity which is readily stored for winter consumption. Now that connections between farmers in southwestern Ontario and the occupants of Bruce county have been established, it is possible to suggest that the dissemination of edible cultigens or the technology of production across this forager/farmer frontier during the late Middle Woodland period may have made both macroband habitation and winter co-habitation more feasible.

One final piece of evidence which may shed light on the changing social relations during the Middle Woodland concerns end-notched net sinkers. This artifact was present on six sites in southern Bruce county in the Middle Woodland period. Net-sinkers were apparently a late addition to the Middle Woodland tool assemblage (Spence et al. 1990), and these artifacts may represent a shift in procurement behaviour toward the communal fishing techniques common to later culture periods (Wright 1966). The presence of these artifacts may therefore reflect changes to the resource procurement strategy and may be associated with acquiring larger staples of fish, perhaps for winter storage.

Unfortunately, not much could be learned about the Nodwell village during the Middle Woodland period, even though the artifact assemblage from this site does suggest a limited utilization of the site at this time.

Nodwell Material Culture and Subsistence Data

Even though radiocarbon dates and material culture demonstrate that the Nodwell site was utilized during the Middle Woodland period, there can be little doubt that the primary occupation of the Nodwell village was during the Late Woodland period, as settlement patterns, material culture, and subsistence remains diagnostic of this era dominate the site. The results from the analyses of material culture and subsistence data from the Nodwell village is now reviewed in light of both the migration and in situ hypotheses.

Differences Between Nodwell and Middle Woodland Assemblages

Wright (1974) noted that the artifact assemblage recovered from the Late Woodland occupation of the Nodwell village was significantly different from those recovered from Middle Woodland sites in the region. Furthermore, Wright (1974) believed that the Nodwell material was indicative of the Ontario Iroquois Tradition, and therefore associated much more closely with the farmers of southern Ontario than Bruce county's foragers. Table 17 details the frequency of the artifact types recovered from Wright's excavation that are associated with the Late Woodland occupation of the Nodwell village (Wright 1974).

The artifact assemblage from the Nodwell village is distinct from the artifact assemblages at Middle Woodland sites in southern Bruce county in a number of ways. Most distinct are the ceramics. The ceramics recovered from the Late Woodland Nodwell village are manufactured using a modelling technique rather than coiling. Unlike coiling, which proceeds by winding and bonding a thin rope of clay to form the pot, modelling begins with a lump of clay which is shaped into a vessel form (Williamson 1990:298).

The design attributes on most of the Nodwell ceramic assemblage are also distinctly Late Woodland, and are associated with Iroquoian pottery types, rather than the pots produced by northern hunter-gatherers (MacNeish 1952; Wright 1966). Psuedo-scallop-shell and dentate stamping have been replaced by a plethora of more sophisticated stamped and incised designs which include horizontals, obliques, verticals and punctates. Most vessels have collars, and some have castellations and carinated shoulders. Decoration is largely confined to the shoulder through lip portion of the pot and vessel bodies are frequently plain.

Ceramics	Ground/Rough Stone	Chipped Stone	Bone/Antler/Shell	Copper
451 rim sherd vessels	16 celts	12 projectile points	55 bone beads	8 awls
679 neck sherds	1 celt blank	9 bifaces	1 bone beamer	1 bar
394 shoulder sherds	13 celt flakes	6 drills	94 bone awls	2 beads
6666 body sherds*	1 chisel	138 scrapers	14 bone projectile points	4 scrap
	2 pendants	4 utilized flakes	4 bone bracelet frags.	1 knife
95 pipe bowls	42 hammerstones	8 rough chipped stone	7 bone netting needles	
84 pipe stems	29 anvil stones	76 wedges	2 bone spatuals	
79 pipe frags.	84 anvil- hammers	2 spoke shaves	1 bone harpoon	
	77 abraders	5893.5 grams of flakes	1 bone handle	
190 lumps of fired/unfired clay	11 manos		1 bone knife	
	7 metates		47 worked deer toe bones	
3 foreign rim sherds	1 netsinker		21 modified bone	
	8 cobble spall scraper		1 worked turtle carapice	
	4 worked pebbles			
	3 adze frags.		14 worked beaver incisors	
	1 axe		2 worked bear canines	
	1 pipe fragment		1 worked dog canine	
	1 pipe blank			
			3 worked antler	
	33 ochre nodules		2 antler projectile points	
			2 shell beads	
			1 shell pendant	
			20 shell polishers	
			1 utilized shell frag.	

Table 17: The Material Culture Assemblage from the Nodwell Village.
(Stewart 1974; Wright 1974)

* Wright (1974) identified 2116 complete body sherds greater than 2.5 cm from the entire site, in my re-analysis of this material I examined 4810 complete body sherds, and 1370 exfoliated body sherds greater than 2.5 from the 12 houses. This number plus the 486 body sherds identified by Wright from locations outside the houses = 6666 body sherds.

Ceramic pipes are abundant at the Nodwell village, along with two fragments of stone pipes. This artifact type is completely absent at southern Bruce county's earlier sites and is associated with the Late Woodland period across southern Ontario (Wright1966). Other additions to the artifact assemblage include the adze, axe and spokeshave, as well as bone netting needles, bracelets, worked or perforated deer toe bones and shell polishers. Again, many of these items are thought to be diagnostic of Late Woodland, and in particular Middle Iroquoian occupations elsewhere in southern Ontario (Wright 1966).

Other artifacts, associated with the Middle Woodland occupation in southern Bruce county are either absent from the Nodwell assemblage or they have altered in form. For example, copper panpipes and antler club spikes are absent. Projectile points, while present, have assumed a different form. The majority of the Nodwell lithic projectile points are small, isosceles triangular points which may have side notches (Wright 1974). Furthermore, chipped lithics are made from a variety of source materials including Kettle Point chert, Lockport chert, and local nodular chert. The presence of Lockport chert reflects the addition of a new source material. Earlier lithic materials such as Selkirk, Collingwood and Bayport cherts are all absent from the Nodwell assemblage.

There were also some distinct differences in the subsistence remains recovered from the Nodwell village when compared to the subsistence material recovered from the Middle Woodland period sites in southern Bruce county. These differences exist primarily within the botanical assemblage. Table 18 demonstrates the presence of maize, a domesticated cultigen which was absent from all earlier sites in the region, which in itself is used to define Late Woodland occupations, particularly those of southern horticulturalists.

The botanical remains listed above were almost all recovered from pits inside houses. Wright (1974:292) believed that the paucity of botanical remains recovered from the Nodwell village, even after extensive flotation to recover floral samples was undertaken, suggested that the pits were filled during periods when edible plants were not readily available. On this basis,

Wright (1974) suggests that the Nodwell village was occupied throughout the winter. Faunal remains, overwhelmingly dominated by species available from spring through fall were used to demonstrate a full annual cycle of habitation at this village, a behaviour not fully recognizable at earlier sites (see Table 20).

Variety	Amount
Maize	384 kernels
Chenopodium	49 seeds
Raspberry	18 seeds
Elderberry	17 seeds
Blueberry	7 seeds

Table 18: Botanical Remains Recovered from the Nodwell Village.

(Wright 1974).

Wright's (1974) belief that the Nodwell village was founded by a migrant community of horticulturalists was based largely on the discontinuity of settlement pattern, artifact assemblages and subsistence practices between the sites occupied during the earlier Middle Woodland period and the Nodwell village. The lack of any other villages with a similar structure within 130 kilometres added weight to this belief. Furthermore, Wright's (1974) seriation of ceramic types was used to situate the Nodwell village temporally to the mid-14th century (Table 19). Wright (1974) used this mid 14th century date to argue that a migration was the only feasible explanation of the village's appearance because the last macroband habitation in southern Bruce county was dated no later than AD 1000, and during the 300 year period between these occupations no local precursors of the Nodwell village's structure had developed. In fact, Wright (1974) suggested that the 300 year gap between the occupation of the Thede site and the Nodwell village meant the region had experienced an occupational hiatus (Wright 1974).

Wright (1974) originally dated the Nodwell village to the 14th century on the basis of a ceramic seriation of pottery types conducted on the 407 analysable rim sherd vessels recovered from the site (44 vessels were too fragmentary to analyse). The seriation analysis grouped pottery types on stylistic elements outlined in MacNeish's (1952) *Iroquoian Pottery Types* which were believed to vary temporally. Table 19 presents the frequency and percentage of these ceramic types from the entire vessel assemblage. Following Wright (1974), rim sherd vessels are defined on an average of five rims per vessel. Therefore, to achieve the number of rims recovered from the site multiply the number of vessels by five.

Wright (1966) claimed that a Middleport sub-stage date hinged on the percentage of vessels typed to Ontario Horizontal, Middleport Oblique and Lawson Incised being greater than 50%. The percentage of these types from the ceramic vessel assemblage recovered from the Nodwell village equals 34.3%. Even when the un-typed vessels are not included in the total assemblage the percentage only equals 38%. Nevertheless, Wright (1974) still believed that a Middleport date for the Nodwell village was justified because the percentage of these Middleport sub-stage varieties was still greater than the percentage of varieties dating to either later or earlier periods.

The final element completing Wright's migration argument concerns determining the source of the Nodwell population. Since the settlement, material culture and subsistence data all suggested the Nodwell village was occupied by a farming society, Wright looked to Iroquoian groups inhabiting other parts of southern Ontario which were experiencing a population increase during the Middleport horizon to determine the source population.

Wright (1974) suggested that the occupants of the Nodwell village had migrated from Simcoe county, 130 km to the east of Nodwell, where the closest cluster of Middleport villages was located. In the years following the publication of the Nodwell report both Smith (1979) and Kapches (1981) undertook comparative analyses of the "typed" rim sherd assemblages from Nodwell and other known Middleport sites in

Pottery Types	Frequency	Percentage
Ontario Horizontal	88	21.6%
Iroquois Linear	27	6.6%
Ontario Oblique	3	0.7%
Pound Necked	81	19.9%
Middleport Oblique	38	9.3%
Middleport Criss-cross	4	1.0%
Lawson Incised	14	3.4%
Lawson Opposed	7	1.7%
Niagara Collared	2	0.5%
Huron Incised	16	3.9%
Black Necked	57	13%
Sidey Crossed	19	4.7%
Warminster Horizontal	8	2.0%
Warminster Crossed	1	0.3%
Aberrant un-typed	42	10.3%

Table 19: Percentage of Iroquois Pottery Types Present at the Nodwell Village.

(Wright 1974).

southern Ontario. Smith (1979:55-61) suggested that the Nodwell assemblage was most closely related to the assemblage from sites in the Toronto area to the southeast of Bruce county. Kapches' (1981:276) more detailed statistical analyses determined that the Nodwell ceramic assemblage was similar to the assemblages from sites in the Campbellville and Grand River regions of southwestern Ontario. Kapches (1981) also determined that the Nodwell assemblage was distinct from the assemblages at Middleport sites in Simcoe county, suggesting that there was no reason to expect the Nodwell population came from this region. However, both Smith (1979) and Kapches (1981) felt that the Nodwell ceramic assemblage was unique from other Middleport assemblages and believed that the sites most similar to Nodwell had yet to be located.

Continuities in the Nodwell Material Culture and Subsistence Data

There are also some striking similarities between the Nodwell village artifact and faunal assemblages and the earlier assemblages from Bruce county. These "continuities" contribute to the unique nature of this village, and may be the primary reason that any explanation of the origin of the Nodwell village population has remained controversial for thirty years (Fox 1990; Kapches 1981).

With regard to the assemblage of subsistence remains from the Nodwell village, the primary difference is the addition of a small quantity of maize. While maize kernels were absent from earlier sites in southern Bruce county, there was indirect evidence that the Middle Woodland population already had access to this resource (Molto 1979). Furthermore, the Nodwell village is unique among Middleport substage villages because there is no evidence of other types of cultigens. Other villages dating to this period generally contain remnants of corn, beans and tobacco (Kapches 1981; Pearce 1984:198-199; Dodd et al. 1990).

The remaining faunal assemblage, detailed in Table 20, is larger, but essentially the same as that recovered from the Middle Woodland Donaldson site (see Table 16). The faunal assemblage continues to be dominated by fish, land mammal and avian resources, with smaller quantities of reptiles and amphibians. All of the fish listed in Table 20 spawn between early spring and late fall. Sucker, which spawns in spring remains the dominant fish species, but Lake Whitefish which spawns in late fall is also important. Woodchuck, beaver, white tailed deer, black bear and <u>Canis</u> species continue to be the most important mammals. The majority of the mammals, as well as all other classes of fauna are most easily hunted from spring through fall given the migration and hibernation

Mammalia	Aves	Osteichthyes*	Amphibia	Reptilia
Cottontail Rabbit=8, MNI=4 Hare=1, MNI=1 Eastern Grey Squirrel=13, MNI=8 Red Squirrel=24, MNI=10 Squirrel sp.=11 Eastern Chipmunk=91, MNI=15 Starred Nosed Mole=1, MNI=1 Woodchuck=623, MNI=49 Beaver=273, MNI=30 Mouse sp.=53, MNI=12 Meadow Vole=5, MNI=2 Muskrat=22, MNI=9 Porcupine=32, MNI=10 Dog=16, MNI=6 <u>Canis</u> sp.=586, MNI=11 Red Fox=9, MNI=6 Black Bear=131, MNI=18 Bear sp.=9 Racoon=81, MNI=15 Mink=3, MNI=2 Marten=3, MNI=2 River Otter=14, MNI=5 Whitetailed Deer=1046, MNI=38 Moose=16, MNI=4	Herring Gull=5, MNI=3 Passenger Pigeon=287, MNI=31 Woodpeckers=5, MNI=5 Canada Goose=16, MNI=4 Ruffed Grouse=14, MNI=6 Common Crow=6, MNI=3 Common Raven=1, MNI=1 Loon sp.=25, MNI=7 Great Blue Heron=8, MNI=3 Whistling Swan=1, MNI=1 Shoveler=2, MNI=2 Oldsquaw=4, MNI=1 Bald Eagle=3, MNI=2 Sandhill Crane=4, MNI=1 Dove sp.=1, MNI=1 Bufflehead=3, MNI=1 Hawk sp.=2 Eastern Kingbird=1, MNI=1 Turkey=1, MNI=1 Great Horned Owl=1, MNI=1 Perching Bird Sp.=5 Red Neck Grebe=1, MNI=1 American Widgeon=1, MNI=1 Yellow Shafted Flicker=1, MNI=1	Lake Sturgeon=136 Lake Whitefish=190 Lake Trout=35 Northern Pike=87 Pike Family (Esocidae sp). =69 Longnose Sucker=5 Sucker family (Catostomidae sp.)=1155 Channel Catfish=71 Brown Bullhead=4 Catfish Family (Ictaluridae sp.)=65 Pumpkinseed=12 Largemouth Bass=2 Sunfish family (Centrarchidae sp.)=17 Sauger=3 Walleye=430 Percidae (<u>Stizostedion</u> sp.)=100 Redhorse (<u>Moxostoma</u> sp.)=35 Minnow family (Cyprinidae sp.)=2 Freshwater Drum=2 Mullet=5 Bowfin=2	Anura sp.=51, MNI=8	Painted Turtle=18, MNI=3 Snapping Turtle=17, MNI=1 Soft shell Turtle=1, MNI=1 Turtle=4

Table 20: Frequency of Identified Faunal Remains Recovered from the Nodwell Site. (Stewart 1974).
*the frequency of fish remains varies from Stewart 1974 due to my own analysis of another 10% of the overall fish assemblage.

71

patterns of most of these species, suggesting warm season occupation. Unlike earlier sites however, the overwhelming distribution of features within houses provides strong evidence to suggest that this village was occupied over the winter.

The distribution of both faunal and botanical material, which is found overwhelmingly within houses, adds support to a winter occupation interpretation (Wright 1974), as does the prevalence of white tailed deer and other mammals like mink, which are available and can be hunted successfully during the winter months. Some birds, including the ruffed grouse, and common crow would also have been available during the winter.

The presence of ten immature deer may also be used to interpret a winter occupation of the Nodwell village. At least six of these deer have either unerupted second molars or deciduous premolars suggesting that they were hunted between November and February if they were born in May as is usual in southern Ontario (Timmins 1997:103). Nevertheless, the faunal data from earlier sites does not negate the possibility of winter habitation as early as AD 700. In fact, the similarities between the faunal assemblages recovered from the Middle Woodland sites and the Nodwell village can be used to argue that Middle Woodland populations had the same potential to survive the winter in a macroband community as the Nodwell population.

Furthermore, it is the natural resources which appear to have been the most important foodstuffs at the Nodwell village. Not only are natural resources abundant at the village, but indirect evidence suggests that horticulture was not the dominant subsistence strategy. Only one axe was recovered from the village. If crops of corn had been grown around the village, a higher frequency of implements which could be used to clear land would be expected. As well, the single dog coprolite recovered from the village was laden with fish bones, but no cultigens.

Six immature dog burials were also identified at the Nodwell village. These remains were not included in Table 20. This practice of burying dogs was also evidenced at the Middle Woodland Donaldson site, and while dog burials occur sporadically at Late Woodland farming sites outside of Bruce county, this practice was always common amongst hunter-gatherers residing around the Bruce Peninsula. Furthermore, this phenomenon is believed to be associated with the ceremonial practices of northern hunter-gatherers during the Late Woodland period (Brizinski and Savage 1983; Fox 1987b; Prevec 1987; Smith 1985; Stewart 1992).

The artifact assemblage from the Nodwell village is also unique when compared to assemblages from Middleport sites elsewhere in southern Ontario. Cobble spall scrapers, chipped lithic scrapers, as well as an abundance of artifacts made from copper and from Kettle Point chert are all unique to southern Bruce county during the Late Woodland period. All of these items were used throughout the Middle Woodland period in this region. Wright (1974) has explained the presence of these artifacts by suggesting that the Nodwell village was located in proximity to northern foraging societies and therefore was able to act as a centre for trade between northern foragers and southern farmers. If this was the case, few items seem to have made it beyond the boundaries of the Nodwell village as both copper and Kettle Point chert are noteworthy, if only for their absence, at other Late Woodland Iroquoian sites (Fox 1990a; Janusas 1984; Kapches 1981). Cobble spall scrapers are diagnostic to the southern Bruce county region, and they were not common in other regions during any time period. Chipped lithic scrapers do occur at other Middleport villages (Kapches 1981). However, the dominance of this item in the overall chipped lithic assemblage is a trait most often associated with early Iroquoian sites and not sites dated to the Middleport substage (Williamson 1990).

It should also be noted that there are a variety of items of material culture common to Middleport villages which are absent or poorly represented in the Nodwell village assemblage. These include sinew stones, net-sinkers and antler chisels (Dodd et al. 1990; Wright 1966). The absence of these items further enhances the differences between the Nodwell village and other Middleport villages in southern Ontario.

The similarities between the Nodwell material culture and subsistence assemblages and those from earlier sites suggest that there may be a greater continuity of population in southern Bruce county than Wright's migration model represents. Furthermore, when the distribution of these remains across the Nodwell village is examined there is further evidence to suggest that the Nodwell village developed locally.

Distributional Variability at the Nodwell Village

The material culture and subsistence data presented above demonstrate that the Nodwell village was occupied during the Late Woodland period by a population who shared a ceramic pot and pipe tradition with Iroquoian farmers who inhabited other regions of southern Ontario. Other artifact traditions were also shared with the Middle Iroquoian populations of southern Ontario, but many of these items are diagnostic of the Uren sub-stage of the middle Late Woodland period, and not the Middleport sub-stage.

The material culture assemblage from the Nodwell village is also distinct from those associated with farming villages elsewhere in southern Ontario. Various artifact types recovered from the Nodwell village are 'continuities' of earlier Middle Woodland traditions which have not been recovered from Middleport villages elsewhere in southern Ontario. Furthermore, some items of material culture which are found at other Middleport villages are absent from the Nodwell collection. Horticultural produce was consumed by the inhabitants of the Nodwell village, but the majority of the foodstuffs appear to have been locally available natural resources. Therefore, there is little evidence to indicate that the subsistence strategy changed significantly between the Middle and Late Woodland periods, particularly because there is indirect evidence to suggest that maize was already utilized in Bruce county by AD 700. In fact, the absence of other cultigens such as beans and squash and the limited number of artifacts associated with the

production of domesticates recovered from the village suggests that the subsistence strategy at the Nodwell village was distinct from the subsistence practices employed at other Middleport villages (Dodd et al. 1990).

The differences between the material culture and subsistence assemblages recovered from the Nodwell village and those from other Middleport villages in southern Ontario challenge Wright's (1974) migration model, and enhance the perception that the Nodwell village developed locally from changes already underway in the region. Furthermore, Wright's (1974) migration model hinges on the abrupt appearance of the Nodwell village on the cultural landscape of southern Bruce county during the 14th century, but the variability of material culture between the Nodwell houses indicates that the village may have developed over a lengthier period of time.

As demonstrated above, Wright (1974) assigned the Nodwell village to the Middleport substage of the Late Woodland period largely due to the percentage of Middleport ceramic types recovered from the village. Nevertheless, the percentage of Middleport substage ceramics at Nodwell was no more than 38%, significantly less than the 50% requirement Wright (1966) has proclaimed necessary to date sites to this era. Instead of proposing a longer period of occupation for the Nodwell village, Wright (1974) suggested that the population inhabiting the village had both conservative and progressive elements: certain potters continued to use older designs while others experimented with new ones. For Wright (1974) the conservative and progressive dichotomy represented in the ceramic vessel assemblage at the Nodwell village was a contemporary phenomenon reflecting the behaviour of individual potters. However, Wright's (1974) own evidence suggests that this dichotomy may be associated with temporal change and the duration of village occupation. For example, Wright (1974) determined that there was a significant difference between the ceramic assemblage recovered from basal midden deposits at the Nodwell village and the ceramic assemblage recovered from the surface of the site, suggesting a stratigraphic change through time.The basal middens had 25% more "earlier" pottery types than the assemblage recovered from the surface, and that the surface collection produced 28% more "late" varieties. Furthermore, Wright (1974) demonstrated that this dichotomy varied spatially by house and he therefore labelled houses conservative, intermediate or progressive.

Given that the radiocarbon dates reflect a lengthy occupation at the Nodwell village and not simply occupation during the Middleport substage, it is possible that the differences between houses represent real temporal change rather than variation in contemporary behaviour. If this is the case, it may be possible to determine the full duration of the Nodwell village occupation. Furthermore, the differences between houses may help to determine the sequence of village development.

Wright (1974) used a variety of criteria to compare the ceramic vessel assemblages from each house, as well as the midden and surface material at the Nodwell village. Wright began by comparing MacNeish's (1952) Iroquoian pottery types but he believed that this classification scheme was better used for making comparisons between sites on a broad scale and was incapable of adequately representing finer grained spatial and temporal change which can occur within a single assemblage. Therefore, Wright (1974:228-244) also examined a variety of stylistic attributes which he recognized as changing temporally between the midden and surface vessel assemblages. The attributes observed were profile form, decorative motif, and shoulder sherd form.

Wright found that the same houses continued to cluster in each of the comparisons (Figure 21). Houses 4, 7, 10 and 11 were grouped as conservative, having much higher rates of "earlier" varieties of pots, a higher frequency of horizontal motifs, incipient shoulder forms and concave profiles. Houses 1 and 8 were continually grouped as progressive, having higher frequencies of "later" varieties of pots, vertical or oblique motifs, carinated shoulders and convex profiles. Houses 6, 9 and 12 were grouped as intermediate, having combinations of horizontal and vertical decorations, straight profiles, incipient shoulder forms and diverse types of pots. Several other analyses were attempted including the examination of

technique of design application, frequency of lip or interior decoration, frequency and type of castellations present, and orientation of motif. Unfortunately, the samples with these attributes were too small to determine any significant variation. Attempts were also made to examine variation on pipe styles but this assemblage was very tiny when divided up among houses. Similarly, no attempt was made to situate Houses 2, 3 or 5 within the conservative through progressive framework as all three houses contained only minimal (less than ten) numbers of vessels.

When observed independently, the ceramic assemblages from the four conservative houses fit the criteria established by Wright (1966) to define the Uren substage of the middle Late Woodland period which include an emphasis on horizontal motifs and greater than 50% representation of Iroquois Linear, Ontario Oblique and Ontario Horizontal pottery types. The Uren substage is an Iroquoian tradition which predates the Middleport substage by at least 50 years and is thought to begin circa AD 1250 (Timmins 1985:163).

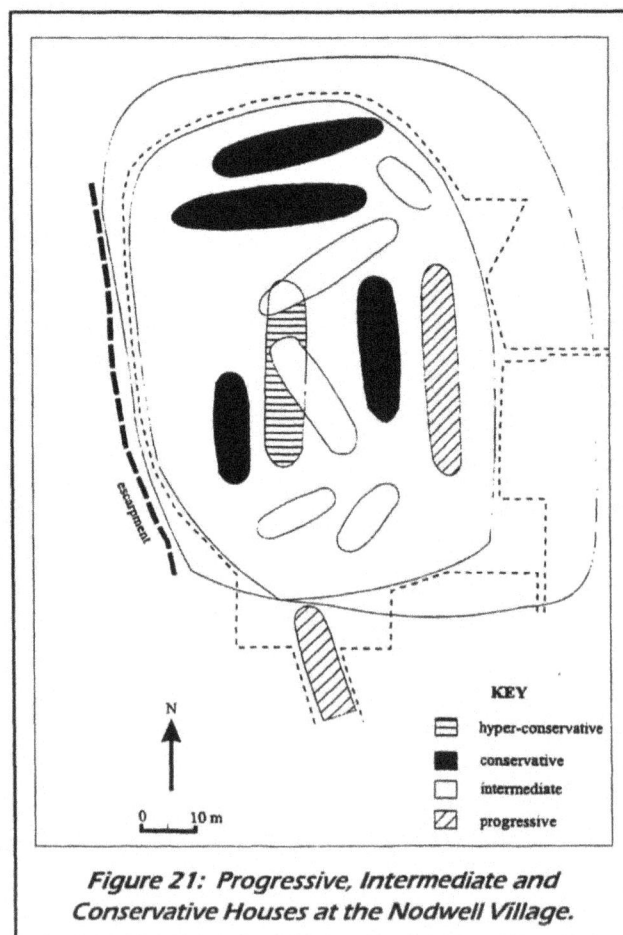

KEY

▤ hyper-conservative
◼ conservative
☐ intermediate
▨ progressive

Figure 21: Progressive, Intermediate and Conservative Houses at the Nodwell Village.

Not only is the ceramic vessel assemblage dominated by traits common to the Uren substage, but these four houses contain material culture common to this stage of the middle Late Woodland such as perforated deer toe bones. No items of material culture recovered from these houses, except for one possible broken netting needle, are diagnostic of the Middleport substage, suggesting that it is unlikely that the four conservative houses were occupied during the Middleport stage. Furthermore, radiocarbon dates from House 7, place the occupation of this house firmly within the Uren substage. Unfortunately, radiocarbon dates from House 10 predate the Uren substage by 90 years. It does seem unlikely that this house would be occupied that long and it is therefore possible that the corn from which this date was taken was left during an even earlier occupation of the village. However, two other explanations of the early radiocarbon date are possible. Either House 10 was occupied for up to 90 years with its initial occupation pre-dating the Uren substage, or the single sigma deviation on which a date of AD1155 was based does not provide an adequate range. No radiocarbon dates are available for either House 4 or 11.

Conversely, both the ceramic assemblage and other material culture from the most progressive houses (Houses 1 and 8) clearly represent a Middleport substage occupation of the Nodwell village, and radiocarbon dates from House 8 also place this occupation during the Middleport substage. There are Uren substage dates from House 8, but the high density of wall posts and pits in this house detailed in the previous chapter suggest that this house was occupied or re-occupied over a long period of time. The intermediate houses (houses 6, 9, and 12) could easily have been occupied anytime between AD 1250 and AD 1350 as the assemblages appear to span both stages. No radiocarbon dates are available from these houses. Unfortunately, Wright (1974) was unable to use the ceramic assemblage from House 5 because it was too small, yet this house is clearly earlier than even the conservative houses because it was torn down and overlain by two later houses.

The results of Wright's (1974) own analysis appear to represent the occupation of the Nodwell village for a much lengthier period than

his migration model allows. However, the statistical validity of Wright's (1974) analysis is questionable. When statistical tests for the equality of percentages were employed to compare the most robust samples used in each of Wright's attribute categories, I found that the variation between the household vessel assemblages was largely insignificant due to the small size of the household samples (Sokal and Rohlf 1969:608-609). Nevertheless, MacNeish's (1952:92) tests on sample variability determined that one hundred rimsherds was adequate to detect real variability between samples. The vessels examined by Wright are made up of five rimsherds each, so a minimum number of 100 is attained in nearly every house assemblage.

Regardless of the statistical validity of Wright's (1974) results, my own analyses on several thousand body sherds recovered from the Nodwell houses shows much the same variation between houses, and the large sample size is not subject to the same statistical problems. The body sherd analysis measured sherd thickness and body decoration for 4810 sherds and recognized a further 1370 sherds as exfoliated (Table 21).

The analysis of body sherd thickness is based on the assumption that pots were more finely constructed through time. Recent analyses of the body sherd assemblage from the Kirche site in the Upper Trent valley of Ontario found that pots from more recent houses were considerably thinner than the pots recovered from earlier houses in the same village (Cannon pers. comm.). Furthermore, the transition from thick to thin pots over time has been recognized in other regions of southern Ontario (Williamson 1990; Murphy and Ferris 1990). The analysis of exfoliated sherds is also derived from the belief that later pots are manufactured better than earlier ones. However, Wright (1981) has also used these data to suggest differences in ceramic manufacturing techniques between ethnic groups. Body sherd decoration also changes temporally.

In each of the three categories of analysis used to compare body sherds between houses my results were similar to Wright's (1974) analyses of rimsherd vessels. Houses 4, 7, 10 and 11 were conservative in each category, Houses 1 and 8 were progressive, and Houses 6, 9 and 12 were intermediate. Given the size of the body sherd assemblage I was also able to situate Houses 2, 3 and 5, which had not been possible in Wright's analysis. Houses 2 and 3 were deemed intermediate and House 5 was so distinct that a fourth category of hyper-conservative was used.

House Number	Sherd Frequency	Average Thickness	Percentage Sherds Fully Exfoliated	Decoration
House 1	a. 287 b. 329	7.5 mm	12.8 %	90.2% plain 9.8% rib paddled
House 2	a. 45 b. 57	9.1 mm	21.1%	84.4% plain 15.6% rib paddled
House 3	a. 105 b. 133	9.0 mm	21.1%	81.9% plain 18.1 rib paddled
House 4	a. 160 b. 231	9.6 mm	30.7%	73.1% plain 20% rib paddled 6.9% corded
House 5	a. 30 b. 47	10.6 mm	36.2%	43.3% rib paddled 40% plain 16.7 % corded
House 6	a. 581 b. 740	8.9 mm	21.5%	81.1% plain 18.9 %rib paddled
House 7	a. 344 b. 500	9.5 mm	31.2%	73% plain 20.1% rib paddled 5.2% corded 1.7% check stamped
House 8	a. 1205 b. 1389	7.6 mm	13.2%	87.2% plain 11.2% rib paddled 0.5 % check stamped 1.1% corded
House 9	a. 1091 b. 1384	9.0 mm	21.1%	83.1% plain 15.7% rib paddled 1.2% corded
House 10	a. 395 b. 568	9.6 mm	30.5%	69.1% plain 22.8% rib paddled 8.1% corded
House 11	a. 512 b. 733	9.7 mm	30.2%	70.7% plain 22.1% rib paddled 7.2% corded
House 12	a. 55 b. 69	8.5 mm	20.3%	81.8% plain 14.6% rib paddled 3.6% corded

Table 21: Body Sherd Variation between Houses.

a. Equals the frequency of body sherds greater that 2.5 cm examined for thickness and decoration. b. Equals the total number of body sherds greater than 2.5 cm which were recovered from each house, including the exfoliated sherds.

The analysis of body sherds appears to show real temporal differences between houses. The body sherd assemblage from House 5 has the thickest sherd width (10.6 mm), highest percentage of exfoliated pottery (32.6%), and the highest percentage of cord maliated or roughened sherds (16.7%). These characteristics are often associated with early Late Woodland period pottery. Furthermore, the few rimsherds from House 5 do not conform to any classic Iroquoian pottery types. Instead they can be associated with the Western Basin Springwell phase pottery tradition, and may pre-date Iroquoian ceramic traditions. Springwell phase pottery was common in southwestern Ontario between AD 1100 and 1200 (Murphy and Ferris 1990). Furthermore, this pottery is associated with a foraging society rather than a farming population (Murphy and Ferris 1990). Among the entire artifact assemblage from House 5 there are no artifacts diagnostic of later time periods.

The results of Wright's (1974) analysis of rimsherd vessels grouped Houses 4, 7, 10 and 11, and I classified these houses as pre-Middleport Late Woodland, or Uren substage houses for reasons outlined above. The analysis of body sherds supports this assumption as body sherds remain quite thick (9.5-9.7 mm), the percentage of exfoliated sherds remains high (30.2%-31.2%), and cord roughened sherds, while present, have decreased to approximately 7% of the assemblage. Both rib paddled sherds and plain sherds now dominate the assemblage. Sutton (1996:111) demonstrated that the corded body sherd treatments represent approximately 8.9% of the collection from Uren substage sites in Simcoe county, Ontario, and this figure is very similar to the assemblages from the conservative houses at the Nodwell village.

Houses 6, 9 and 12 remain intermediate and have diverse artifact assemblages which indicate they could be occupied anywhere between AD1250 and AD 1350. Houses 2 and 3 can now be deemed intermediate as well given that the body sherd assemblages from these two houses are so similar to those from Houses 6, 9 and 12. The body sherd assemblages from intermediate houses have thinner constructions (8.5-9.1 mm), a smaller percentage of exfoliated sherds (20.3%-

21.5%), and few, if any, cord wrapped sherds (they are only present in Houses 9 and 12, at 1.2% and 3.7%). The Middleport body sherd assemblages from several sites in the Markham, Ontario area analysed by Kapches (1981) show approximately 1% cord maliated or roughed decoration, with larger amounts of rib paddling, and a majority of plain sherds. The body sherd assemblage among intermediate houses at the Nodwell village is predominantly plain (approximately 83%), with approximately 16% rib paddled. It is probable that these houses were occupied during the Middleport sub-stage. Furthermore, radiocarbon dates from House 3 suggest that this house was occupied in the 14th century.

Houses 1 and 8 continue to be progressive, and while a variety of diagnostic artifacts demonstrate that these two houses were occupied during the Middleport substage, these houses are quite distinct from the intermediate houses. Wright (1974) found that the rimsherd vessels had the most progressive traits in these two houses. Similarly, the analysis of body sherds found that the sherd thickness was very thin (7.5-7.6 mm), the percentage of exfoliated sherds was low (12.8%-13.2%), and plain sherds dominated the collection (87.2%-90.2%). Aside from having a very distinct ceramic assemblage, Houses 1 and 8 were also unique in terms of their settlement features. House 1 was located outside of the village palisade, and House 8 was a very busy structure with large numbers of wall-posts and interior pits, and a clear extension.

Given that there are clear differences between houses with regard to the artifact assemblages, and in particular the ceramic vessel assemblages, it is improbable that the entire Nodwell site was occupied contemporaneously, but developed incrementally, with certain houses being occupied before others and perhaps even periodic village abandonment. This assumption is supported by the diverse radiocarbon dates from the site. The sequence of occupation suggested follows Wright's conservative-progressive dichotomy. House 5, labelled hyper-conservative, was occupied early, probably during the early Late Woodland period.

Houses 4, 7, 10 and 11, labelled conservative, were occupied in the middle Late Woodland and may be associated with the Uren substage of the Ontario Iroquois Tradition. Houses 2, 3, 6, 9, and 12, labelled intermediate were occupied later, probably during the Middleport substage of the middle Late Woodland period. Finally, Houses 1 and 8, the progressive houses, were either occupied just after the intermediate group, but still during the Middleport substage, or some other cultural factors must account for their distinct ceramic assemblages. Given that House 1 and House 8 have unique settlement features this is a real possibility.

Population estimates outlined in Chapter 2 demonstrate that the original population which inhabited House 5 was quite small. The population estimate for House 5 was only 11 persons. However, later construction on top of this house may have destroyed the hearth features on which this estimate was based, and it is possible that the population was larger. Population estimates for the Uren phase occupation at the Nodwell village shows an increase in population to approximately 110. Similarly, the Middleport population inhabiting the Nodwell village was approximately 105.

At this point it is still very difficult to determine when the palisade was constructed around the Nodwell village, or even if both palisades were constructed at the same time. It is unlikely that a small population constructed a large palisade around a single longhouse during the early Late Woodland period. Therefore, the palisade construction probably began once the population increased and numerous houses were constructed during the Uren phase of the Late Woodland period. Furthermore, now that the duration of village occupation has been increased, I believe that the second palisade was added during the Middleport stage of occupation as a necessary replacement for the original palisade which may have deteriorated over time.

One final vessel sherd analysis was undertaken on the Nodwell material by Trigger et al. (1980). Trigger et al. (1980:123) undertook a trace element analysis on 90 pot sherds from the Nodwell village, randomly selected from Houses

6, 7, 8, 9 and 11. The results of this study indicate that the chemical makeup of the clay used to make pots in House 8 was distinct from all the other sherds examined because it showed a high percentage of calcium (Trigger et al. 1980:130). Other differences were between Houses 7 and 11, and House 9. This corresponds well with Wright's (1974) distinction between Houses 7 and 11 as conservative, and House 9 labelled intermediate, and suggests that the occupants of these houses were using different clay sources. House 6 showed similarities to both Houses 7 and 11, and House 9 (Trigger et al. 1980:130). With the evidence of temporal differences between houses provided by the body sherd analysis, it makes sense that over the duration of Nodwell's occupation various sources of clay were used.

Faunal material can also be used to test the sequence of Nodwell village development proposed above. For example, if all of the houses in the Nodwell village were occupied at the same time, then it would be expected that most households would have had a similar diet. Given that subsistence practices change through time in southern Ontario, especially after the introduction of cultigens, if the houses were occupied during different time periods there may be some variation in household diet.

However, the differences between the subsistence assemblages at the Nodwell village are minimal. The primary difference concerns the distinct nature of the House 5 subsistence assemblage when contrasted to all other houses. The House 5 assemblage has twice as many bird (7.5%) and fish remains (58.7%) as any other house and considerably fewer mammals (31.7%) are represented (Wright 1974:281). The subsistence strategy represented in this house is similar to the late Middle Woodland sites in the region. This is not surprising given that this house probably dates to the early Late Woodland period. Nevertheless, the frequency of fish and birds (primarily loon), may be used to suggest that House 5 was occupied predominantly during the spring through fall period.

Houses 7 and 11 have both large numbers of fish remains and large quantities of mammals. The

most recent houses have the largest quantities of mammal remains, but overall the subsistence assemblage from houses labelled intermediate and progressive are very similar (Wright 1974:281). Nevertheless, the increasing frequency of mammal bones through time may suggest that the seasonal use of the Nodwell village changed through time, and only during the latter stages of occupation became the focus of year-round settlement. The changes in the seasonal use of the village through time were not recognized by Wright (1974) who used the distribution of external pit features to suggest that the village was occupied during the winter months. Now that it has been determined that the village was constructed incrementally, there is a possibility that exterior pits used by earlier populations were overlain by later longhouse structures. Therefore, the distribution of pits examined by Wright may only reflect the most recent occupation.

The results of the analysis of subsistence and material culture remains demonstrate that there are real differences between household assemblages and the best interpretation of these differences suggests that the Nodwell village developed over a long period, perhaps as much as 250 years. It is therefore unlikely that the Nodwell village was the result of a migration of Iroquoian farmers into Bruce county during the 14th century as Wright (1974) originally suggested, but developed incrementally as the indigenous inhabitants of southern Bruce county experimented with a new form of community settlement from the early Late Woodland period through the Middleport substage of this period.

This is not to say that the development of the Nodwell village was not influenced by events elsewhere in southern Ontario during the Middleport stage and earlier. Rather, the Nodwell village was probably the culmination of changes to local social and economic structures which began during the late Middle Woodland period in southern Bruce county, and these changes probably precipitated from ongoing interaction between the inhabitants of Bruce county and the farming communities of southern Ontario. The introduction of cultigens and the transfer of information between these societies is no doubt responsible for the similarity of both form and content of this village to other sites in southern Ontario. However, local traditions are also an important element of the Nodwell's structure, and produce the strong variability between this village and other villages in southern Ontario. It would appear that interaction, rather than direct migration, is a more significant variable for explaining culture change in southern Bruce county.

Interaction

There is evidence to suggest that the interaction with outside societies which was noted during the late Middle Woodland period in southern Bruce county continued throughout the Late Woodland occupation of the Nodwell village. Every house at the Nodwell village contains foreign cherts, and most houses contain copper. None of the copper recovered from the Nodwell village has been sourced, but all copper is native. This copper could have come from almost any direction (Turff 1997). However, it is probable that this copper came from one of the numerous large copper mining locales located along the north shores of Lake Huron or Lake Superior. Because there is no evidence of copper tool manufacturing at the Nodwell village, and because the tools found resemble those tools recovered prehistorically on sites in northern Ontario, it is probable that the tools were traded into Bruce county from the north (Wright 1967; 1969; 1974).

The foreign chert recovered from the Nodwell village was limited to Lockport and Kettle Point cherts. Unlike the Middle Woodland assemblages there is no longer evidence for Bayport, Fossil Hill, or Selkirk chert. The importance of Kettle Point chert continues from the Middle Woodland occupation of southern Bruce county, although at most other Late Woodland sites in southern Ontario this chert is no longer significant (Janusas 1984). This chert may have remained an important lithic source for the occupants of southern Bruce county because of the ease with which it could be collected.

The presence of Lockport chert in the Nodwell village assemblage is a Late Woodland addition, not recovered from any Middle Woodland sites. This chert can be quarried at various outcrops in southern Ontario from Grimsby to Ancaster (Eley and von Bitter 1989:19-20). The presence of this chert suggests that the people of the Nodwell village were either travelling to a new location to quarry chert or were interacting with a regional population that was insignificant to the occupants of the Middle Woodland period sites. However, Lockport chert is frequently mistaken for Onondaga chert (Eley and von Bitter 1989:20), and during a cursory examination of this chert from the Nodwell collection, I was unable to distinguish from which host formation the chert came.

If the chert from the Nodwell village is in fact Onondaga chert, there may be a greater continuity of interaction spheres between the Middle and Late Woodland habitation of southern Bruce county than previously acknowledged. Onondaga chert can be quarried from various locales, most of which are located along the northern shores of Lake Erie near the mouth of the Grand River (Eley and von Bitter 1989:17). During the Middle Woodland period, Selkirk chert was quarried from sources in the same region. If the chert recovered from the Nodwell site is Onondaga chert, then there is a continuity of interaction between these two regions from the Middle Woodland period through the Middleport substage of the Late Woodland period.

Support for this hypothesis can be found in Kapches (1981) and Wright (n.d.). Kapches' (1981:310) typological analysis of ceramics from Middleport periods sites across ten local regions in southern Ontario determined that there was a higher statistical co-efficient of similarity between the Nodwell ceramic assemblage and the assemblage from the Middleport village, located along the Grand River, than between Nodwell and any other Middleport village. More recently, Wright (n.d.:100) compared motif attributes from both pots and pipes from seven Middleport villages and found a strong correlation between the Nodwell and Middleport village assemblages. Unfortunately, the statistical significance of these investigations may be unreliable. Given that the collections from these two villages were larger than any other collections examined by these two researchers, the similarities between these two sites may simply result from the size of the collections, which were probably more variable than the other assemblages which were examined.

Nevertheless, the earliest interaction between the foragers of southern Bruce county and farmers occurred with the farmers of the Grand valley. This initial forager/farmer frontier can be considered very basic: characterized by the exchange of commodities between the two societies. However, prolonged interaction between southern Bruce county and the Grand River region over several generations would have resulted in the exchange of ideas and information and may account for the eventual similarity between the structure and contents of the Nodwell village and Late Woodland Middleport villages in southwestern Ontario (Kapches 1981).

However, the structure of the forager/farmer frontier in southern Ontario altered through time as a result of changes outside of southern Bruce county. By the Uren stage, when Nodwell assumes village status, much of southern Ontario is occupied by farmers. Therefore, the forager/farmer frontier no longer exists strictly between Bruce county and the Grand River valley, but between Bruce county and most of southern Ontario. The shifting of this frontier suggests that the Bruce county foragers had to adapt to a significantly different cultural landscape by the middle Late Woodland period, and the structure and form of the Nodwell village may reflect not only internal socio-economic change, but the manner in which Bruce county foragers were able to negotiate this much larger frontier. By assuming the form of a farming community, but not necessarily the economic strategy, the occupants of the Nodwell village may have been both protecting their rights to their territory and strengthening their bonds with various farming communities inhabiting the fringes of this territory.

Furthermore, a shift in the operation of the forager/farmer frontier appears to coincide with the shift in location of this frontier during the Late Woodland period. For example, it is probable that the ceramic collections from the most progressive houses at the Nodwell village (Houses 1 and 8) reflect intensive interaction with outside Iroquoian farming populations. As stated above, House 1 and 8 were occupied during the Middleport stage. Intermediate houses may also have been occupied during this period, but the percentage of progressive traits was even higher in Houses 1 and 8 and it was suggested that social rather then temporal differences may have contributed to the distinction.

Kapches (1984:307) suggests that there is evidence for population increase in many regions inhabited by Middleport populations, and that these villages were more likely to fission in response to population growth than to conglomerate into large cosmopolitan villages because social organization was not sophisticated enough to control large populations. I therefore suggest that the appearance of a very progressive house outside the palisades of the Nodwell village during the Middleport substage probably came about when a Middleport village elsewhere in southern Ontario was forced to fission. The low population of the Nodwell village and the entire Bruce region, combined with the abundance of natural resources in this region, as well as a long history of interaction between Bruce county and outside farming populations probably made the Nodwell village a prime candidate for the acceptance of immigrants.

Furthermore, the wall post density of House 1 was very low, indicating that this house was not occupied for very long. Therefore, the extension built on the end of House 8 located inside the village may have been built to accommodate this immigrant population and formally accept them into the village. The large number of pit and hearth features inside House 8 indicates that this house was inhabited by a larger population than any other house. The immigration of a farming population to the Nodwell village during the Middleport stage would explain both the distinct settlement pattern of these two houses, and the distinct nature of their ceramic assemblages: suggesting that outside influence provided by an immigrant Iroquoian population introduced more progressive ceramic styles at this time. Furthermore, a migration of farmers into the

Nodwell village suggests that the function of the forager/farmer frontier had altered considerably from its initial form when the exchange of commodities dominated the interaction across the frontier.

Interaction may also have continued between southern Bruce county and foraging populations in Michigan, 200 km across Lake Huron during the Late Woodland period. Two pots recovered from the basal middens at the Nodwell village were identified by Wright (1974:212) as being of the style produced in Michigan during a culture phase contemporaneous with Middleport (Fitting 1970). However, more recent research has demonstrated that Younge Phase pottery was produced by communities on both the east and western shores of Lake Huron over a lengthy temporal period (Murphy and Ferris 1990). Therefore, these pots may indicate continued interaction with Western Basin foragers identified by the presence of Springwell pottery in House 5.

Interpretation

Wright (1974) used artifact and subsistence data from the Nodwell village to establish the similarity of the village to Iroquoian farming villages elsewhere in southern Ontario and to date the Nodwell village to the Middleport substage of the Late Woodland period. By assigning the Nodwell site to this date Wright (1974) was unable to explain the Nodwell village as anything other than a migratory event, because there were clearly no antecedents to the culture pattern typified by this village at any of Bruce county's previous habitations. Nevertheless, the distinct nature of the Nodwell subsistence and material culture made it impossible to determine where the immigrants had come from.

The results of a systematic re-analysis of the artifact and subsistence data from the Nodwell village, building on the analyses conducted by Wright (1974) now suggests that the Nodwell village developed incrementally, with certain houses being abandoned before others were constructed, and that this procedure had been underway for a long temporal period, perhaps beginning in the early Late Woodland, soon

after longhouses were constructed at the Middle Woodland Donaldson site. Not only are houses of different periods distinct from one another in terms of their artifact assemblages, but groups of houses share the same types of artifacts and artifact attributes, so it is possible to determine which portion of the village was occupied during different periods. These data also help to explain both the radiocarbon dates from the Nodwell village and the incoherency of the settlement plan. House 5 appears to have been occupied first. Following the occupation of House 5 it is probable that there was a period of abandonment. Timmins (1997) demonstrates that it was not uncommon for early late Woodland populations to periodically abandon longhouse sites and return to a more traditional foraging strategy. During the Uren sub-stage of the Late Woodland period Houses 4, 7, 10 and 11 were constructed, followed soon after by Houses 1, 2, 3, 6, 8, 9 and 12. These households continue to cluster no matter how the data are examined.

By suggesting a much longer period of occupation for the Nodwell village it is possible to explain all of the unique elements of the subsistence and material culture assemblage as regional traditions which continue from the Middle Woodland period. Interaction with farmers is very much part of the local tradition, and its origins are firmly established by the end of the Middle Woodland period. The process of interaction helps account for the differences between Middle Woodland artifact and subsistence assemblages and those recovered from the Nodwell village. The occupants of the Nodwell village appear to have adopted ceramic traditions, a pipe complex, corn subsistence and other elements from their farming neighbours.

Interaction with farming groups elsewhere in southern Ontario also helps to explain the "progressive" nature of the ceramic vessel assemblage recovered from Houses 1 and 8. These two houses appear to have been occupied during the Middleport substage of the Late Woodland period along with other houses in the village, but were still quite distinct. I have suggested that House 1, located outside the village, was occupied by immigrant farmers. Once accepted by the Nodwell community this group moved inside the village and was housed in House 8, which was expanded to accommodate a new population, and appears to have been overcrowded. This explanation is not only supported by the similarity of material culture within these two houses, but helps to explain the unique settlement features of both houses.

The subsistence and artifact data from the Nodwell village have therefore helped to define both the origin and sequence of occupation of the Nodwell village, and in essence suggest that local culture change, interaction and migration all played a role in the formation of this village.

Late Woodland Material Culture and Subsistence

Pre-Iroquoian Late Woodland

At least five sites in southern Bruce county may be associated with the early Late Woodland period. These sites are defined on the presence of cord-wrapped-stick impressed rimsherds with exterior annular punctates forming bosses on the interior profile. This assemblage was also outlined in the Middle Woodland section because this pottery is present at the Donaldson site prior to AD 710 and it remains uncertain exactly when pots from other sites were manufactured.

In southwestern Ontario the appearance of this pottery coincides with the transition to farming and is associated with the early Late Woodland period (Smith and Crawford 1997). The presence of this pottery at the Donaldson site by AD 700 marks the earliest appearance of this pottery style outside of southwestern Ontario (Fox 1990a) and it is therefore probable that this pottery was incorporated into the Middle Woodland ceramic assemblage as the result of interaction between the Bruce county foragers and the farmers of southwestern Ontario.

It is also probable that this ceramic style continued to be used throughout the pre-Iroquoian Late Woodland period in Bruce county because a radiocarbon date taken from charred organic remains inside a vessel recovered from the Hunter/Frenchman's Bay site dated to AD 928±138 (Ferris 1988). If this is the case, the small numbers of rimsherds recovered from only five sites could be used to suggest that the pre-Iroquoian occupation of Bruce county was ephemeral, and that the region was largely depopulated.

However, a large number of corded body sherds have been recovered from ten sites in southern Bruce county. Corded body sherds were common from the late Middle Woodland through the early Late Woodland period and may be associated with the same time period as the cord-wrapped-stick rim sherds. The frequency of the rims and body sherds from these sites is outlined in Table 22. If corded body sherds were being used at the same time as the cord-wrapped-stick impressed rim designs, then there is evidence to suggest much more activity in southern Bruce county during the early Late Woodland.

Given that corded body sherds have been recovered from nine of the thirteen known Middle Woodland occupations, there appears to have been a strong continuity in the regional settlement pattern between the Middle and Late Woodland periods in Bruce county. Furthermore, a large number of corded body sherds were recovered from the Nodwell village, most of which were associated with House 5 - the earliest house in the village. It is therefore probable that Nodwell became an important settlement during the early Late Woodland period. Unfortunately, there is no other material culture or subsistence data which can be directly

Site Name	Cord-Wrapped-Stick Impressed Rimsherd with Annular Punctates	Cord Maliated Body Sherds
Hunter/Frenchman's Bay (BdHh-5)	1 vessel	
Shutt (BcHi-6)		11 corded sherds
Port Elgin Cemetery (BcHi-2)	1 rimsherd	4 corded sherds
North Elgin		1 corded sherd
Nodwell (BcHi-3)		131 corded sherds
Boiled Baby (BcHi-16)	4 rimsherds	206 corded sherds
Thede (BcHi-7)		10 corded sherds
Donaldson (BdHi-1)	27 rimsherds	176 corded sherds
Busch (BcHh-6)	1 rimsherd	
Kirkland Farm		10 corded sherds

Table 22: Frequency of Pre-Iroquoian Late Woodland Ceramics.
(Finlayson 1977:142, 287, 363; Fox 1989; Wright and Anderson 1963:31-35).

associated with this period at any site but Nodwell. However, given the locations and sizes of the other sites it is probable that most sites functioned as resource extraction locations between spring and fall. House 5 of the Nodwell site, however, was probably the focus of macroband habitation.

The subsistence data from House 5 at the Nodwell village included a small amount of maize, as well as large quantities of fish, birds and some mammal bones. The Nodwell site is located at some distance from the nearest fish-spawning river, so fish resources would have had to have been brought back to Nodwell from smaller extraction sites. The shift to the inland Nodwell location for macroband habitation may reflect a concern for defence and the need to protect stored resources. Furthermore, the construction of a longhouse at the Nodwell site, continues the transition toward larger communal settlement organization which began during the Middle Woodland period.

Given the similarities between the late Middle Woodland and early Late Woodland settlement system in southern Bruce county it would appear that there is a continuous occupation from the Middle Woodland through early Late Woodland period, and that the socio-economic change evidenced by the construction of a house at the Nodwell village at this time was a natural outgrowth of earlier changes. The interaction between the southern Bruce county foragers and the farmers of southwestern Ontario which occurred at this time, and is demonstrated by the manufacture of a new pottery style, may have also stimulated further changes to the traditional pattern of life in Bruce county.

Middle Late Woodland Material Culture and Subsistence Data

Aside from the Nodwell village, eleven smaller sites have been identified in southern Bruce county during the middle Late Woodland period. These sites were originally classified as Middleport campsites (Wright 1974), and were thought to function as special purpose campsites associated with the Nodwell village. Now that the occupation of the Nodwell village appears to begin somewhat earlier than the Middleport substage of the Late Woodland period, it is

unlikely that these sites were utilized only during the Middleport substage. In fact, these sites include diagnostic material from many different cultural eras and were probably used continually from the Middle Woodland period throughout the Middleport substage of the Late Woodland period. Therefore, these sites have now been re-classified more generally as middle Late Woodland period occupations. Furthermore, none of these sites have been radiocarbon dated, and only one site has been subject to a limited excavation, so the diagnostic material culture assemblages are too small to use seriation analyses to assign these sites to a more specific temporal period. Like the Nodwell site though, the middle Late Woodland ceramics recovered from these sites can be associated with the Iroquois tradition.

Table 23 details the frequency of diagnostic artifacts recovered from middle Late Woodland sites in southern Bruce county other than Nodwell. Furthermore, diagnostic items are limited to ceramic and lithic materials, as no diagnostic bone artifacts have been recovered. When compared to the Nodwell village, the assemblages of material culture from the sites listed in Table 23, are small. Since the size of most of these sites are also small, this is probably a factor of site function rather than the lack of excavation. In contrast to the Nodwell village, these settlements lack many diagnostic tools. No bone netting needles, perforated deer toe bones, or bone bracelets have been recovered. Similarly, the diagnostic stone assemblage does not include axes, adzes or spokeshaves, and projectile points are infrequent. Even the ceramic assemblage is much smaller. This suggests that the sites were used on a more limited basis than the Nodwell village, and that a smaller range of activities took place at these sites.

Nevertheless, the diagnostic assemblages do vary in size. The most significant collections were made at the Busch site and BcHi-16 which settlement data suggest were larger than the other middle Late Woodland campsites. The Busch site, located on the shores of inland Lake Arran is the most substantial campsite which has been located, and the only site which contained numerous hearths and artifact clusters (Shutt 1952; Wright 1953a). For this reason it was suggested earlier that this site was used by a larger population than the other campsites. The linear arrangement of features along the shoreline suggested the annual re-occupation of this site, and the lack of evidence for substantial dwelling structures was used to interpret this site as a summer habitation, perhaps even a summer village. The larger quantity of

Site Name	Ceramics	Stone
North Shore (BdHi-2)	2 Ontario Horizontal rimsherds 1 Lawson Incised rimsherd 1 Ontario Oblique rimsherd	
Shutt (BcHi-6)	8 Middleport Oblique rimsherds 3 Ontario Horizontal rimsherds 1 Iroquois Linear rimsherd	7 Onondaga flakes 1 net sinker
Mirimachi Bay (BcHi-4)	2 Ontario Horizontal rimsherds 2 Iroquois Linear rimsherds 1 pipe bowl	1 isosceles triangular point 1 net sinker
North Elgin	2 Middleport Oblique rimsherds	
Port Elgin Cemetery (BcHi-2)	1 Middleport Oblique rimsherd 5 Ontario Horizontal rimsherds 3 Lawson Incised rimsherds 1 Iroquois Linear rimsherd 1 Black Necked rimsherd 1 pipe bowl	
Boiled Baby (BcHi-16)	3 Middleport Oblique rimsherds 19 Ontario Horizontal rimsherds 5 Lawson Incised rimsherds 1 Iroquois Linear rimsherd 2 Pound Neck rimsherds 1 pipe stem 1 pipe bowl 1 pipe fragment	1 net sinker
Indian Church	1 pipe fragment	1 isosceles triangular point
Donaldson (BdHi-1)	2 Middleport Oblique rimsherds 1 Ontario Horizontal rimsherd 2 Ontario Oblique rimsherds	
Thede (BcHi-7)	1 Middleport Oblique rimsherd 1 Ontario Horizontal rimsherd 2 Lawson Incised rimsherds	
Kirkland Farm	3 Ontario Horizontal rimsherds 1 pipe stem	
Busch (BcHh-6)	12 Middleport Oblique rimsherds 16 Ontario Horizontal rimsherds 8 Lawson Incised rimsherds 2 Ontario Oblique rimsherds 1 Iroquois Linear rimsherd 1 Pound Necked rimsherd 3 pipe bowls 1 pipe stem	2 isosceles triangular points

Table 23: Middle Late Woodland Diagnostic Material Culture.
(Knechtel 1955; Lee 1960:18, 25-26; Shutt 1952; Wright 1953a:1, 3; 1953b:3; Wright and Anderson 1963:30).

diagnostic material culture recovered from this site adds some support to this interpretation.

BcHi-16 was also considered a substantial campsite and cemetery (see Chapter 2). Non-diagnostic items of material culture recovered from this site include two utilized flakes, one piece of lithic debitage, one stone bead, a possible axe, one bone awl and one bone bead (Wright 1953b:3). Given that this site contains the only known middle Late Woodland cemetery in the region, and is the only site which has been subject to excavation it would be expected that this site would be distinct from the other small sites. The hearth floor does suggest that this site also functioned as a campsite and the presence of a single netsinker in the artifact assemblage (Table 23) suggests that it was a fishing location. BcHi-16 is located alongside Mill Creek which today has runs of spring spawning fish, including sucker. The proximity of this site to the Nodwell village suggests that this may have been an important location for accessing spring spawning fish in the early spring when stored resources had been depleted.

The Port Elgin Cemetery site and the Shutt site have also been subject to more intensive investigation than the other small sites in southern Bruce county (Knechtel 1955; Shutt 1951; 1952; Wright 1953a). This probably accounts for the diagnostic assemblages from these sites being slightly larger. In reality though, these sites were both small, and like the other small sites in the region were located at strategic positions for exploiting naturally occurring resources. The North Shore, Shutt, Indian Church, Donaldson and Thede sites are all located along the Saugeen River at sets of rapids, in ideal places for harvesting fish. Important fish spawns occur throughout the warmer seasons in the Saugeen River, beginning with the sucker and pickerel spawn in the early spring and ending with the Whitefish spawn in December (Burns 1973:43-44). The presence of a net sinker at the Shutt site suggests that these fish may have been harvested in large quantities.

The North Elgin, Port Elgin Cemetery and Kirkland Farm sites are located along smaller streams, each with small fish runs today. These sites could also have been used as small hunting camps. Both the North Elgin and Port Elgin Cemetery sites are located in proximity to the Nodwell village and if corn had been grown in any quantity around the village, the modified environment may have attracted grazing species such as white tailed deer, making these two sites prime hunting locations (Kapches 1981:219).

The Mirimachi Bay site, located on a shallow sheltered bay along the Lake Huron shoreline and close to the Nodwell village would have been ideal for fishing both Lake Trout and Northern Pike. Both species spend long periods of time around the spawning season in lake shallows and both fish are widely represented at the Nodwell site. Northern Pike would have been most accessible in the summer months and Lake Trout congregate inshore from November until spring (Burns 1973:43-44). The presence of a netsinker at this site suggests that it functioned as a fishing station. The accessibility of Lake Trout during the winter months may have made it a valuable resource and this species is well represented in the Nodwell village faunal assemblage (see Table 20).

I believe that most of these sites functioned the same way for centuries, as small resource extraction locations, and settlement pattern data in combination with the material culture support this interpretation. Because most natural resources would have been available in southern Bruce county between spring and fall, these sites were occupied primarily during the warmer seasons, although some sites, specifically those closer to the Nodwell village may have been winter hunting camps. Given that the Middleport occupation of the Nodwell village appears to have had its primary occupation during the winter months, most of these small sites were probably occupied by small groups from the Nodwell village, perhaps households or some other special work groups, who harvested the abundant fish resources spawning in the Saugeen River and surrounding drainages in the warmer months, processing and storing these fish for winter consumption.

It should be pointed out that there is no evidence to suggest that any of the middle Late Woodland sites in southern Bruce county served as horticultural cabin sites. None of the regional sites contained horticultural remains and none provided material culture associated with growing or processing horticultural produce. For this reason, I believe that corn horticulture was used in a limited fashion by the occupants of the Nodwell village. This is not surprising given the short growing season and poor soils of the region. Instead, the subsistence pattern appears to have revolved around the exploitation of the abundant natural resources of the region.

Subsistence

Direct evidence of the middle Late Woodland subsistence strategy from the small sites in southern Bruce county was extremely limited. No cultigens are present at any sites, but to date no effort has been made to collect botanical data. Furthermore, artifacts associated with hunting and fishing are limited to a tiny number of netsinkers and projectile points. BcHi-16, was the only site to produce any faunal remains which can be directly associated with the middle Late Woodland. Wright (1953b:3) claims that burnt mammal and fish bones were recovered from this site. A closer investigation of the scattered collections from this site which may not be associated with the middle Late Woodland occupation included the remains of a single white tailed deer, one passenger pigeon, as well as sturgeon and sucker bones. It is improbable that these species were all caught at the site because sturgeon does not spawn in the small stream near this site. The other species present are available during different seasons: deer can be caught year round, sucker is available in the spring and passenger pigeon migrates in the fall.

The Shutt and Mirimachi Bay sites also had small collections of fauna that cannot be directly associated with the middle late Woodland period, but which may help to determine the function of these sites. At the Shutt site at the mouth of the Saugeen River, the remains of white tailed deer, beaver, duck, sturgeon and sucker were recovered. At the Mirimachi Bay site, on Lake Huron, both Lake Trout and Northern Pike were identified. Given that no other remains aside from fish were recovered from Mirimachi Bay, it is probable that this site functioned as a fishing camp. The Shutt site had a greater diversity of faunal remains including spring spawning fish, mammals, which could have been hunted anytime, and duck, which was available from spring through fall.

The lack of faunal remains is not unusual at Iroquoian special purpose sites. In fact, only village sites contain a variety of faunal remains, while special purpose sites may contain no remains at all (MacDonald and Cooper 1992; Williamson 1983). The absence of faunal remains suggests that most of the resources harvested at these locations were taken back to the Nodwell village for consumption. The diversity of faunal remains recovered from the Nodwell village support this interpretation. Furthermore, large quantities of fish were recovered from every house at the Nodwell village, and yet the Nodwell village is not situated in proximity to any river with a major fish spawn.

Interaction

The middle Late Woodland campsites in southern Bruce county provide almost no evidence of inter-regional interaction. This is because the exotic material recovered from these sites, which includes both copper and foreign chert, are not temporally diagnostic in this region. However, the presence of Kettle Point chert and copper at the Nodwell village suggests that items made from these materials recovered from the surrounding sites may be related to the middle Late Woodland occupations of these sites.

Onondaga chert was recovered from the Shutt site, and may be diagnostic of the Late Woodland occupation of this site because no Onondaga chert was directly associated with the earlier sites in the region. The presence of Onondaga chert suggests there was interaction between southern Bruce county and populations inhabiting southwestern Ontario.

The Late Woodland Post-Middleport Material Culture and Subsistence Data

Four sites can be associated with the post-Middleport occupations of southern Bruce county, but one of these sites is an individual burial which contains no artifacts or subsistence

remains (Clark-Wilson and Spence 1988). Furthermore, the Nodwell site contains no post-Middleport material, but a single radiocarbon date suggests that this site may have been sporadically occupied toward the end of the Late Woodland period. Only the Hunter/Frenchman's Bay and the Donaldson sites contain material which is reviewed here.

The post-Middleport occupation of the Hunter/Frenchman's Bay site has been dated to the terminal Late Woodland period or the early Historic period on the presence of three ceramic vessels with decorative attributes diagnostic of this time period (Fox 1989:5-6). The post-Middleport occupation of the Donaldson site has been dated to the historic period since fragments of three European trade silver bangles were recovered here (Finlayson 1977:257). No other sites have been located which were occupied after the Middleport period and it appears that southern Bruce county was occupied only sporadically at this time.

At the Hunter/Frenchman's Bay site no faunal remains can be directly associated with this occupation. However, the location and size of the site, as well as the presence of fish bone from an earlier period suggests that this site was used briefly as a fishing station by a small population.

The historic material identified at the Donaldson site was confined to a single hearth feature within a poorly constructed longhouse (Finlayson 1977:257). The only other material culture associated with this longhouse was a single bone netting needle recovered from the same hearth pit. No other artifacts or fauna can be directly associated with this period, but it is probable that this occupation of the Donaldson site was an early historic fishing station.

It would appear that southern Bruce county was largely abandoned after the 14th century. One can only speculate on the reason. By the end of the 14th century the Little Ice Age was probably beginning to affect southern Bruce county. Corn horticulture, which was never suited to the environment of Bruce county, may have failed and forced the population to move elsewhere. Furthermore, the Nodwell village may have become unliveable after several centuries of occupation. Sites located to the north on the Bruce peninsula may have been inhabited by the Nodwell population until the 15th century when the population re-location in southern Ontario was widespread (Kapches 1984; Kenyon 1959).

Chapter Summary

The material culture and subsistence data from each of thirteen Middle Woodland sites was used to suggest that the population of southern Bruce county occupied a series of small campsites in nuclear family units for much of the year, and then congregated in macroband habitation sites, located at prime fishing locales between spring and fall. As with the settlement data detailed in Chapter 2, the material culture and subsistence assemblages provided evidence to suggest that the traditional forager lifeway in southern Bruce county was changing toward the end of the Middle Woodland period, when the population of southern Ontario increased, and band territories were constricted (Spence et al. 1990). The evidence of change was most abundant at the Donaldson site where two longhouses were constructed. Material culture recovered inside these houses indicated that they were used for a wide variety of activities including cooking, storage and flint knapping, an activity more conveniently undertaken outside. This suggested that houses may have been occupied during the winter months.

The two Donaldson longhouses signify a shift in socio-economic behaviour toward a larger, more communal group strategy, replacing an earlier emphasis on nuclear family organization. Netsinkers, found at the Donaldson site suggested that the community was harvesting large numbers of fish, which they may have dried for later consumption. Furthermore, skeletal material from the Donaldson site contain distinct dental pits and lesions associated with eating domesticated cultigens (Molto 1979). It is therefore probable that the late Middle Woodland occupants of the Donaldson site had access to both natural and domestic stores and these foodstuffs may have been stored for winter.

If maize was available to the occupants of the Donaldson site, then this population must have been interacting with farmers either directly or indirectly as early as AD 700. A number of foreign items present in the material culture assemblages from Middle Woodland sites was used to demonstrate that the Bruce county foragers were interacting with populations from many other regions. Furthermore, rimsherds recovered from the Donaldson site were of a type commonly associated with the first farmers in southern Ontario who inhabited the Grand River valley as early as AD 600 (Smith and Crawford 1997). The presence of ceramics and perhaps maize at the Donaldson site suggests that commodities were being exchanged across this forager/farmer frontier before AD 700.

It is entirely possible that direct interaction between the Bruce foragers and the Grand River farmers was desired by both groups. Curiosity may have incited the Bruce population to find out more about the farming population (Dennell 1986). But, farming groups, who are generally more sedentary than foragers, may have desired interaction with the Bruce population in order to access exotic items of material culture and valuable meat protein that are more difficult to accumulate when mobility is decreased (Gregg 1988; Spielmann 1986). Maize and pottery could have been introduced to the Bruce foragers as a result of this interaction. Furthermore, interaction across the forager/farmer frontier generally results in the exchange of ideas and information, which may effect long-term changes to the internal structures of both groups (Dennell 1985; Gregg 1988). It is not surprising that the appearance of this new pottery style, common only to the Princess Point farmers at this time, appears in Bruce county during a period of social and economic change. In fact, interaction with farmers from southern Bruce county may have precipitated other social changes within Bruce county which are recognizable by the early Late Woodland period.

Early Late Woodland ceramics were recovered from several sites in southern Bruce county. These ceramics have cord-wrapped-stick impressed rims with annular punctates which form interior bosses. The only complete vessel also has a corded body, and large frequencies of corded body sherds have been recovered from nine sites in southern Bruce county. Large numbers of corded body sherds were found at the Nodwell village where they constituted close to 20% of the body sherd assemblage from House 5, the earliest house in the village. I therefore suggested that House 5 was occupied during the early Late Woodland period. Further evidence, in the form of Springwell phase rim sherds from House 5 was used to support this suggestion.

There appears to have been a great deal of continuity between Middle and Late Woodland settlement patterns. Most sites occupied during the early Late Woodland period appear to represent seasonally occupied resource extraction sites. Furthermore, the function of the Nodwell and Donaldson sites appears to have reversed. Longhouses are no longer used at the Donaldson site, but the presence of House 5 at the Nodwell village indicates that this strategy was not abandoned. In fact, the Nodwell village was perhaps a better location for a macroband habitation than the Donaldson site because it is situated in a more defensible location, something a population that stores surplus resources would consider. Furthermore, if the population of the Nodwell village was experimenting with horticulture during the early Late Woodland period, then the location of the Nodwell site on the only sandy soil in the region would also be more appropriate than the Donaldson site. However, the subsistence assemblage from House 5 at the Nodwell site was comprised predominantly of fish. This suggests that the other sites in the region continued to be used between spring and fall so that fish could be harvested, but that the focus of community settlement was at the Nodwell site.

Wright's (1974) migration model to explain the appearance of the Nodwell village was premised on several assumptions: 1) that southern Bruce county had experienced an occupational hiatus during the early Late Woodland period, 2) that there were no local precursors to the culture pattern represented by the settlement, artifact and subsistence data at the Nodwell village, 3) that there were no similar villages within a 130 kilometre radius, and 4) that the site appeared on the cultural landscape of southern Bruce county abruptly in the 14th century.

However, artifact and subsistence data have demonstrated that there was never an occupational hiatus in Bruce county. If anything, the early Late Woodland culture pattern is so similar to that employed during the Middle Woodland period that previous researchers merely failed to recognize it. Furthermore, the artifact and subsistence data have demonstrated that there was a wide range of continuities between the Middle and Late Woodland periods in southern Bruce county.

There is no doubt that the material culture and subsistence assemblage recovered from the Nodwell village is distinct from assemblages recovered from earlier sites. At the Nodwell village we witness the introduction of new artifact types and styles, as well as the first indisputable evidence of corn horticulture. Furthermore, each of these items were characteristic of the Late Woodland Iroquoian tradition, and therefore closely associated with the farmers from southern Ontario. However, there were also strong continuities in the overall artifact and subsistence assemblage from the Nodwell village with the earlier Middle Woodland occupations, and these continuities have always made the Nodwell village appear distinct from other Iroquoian villages.

Since it is now possible to trace the origin of interaction between the inhabitants of Bruce county and the farmers of southern Ontario back to the Middle Woodland period it would make sense that the Nodwell village developed locally as a result of both internal change and interaction. This would explain both the similarity of the Nodwell village to other Iroquoian villages, and the continuity of local traditions. However, it is not easy to negate Wright's (1974) final assertion: that the Nodwell village appeared abruptly in southern Bruce county during the 14th century. The radiocarbon dates from the site indicate that the site was occupied throughout the Late Woodland period and not simply during the Middleport substage, but because the village is so distinct from earlier occupations, and because there are few settlement features at the Nodwell site which can be used to identify either the sequence of village development or the duration of the occupation, it is easy to dismiss these dates as errors as Wright (1985) did.

In order to determine exactly how long the Nodwell village was occupied, an extensive analysis of the ceramic assemblage from each house was undertaken. The analysis of the ceramic assemblage combined Wright's (1974) analyses of rimsherds with an analysis of approximately 6000 body sherds. As a result of this analysis I was able to demonstrate that there were three periods of occupation at the Nodwell village. The first occurred during the early Late Woodland period when House 5 was occupied. Sometime after this, perhaps following a short-term abandonment of the village Houses 4, 7, 10 and 11 were occupied. This seems to have occurred during the Uren sub-stage of the middle Late Woodland. Finally, Houses 1, 2, 3, 6, 8, 9 and 12 were occupied during the Middleport sub-stage of the Late Woodland period. Once this sequence was established, the distribution of radiocarbon dates, subsistence remains, other items of material culture, and the results of earlier trace element analysis were used to demonstrate the validity of this sequence (Stewart 1974; Trigger et al. 1980; Wright 1974; Wright 1985).

It now appears that the Nodwell site was occupied for approximately 250 years, developing incrementally as certain houses were abandoned and others were constructed. Viewed historically, there seems little reason to assume that the Nodwell village began as the result of a migration, but rather developed locally as a natural outgrowth of social changes already underway in southern Bruce county during the Middle Woodland period. Furthermore, these changes were influenced by interaction and the exchange of ideas, information and commodities with Iroquoian groups inhabiting other regions of southern Ontario. There is both subsistence and material culture evidence to suggest that this interaction began during the Middle Woodland period and continued until the Nodwell site was abandoned at the end of the 14th century.

The form and contents of the Nodwell site, not only reflects local traditions, but also integrates ideas which developed outside of Bruce county in other parts of southern Ontario. There is direct evidence of interaction in the form of exotic materials not available in southern Bruce county. Interaction was also used to explain the distinct nature of the ceramic assemblages from Houses 1 and 8 at the Nodwell village. These houses were occupied during the Middleport substage along with several other houses at the Nodwell village, but the ceramic assemblages from these two houses were unique and obviously related. I suggested that House 1, which was located outside the palisade walls, was established by an immigrant Iroquoian population from outside southern Bruce county. Furthermore, it appears as if House 8, which was the only house which was modified by an extension, may have ultimately housed this population when they were formally accepted into the village. The complex history of the Nodwell village therefore results from numerous processes including local culture change, interaction, and migration.

The material culture and subsistence data from other sites in southern Bruce county which date to the middle Late Woodland was also examined. The analysis of this material was used to demonstrate that these sites were used seasonally for specific functions by small populations. Most sites appear to be fishing locations, but all sites can be considered resource extraction locations. Most sites appear to have been occupied between spring and fall, probably to take advantage of the abundant natural resources which could be dried and stored for winter consumption at the Nodwell village. There was no evidence of cultigens at any of these sites, nor was there any indication that these sites were used as field houses from which to tend horticultural produce. If anything, the presence of these sites at strategic locations for accessing natural resources diminished the value of corn horticulture in Bruce county's subsistence economy. This is really not surprising, as the limited growing season and poor soils in Bruce county would have made growing corn a difficult and unpredictable undertaking. Every site used during the middle Late Woodland period was used by the inhabitants of Bruce county during earlier cultural periods, a fact which provides even more weight to the in situ model of culture change in this region. Furthermore, the fact that these sites continue to be used suggests that corn horticulture was a more tenuous proposition in Bruce county than in other parts of southern Ontario, and that the inhabitants of the Nodwell village continued to utilize a relatively traditional subsistence pattern in comparison to other Iroquoian communities inhabiting southern Ontario.

An attempt was also made to examine the material culture and subsistence assemblages from sites in southern Bruce county which were occupied after the Nodwell village was abandoned. The only two sites in southern Bruce county which included material known to date to this period appear to have functioned as small fishing stations. Following the Middleport stage occupation of the Nodwell village, southern Bruce county was largely, if not completely, abandoned.

Chapter 4
Interpretations and Conclusions

Introduction

The primary goal of this study was to re-evaluate the process of regional socio-economic change from foraging to farming which culminated with the appearance of the Late Woodland period Nodwell village site in southern Bruce county, Ontario. The near complete excavation of this village by Wright (1974) determined that the Nodwell site had both the form (settlement pattern) and contents (material culture and subsistence remains) representative of a small-scale farming community, and was therefore distinct from any of Bruce county's earlier Middle Woodland period forager habitations. The most recent of the absolute dates taken from Middle Woodland sites in this region dated that phase to the late 10th century (Finlayson 1977; Fox 1989). Relative dating of the Nodwell village via ceramic typology placed the occupation of this site in the mid-14th century (Wright 1974).

Prior to the construction of the Nodwell village, the inhabitants of southern Bruce county had employed a socio-economic strategy based on mobile foraging. These foragers followed an annual cycle, inhabiting numerous small sites, probably in nuclear family units, for much of the year and congregating at macroband habitation sites during the spring fish runs along the banks of the Saugeen River. This strategy allowed the foragers of Bruce county to exploit numerous naturally occurring resources throughout the region during the course of the year, and brought families together only when natural resources were most abundant. In contrast, the Nodwell village was occupied by a much more sedentary community of people living in extended family groups, and producing domesticated crops. Therefore, the Nodwell village represented a significant shift in regional socio-economic behaviour. Furthermore, this change occurred over a maximum of 350 years. In order to explain this change in cultural behaviour, Wright (1974) advocated a migration model, claiming that a horticultural community which had resided 130 kilometres east of Bruce county had migrated into southern Bruce county during the mid-14th century bringing with it an intact socio-economic system based on small-scale village farming which was distinct from that employed by the indigenous foragers. This explanation was accepted at the time for numerous reasons. Primarily, this explanation was able to account for the obvious changes in settlement and subsistence behaviour reflected in the archaeological record of southern Bruce county, which seemed to appear abruptly and without local precursors. Furthermore, this interpretation was in line with the overarching model of horticultural expansion elsewhere in southern Ontario which suggested that around the first millennium horticulture became the dominant economic strategy in the extreme southern portion of the province and that village based, tribally organized, horticultural communities replaced mobile, band foragers as the dominant population in this region (Fox 1990). This farming population was believed to have grown rapidly, exerting pressure on natural resources and necessitating increased crop growth which depleted soils (Wright 1972). As a result, village fissioning and abandonment was thought to occur every ten to fifty years creating a regional settlement pattern which radiated out of the southern extremes of the province to areas further north. This population is thought to have reached southern Bruce county in the 14th century and settled at the Nodwell village (Wright 1974).

However, in the years since the publication of the Nodwell report, Wright's (1974) interpretation of Nodwell's origins has become increasingly controversial: facing challenges on both theoretical and practical grounds (Dennell 1985; Fox 1990b; Gregg 1988; Kapches 1981).

Chapter 1 discussed how the migration theory over-simplified the process of culture change by failing to explore adequately the complex historical, cultural, regional or ecological context in which this event occurred. Chapters 2 and 3 outlined a series of archaeological data sources which Wright's (1974) model was unable to explain (Fox 1990b; Wright 1985). Furthermore, the challenges to Wright's explanation intimated that the socio-economic transition in southern Bruce county represented by the Nodwell site may have been initiated locally.

In contrast, this research situated the Nodwell event within a much broader historical and regional context and demonstrated that the socio-economic transition from foraging to farming in Bruce county was a long-term process influenced by events occurring both internally, at the local level, and externally, through inter-cultural interaction. The historical approach utilized allowed a comprehensive re-evaluation of the transition from foraging to farming in this region which incorporated an active role for the indigenous foraging population

Synthesis

This study employed a multi-scalar temporal and spatial framework to develop a regional and historical context in which to situate the socio-economic change from foraging to farming in Bruce county represented by the Nodwell village. Archaeological data, including settlement patterns, material culture, and subsistence remains were analysed from a series of sites believed to represent the settlement system of the occupants in southern Bruce county over two temporally distinct cultural periods, known as the Middle and Late Woodland. Change and continuity within the region was then observed by comparing archaeological data from sites dating to the different periods (Figure 22).

Settlement Data

The settlement analysis proceeded at two spatial scales: regional, and site based. The distribution, size, location and number and types of settlement features from sites occupied during the Middle Woodland period were used to demonstrate that southern Bruce county was occupied by a mobile foraging population as

recently as AD 1000. This population followed an annual round similar to other foraging groups in southern Ontario, inhabiting small nuclear family based campsites for much of the year and gathering in macroband habitation sites in the spring to exploit abundant natural resources provided by the spring fish spawns in the Saugeen River.

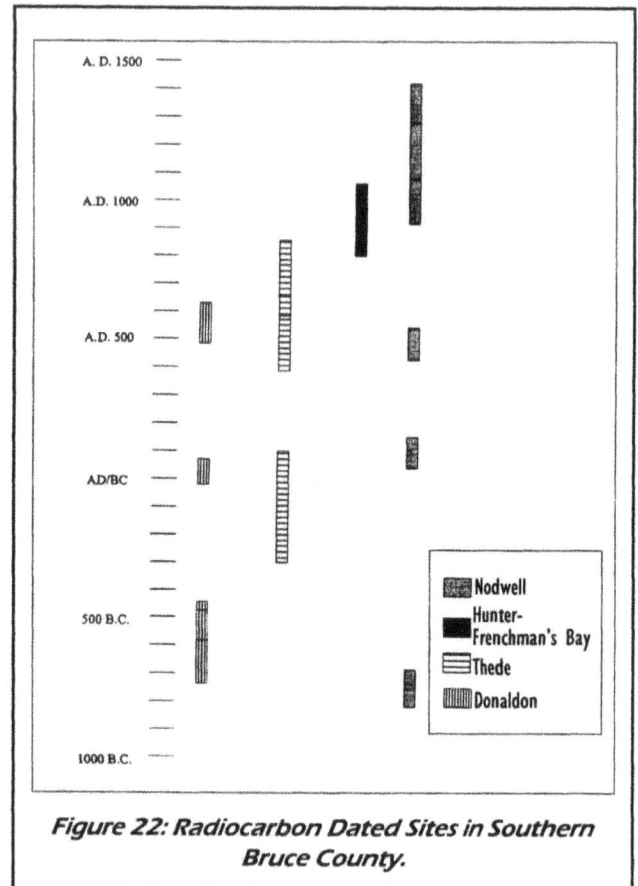

Figure 22: Radiocarbon Dated Sites in Southern Bruce County.

Evidence from southern Ontario in general, and the Donaldson site in particular, indicates that toward the end of the Middle Woodland period this pattern intensified as foragers faced territorial constraints brought about through population increases. By the end of the Middle Woodland period significant changes to the socio-economic system of the southern Bruce county foragers, perhaps in response to territorial constraints, are evidenced in the settlement pattern. The Donaldson site is much larger than previous occupations, and included greater numbers and types of settlement features, suggesting that a larger population was spending longer periods of time in one place. The increased period of communal living during this period appears to have necessitated the realignment of group socio-economic relations. The appearance of longhouses with numerous internal features at the Donaldson site late in the Middle Woodland period emphasizes the social changes brought about through increased sedentism, suggesting that larger social groups were replacing the nuclear family as the primary social and economic units. These houses may also represent a trend toward multi-family winter habitations common to later periods.

In southern Ontario the early Late Woodland period is represented by a movement toward large multi-family villages and the blending of horticultural practice with the traditional hunting, fishing and foraging economy of the Middle Woodland period (Fox 1990a; Smith and Crawford 1997; Timmins 1997). The supposed absence of similar villages dated to this period in southern Bruce county had led previous researchers to suggest that this region experienced an occupational hiatus (Finlayson 1977; Wright 1974). However, my investigation revealed that sites used during the Middle Woodland period continued to be occupied during the early Late Woodland period, albeit in a somewhat different fashion.

Throughout the early late Woodland the inhabitants of southern Bruce county occupied several small campsites located at key natural resource extraction locations primarily along the Saugeen River, including the Donaldson site which no longer appears to have been the focus of a macroband habitation. In order to explain this change in settlement strategy during the early Late Woodland period, I proposed that the Nodwell site had become the focus of macroband habitation, and that the foragers of southern Bruce county were now exploiting the abundant fish resources of the Saugeen River in smaller work parties and storing these resources at the Nodwell site for consumption by the larger community.

Support for this proposition was drawn from both radiocarbon dates and settlement data. Radiocarbon dates clearly indicate that the Nodwell village was occupied during the early Late Woodland period (Wright 1985). Furthermore, settlement data indicate that the

Nodwell site was the only large site in southern Bruce county at that time, and therefore the only site likely to have been the focus of macroband habitation. I also suggested that the shift in macroband settlement location from the Donaldson site to the Nodwell site was precipitated by a need to protect the stored resources.

By the middle Late Woodland period the regional settlement data indicate that the Nodwell village was the focus of winter communal living but that the same regional campsites continued to be used during the warmer months for the purposes of resource extraction. Furthermore, a full analysis of the Nodwell settlement data suggested that while the Nodwell village did resemble the farming villages of southern Ontario, Nodwell was also quite distinct from the other known Middleport substage villages. The Nodwell village was smaller in terms of area and population, and the internal settlement pattern lacked the coherent internal organization associated with other Middleport farming sites. It was therefore suggested that the occupants of the Nodwell village were interacting and exchanging ideas and information with the farmers of southern Ontario and this network was responsible for the similar appearance of the Nodwell village and other sites. However, the differences between the Nodwell village and the farming villages in southern Ontario were probably the result of both the local history and the lengthy period of occupation of this site as demonstrated by radiocarbon dates (Wright 1985).

The analysis of settlement pattern data from southern Bruce county suggests that the Nodwell village developed locally, as the result of long-term socio-economic changes already underway in the region by the late Middle Woodland period, and in response to contact and interaction with farming communities inhabiting other regions of southern Ontario. Both Middle Woodland macroband settlements, and longhouse construction can be used to suggest that the socio-economic structures associated with village settlements were developing locally by AD 700. Changes to the regional settlement system in southern Bruce county follow the appearance of longhouses at the Donaldson site, and appears to have begun during the early Late Woodland period. The shift in macroband site location from Donaldson to Nodwell at this time would be a logical outcome of this change and reflects the need to protect stored resources. The re-occupation of the Nodwell village over several centuries would also explain the differences between the Nodwell village settlement pattern and other Middleport villages in southern Ontario. Finally, the number and location of sites in southern Bruce county remained relatively constant from the Middle Woodland period through the 14th century abandonment of the Nodwell village, suggesting that the inhabitants of Nodwell continued to use natural resources for subsistence and collected these resources from the locations they were most familiar witb.

If migrants had constructed the Nodwell site during the 14th century all evidence should point to the rapid establishment of the village at this time. Not only would radiocarbon dates have to be overlooked, but the historical trend in southern Bruce county toward larger social and economic group relations would have to be ignored, as would the stability of the local settlement system which remained relatively constant through time, even though sites were used differently. If an outside population had suddenly appeared in southern Bruce county there would likely have been rapid changes to this settlement system as the new population altered the local environment through both village construction and resource exploitation.

Subsistence Data

The analysis of subsistence data recovered from the Middle and Late Woodland period sites in southern Bruce county also provided evidence that was used to explain the process of culture change in the region. The type and frequency of faunal and botanical remains recovered from Middle Woodland period sites supported the interpretation of the settlement data and suggested that during the Middle Woodland period the foragers of Bruce county occupied a series of small campsites throughout much of the year and gathered at macroband habitation sites during the spring when the fish spawns in the Saugeen River provided access to abundant resources.

The large assemblages of subsistence remains from the Thede and Donaldson sites were used to elucidate the changes to the indigenous economic strategy between the early and late Middle Woodland period, which were observed in the analysis of the settlement patterns. The subsistence assemblages recovered from the Donaldson and Thede sites were larger and more diverse than that recovered from smaller sites (Finlayson 1977). Fish were more abundant than any other class of fauna or flora.

The Donaldson site assemblage also included species of fish which spawn during the autumn, and these data were used to support a trend toward increased sedentism during the late Middle Woodland period. Netsinkers were also recovered from the Donaldson site and their appearance was used to suggest that fish harvesting intensified at this time. Given that the longhouses were constructed at the Donaldson site during the late Middle Woodland period, fish may have been dried for winter consumption.

The analysis of Middle Woodland skeletal remains by Molto (1979) was used to provide indirect evidence of maize consumption by the occupants of the Donaldson site. This v·as the first indication that the foragers of Bruce county were not only aware of farmers inhabiting southern Ontario but interacting with them prior to AD 700. Whether or not maize was integrated into the economic strategy employed by the Donaldson inhabitants directly (through production) or indirectly (brought in through trade) there is reason to suspect that this additional foodstuff would have been a welcome addition, as the foragers of Bruce county faced territorial constrictions, increased sedentism and intensified their subsistence practices during the late Middle Woodland period. The possibility of preserving maize for winter consumption would also have made this a valuable foodstuff, and the settlement shift inland to the Nodwell site and away from the Saugeen River during the early Late Woodland period may have been stimulated by both the need to protect stored resources and the need to move to a location with soils more conducive to the production of maize.

Maize kernels were recovered from House 5, the first house to be occupied at the Nodwell village, and the house occupied during the early Late Woodland period. However, traditional subsistence practices were not abandoned at this time, or any time during the Late Woodland period. The Nodwell village subsistence collection is overwhelmingly dominated by fish. In fact, horticultural produce, while present, was recovered in small quantities (Wright 1974). Unlike other farming villages in southern Ontario there is no evidence that other crops such as beans, squash or tobacco were produced by the inhabitants of the Nodwell village. Furthermore, few tools associated with the production and processing of domesticated crops were recovered from the Nodwell village, and unlike other farming villages in southern Ontario there appears to be no field cabins which would have been used when tending horticultural produce. Therefore, it was suggested that the poor soils and short growing season in southern Bruce county made corn horticulture a risky venture, and that the inhabitants of this region continued to rely largely on naturally occurring resources.

The analysis of the subsistence data recovered from the sites in southern Bruce county also suggests that the socio-economic change in southern Bruce county, which culminated with the appearance of the Nodwell village, developed locally. The subsistence data from the Donaldson site was used to demonstrate that significant economic change was already occurring in the region by the end of the Middle Woodland period. Not only do the data indicate that natural resources were being exploited more intensively, they suggest that maize was introduced to the diet at this time. Maize, which must have been introduced through interaction with farmers, also provides evidence needed to demonstrate that interaction between the occupants of southern Bruce county and the farmers of southern Ontario began prior to AD 700. This interaction would have also resulted in the exchange of ideas and information across this frontier and further changes to the socio-economic system may have resulted. For example, the shift in settlement from the Donaldson site to Nodwell may represent an attempt to produce maize within Bruce county.

The form of the village, which is similar to those occupied by farming communities elsewhere in southern Ontario, no doubt reflects the continuity of interaction with these groups.

Nevertheless, there is also a strong continuity in regional subsistence practices through time. Fish remained the primary subsistence food, and, as stated above, they were harvested from the same locations used for at least a millennium. Furthermore, maize does not appear to have become a primary subsistence food in Bruce county at any time during the Late Woodland period.

Material Culture

The amount and type of material culture recovered from sites dating to both periods in southern Bruce county was extensive. Material culture assemblages from the Middle Woodland sites included numerous exotic items including copper and several types of foreign chert which suggests that the foragers of Bruce county had connections to numerous communities outside of their territory. Most of these groups were similar foraging societies. However, the presence of ceramics diagnostic of the earliest farmers in southern Ontario suggests that a forager/farmer frontier was already established and traversed before AD 700. Furthermore, the frequency of these ceramics increased during the early late Woodland period and it was suggested that the occupants of Bruce county had begun to replicate this ceramic style.

By the middle Late Woodland occupation of the Nodwell village many other items of material culture, considered to be part of the "Iroquoian tradition" and therefore part of the material culture assemblage associated with Iroquoian farmers in other regions of southern Ontario, were recovered in abundance. The presence of these items had been the crux of Wright's (1974) migration argument. However, many other artifacts recovered from the Nodwell site such as copper, lithic material, and a particular type of scraper showed strong continuity with the material culture assemblages common to the Middle Woodland occupation of Bruce county, and such items were unique to Bruce county in the Late Woodland period.

A full analysis of the substantial ceramic vessel assemblage was also used to determine exactly how long the Nodwell site was occupied. Radiocarbon dates from the site had indicated that Nodwell was occupied, or re-occupied, throughout the Late Woodland period, and not simply during the Middleport substage, but Wright (1985) had dismissed these dates as errors. The ceramic assemblage was chosen because it was the only class of material culture large enough to be examined on a house by house basis, and it is well documented that ceramics are subject to temporal change (MacNeish 1952; Wright 1966; 1974). Furthermore, Wright (1974) himself had already recognized a great deal of variation between the ceramic assemblages from various Nodwell houses, and between midden and surface deposits. Rather than viewing this variation as a factor of time, Wright suggested that certain houses had more conservative potters than others.

The analysis of the ceramic assemblage combined Wright's (1974) analyses of rimsherds with an analysis of approximately 6000 body sherds. As a result of this analysis I was able to demonstrate that there were three periods of occupation at the Nodwell village. The first occurred during the early Late Woodland period when House 5 was occupied. A period of abandonment may have followed this occupation. Following this, Houses 4, 7, 10 and 11 were occupied during the Uren sub-stage of the middle Late Woodland, and then Houses 1, 2, 3, 6, 8, 9 and 12 were occupied during the Middleport sub-stage of the Late Woodland period. Once this was established, the distribution of radiocarbon dates, subsistence remains, other items of material culture, and the results of earlier trace element analysis were used to demonstrate the validity of this sequence (Stewart 1974; Trigger et al. 1980; Wright 1974; Wright 1985).

It appears that the Nodwell village was occupied, perhaps with small periods of abandonment, for approximately 250 years, developing incrementally as certain houses were torn down and others were constructed. Viewed historically, there seems little reason to assume that the Nodwell village began as the result of a migration, but rather developed locally as a natural outgrowth of social changes already underway in southern Bruce county during the Middle Woodland period. Furthermore, these changes were influenced by interaction and the exchange of ideas, information and commodities with Iroquoian groups inhabiting southern Ontario.

The presence or absence of certain types of material culture was also used at a regional scale to determine the function of each of the different sites in southern Bruce county as part of the greater settlement system. As with other analyses, the study of material culture suggested that during the Middle Woodland period, most sites were used as campsites by small groups, but that the Donaldson and Thede sites had been the focus of macroband habitation. In contrast, the Late Woodland occupation of the Nodwell site was the focus of winter habitation for the community and other sites were used as campsites by smaller groups during the warmer months.

Interaction

Settlement patterns, subsistence remains and material culture can all be used to suggest that interaction between the inhabitants of southern Bruce county and the farmers of southern Ontario began during the late Middle Woodland period and continued through to the abandonment of the Nodwell village during the 14th century.

By AD 600 farmers inhabited a limited region in southwestern Ontario including the Grand River valley, Cootes Paradise and Long Point (Crawford et a. 1998; Smith and Crawford 1997). A forager/farmer frontier was established at this time, and the foragers of southern Bruce county interacted with these farmers. Both ceramics and indirect evidence for maize consumption from the Donaldson site indicate this. However, the interaction which was initiated during the Middle Woodland period continued over several centuries, and appears to have intensified and taken on a different form during the Late Woodland period.

During the early stages of the forager/farmer frontier, commodities such as maize and pottery were exchanged, but by the Late Woodland period ideas, information and even communities readily crossed this frontier. The form and contents of the Nodwell village demonstrate the transmission of various cultural traits. It appears that the structure of the forager/farmer frontier itself changed through time, as did the rules which governed the way foragers negotiated this frontier.

By AD 1250, when Nodwell assumes village status, Iroquoian farming societies had expanded into most of southern Ontario. The forager/farmer frontier had altered such that it existed between Bruce county and most of southern Ontario. This implies that the Bruce county foragers had to adapt to a significantly different cultural landscape by the middle Late Woodland period, and the form and contents of the Nodwell village reflect the manner in which Bruce county foragers were able to negotiate this new situation. By assuming the form of a farming community, but not necessarily the economic strategy, the occupants of the Nodwell village may have been both protecting their rights to their territory and strengthening their bonds with various farming communities inhabiting the fringes of their territory.

Furthermore, it is only just before the abandonment of the Nodwell village, several hundred years after contact with farmers was first initiated, that we have the first evidence of face to face interaction between these groups. At this time a single longhouse was constructed outside the palisade of the Nodwell village and occupied by a much more "progressive" population than that which lived inside the village. I have proposed that the construction of this house represents the migration of a small population of farmers into Bruce county. Ultimately, it would appear that this population was adopted into the Nodwell village, occupying an extended portion of House 8. However, upon their arrival this population was treated as outsiders, suggesting that the inhabitants of the Nodwell village did not think of this population as part of their kin group.

Nevertheless, throughout its 250 year development the Nodwell village remained distinct from other farming villages, exhibiting strong continuities with local cultural antecedents. Settlement, subsistence, and material culture data unique to the Nodwell village demonstrate the historical connections between the Middle Woodland foragers and the Late Woodland occupants of the Nodwell village, suggesting that this population maintained a strong regional identity which made them distinct from farming populations. Perhaps the most significant example of this continuity comes from the analysis of the Late Woodland subsistence strategy used by the inhabitants of the Nodwell village. Corn horticulture does not appear to have been a dependable subsistence strategy for the occupants of the Nodwell village: only small quantities of maize were recovered from the site. Furthermore, no other classes of cultigens, and few tools associated with the production and processing of domesticates were recovered. In contrast, large quantities of fish and other natural resources were recovered from this site. These resources appear to have been harvested at the same locations which were always used in this region. Therefore, it appears that the inhabitants of the Nodwell village maintained a relatively traditional foraging lifestyle, while presenting the outward appearance of a farming community.

In southern Bruce county, the accoutrements of village settlements, including longhouses and protective palisades cannot be directly associated with a farming strategy. However, these attributes do reflect social and economic changes which were initiated by the late Middle Woodland period. That the physical evidence of these changes took the characteristics of Iroquoian farmers reflects the familiarity of the southern Bruce county's population with their farming neighbours, and suggests that the inhabitants of Bruce county perceived some benefit from sharing certain cultural traditions with their farming neighbours.

Summary

Wright's (1974) migration model to explain the appearance of the Nodwell village, and the process of culture change that this site embodied was premised on several assumptions: 1) that southern Bruce county had experienced an occupational hiatus during the early Late Woodland period, 2) that there were no local precursors to the culture pattern represented by the settlement, artifact and subsistence data at the Nodwell site, 3) that there were no similar villages within a 130 kilometre radius, and 4) that the site appeared on the cultural landscape of southern Bruce county abruptly in the mid 14th century.

The re-evaluation presented in this study demonstrated that a migratory episode was not the only potential explanation of these events, and that local culture change was in fact a more feasible explanation of the appearance of the Nodwell village. As a result of my analyses, the four assumptions made by Wright were demonstrated to be either incorrect, or to have little bearing on the process of culture change in southern Bruce county.

It was not the goal of this study to negate Wright's (1974) explanation. Instead the focus of this research was to create a more sophisticated theory and methodology with which to evaluate the process of culture change in this region. By situating the transition from foraging to farming in Bruce county into a regional and historical framework I demonstrated that the socio-economic transition in Bruce county represented by the Nodwell village was part of a long-term process influenced by events occuring both internally, at the local level, and externally, through inter-cultural interaction, and I have concluded that this transition resulted from numerous complex processes including local culture change, interaction, and immigration.

Conclusion

The study of the transition from foraging to farming in the prehistoric period has, until recently, been governed by over-generalized assumptions: that one can explain cultural behaviour simply by observing cross-cultural regularities, and that foraging and farming occupy separate ends of an evolutionary continuum. As a result of these assumptions, it was believed that farmers who had more complex cultural systems and advanced technology easily replaced or assimilated foraging populations as they swept across the landscape in a "wave of advance" precipitated by the need to access additional arable land. In turn, this assumption has led to both a theoretical and methodological impasse which has segmented the study of foraging societies from the study of farming societies, and limited the number of causal variables we could draw on to explain the process of culture change.

However, recent research has demonstrated that foraging and farming are not always mutually exclusive endeavours, and that there is a much greater variability of human behaviour reflected in the archaeological record than once believed (Gregg 1988; Kent 1989c). This has brought into question the reliability of generalizing explanations and highlighted the need to explore a greater diversity of causal factors in the process of culture change, including those variables of change which are particularistic and motivated by historical and cultural circumstances.

In this study I have examined the process of culture change from foraging to farming in one region. By situating the process of culture change in Bruce county in a broad temporal and regional context I was able to demonstrate that change resulted from both general, externally induced processes, and particular, culturally dependant variables. Only by using an historical approach could I begin to comprehend the dynamics of change which were set into motion at a much earlier period, and observe how change was integrated into the pre-existing social system.

The process of change from foraging to farming will no doubt vary in other regions, but the historical approach used here provides a format which can be used to explore this diversity. Not only does this approach re-unite the study of foragers and farmers within a single explanatory framework, it gives the archaeological data primacy in explanations of culture change, and therefore infuses the archaeological record with a new dynamic.

References Cited

Ammerman, A.J., and L.L. Cavalli-Sforza, 1971. Measuring the Rate of Spread of Early Farming in Europe. *Man* 6, 674-688.

Ammerman, A.J., and L.L. Cavalli-Sforza, 1973. A Population Model for the Diffusion of Early Farming in Europe. In *The Explanation of Culture Change*. Ed. Colin Renfrew. Duckworth Press, London. Pp. 343-359.

Ammerman, A.J., and L.L. Cavalli-Sforza, 1979. The Wave of Advance Model for the Spread of Agriculture in Europe. In *Transformations: Mathematical Approaches to Culture Change*. Ed. K. Cooke and Colin Renfrew. Academic Press, New York. Pp. 275-293.

Anders, Martha B., 1990. *Historia y Etnografía: Los Mitmaq de Huánuco en Las Visitas de 1549,1557 y 1562*. Instituto de Estudios Peruanos, Lima.

Anthony, D.W., 1990. Migration in Archaeology: The Baby and the Bathwater. *American Anthropologist 92(4)*:895-914.

Ashbee, P., 1982. A Reconsideration of the British Neolithic. *Antiquity* 56(217):134-138.

Bender, Barbara, 1978. Gatherer-Hunter to Farmer: A Social Perspective. *World Archaeology 10(2)*:204-222.

Bernabo, Christopher J., 1981. Quantitative Estimates of Temperature Changes Over the Last 2700 Years in Michigan Based on Pollen Data. *Quaternary Research 15*:143-159.

Berry, Claudia F., and Michael S. Berry, 1986. Chronological and Conceptual Models of the Southwestern Archaic. In *Anthropology of the Desert West: Essays in Honour of Jesse D. Jennings*. Eds. C.J. Condie and D.D. Fowler. University of Utah Anthropological Papers No. 110, Salt Lake City. Pp. 253-327.

Blanton, Richard E., Stephen A. Kowalewski, Gary Feinman and Jill Appel, 1981. *Ancient Mesoamerica; A Comparison of Change in Three Regions*. Cambridge University Press, Cambridge.

Brizinski, Morris and Howard Savage, 1983. Dog Sacrifices Among the Algonkian Indians: An Example from the Frank Bay Site. *Ontario Archaeology 39*: 33-39.

Burns, James, 1973. *An Analysis of the Faunal Remains from the 1971 Excavations at the Donaldson Site*. Report on file, London Museum of Archaeology, London.

Casselberry, S.E., 1974. Further Refinement of Formulae for Determining Population from Floor Area. *World Archaeology 6*:117-122.

Chapdelaine, Claude, 1993. The Sedentarization of the Prehistoric Iroquoians: A Slow or Rapid Transformation. *Journal of Anthropological Archaeology 12*:173- 209.

Chapman, L.J. and D.F. Putnam, 1966. *The Physiography of Southern Ontario*. University of Toronto Press, Toronto.

Clark, J. G. D., 1980. *Mesolithic Prelude. The Palaeolithic-Neolithic Transition in Old World Prehistory*. Edinburgh University Press, Edinburgh.

Clark, Susan, Cynthia Cornell and Cathy Donnelly, 1980. The Physical Landscape. In *Environmentally Significant Areas of Southern Bruce County.*, Eds. S. Hilts and M. Parker. The University of Guelph, Centre for Resource Development Publications, Guelph. Pp. 10-28.

Clark-Wilson, Elizabeth and Michael Spence, 1988. The Port Elgin Burial. *Kewa 88* (7):11-19.

Clarke, David L., 1976. Mesolithic Europe: The Economic Basis. In *Problems in Economic and Social Archaeology*. Eds. G. de G. Sieveking, I.H. Longworth and K.E.Wilson. Duckworth Press, London. Pp. 449-481.

Clarke, David L., 1977.Spatial Information in Archaeology. *Spatial Archaeology*. Ed. David L. Clarke,. Academic Press, New York. Pp. 1-32

Cleland, Charles E., 1966. *The Prehistoric Animal Ecology and Ethnozoology of the Upper Great Lakes Region*. Museum of Anthropology, University of Michigan, Anthropological Paper No.29, Ann Arbour.

Cleland, Charles E., 1982. The Inland Shore Fishery of the Northern Great Lakes: Its Development and Importance in Prehistory. *American Antiquity* 47 (4):761-784.

Crawford, G., D. Smith, J. Desloges and A. Davis, 1998. Floodplains and Agricultural Origins: A Case Study in South-Central Ontario, Canada. *Journal of Field Archaeology* 25:123-137.

Cribb, R., 1991. *Nomads in Archaeology*. Cambridge University Press, Cambridge.

Crumley, C.L. and W.H. Marquardt, 1990. Landscape: A Unifying Concept in Regional Analysis. In *Interpreting Space: GIS and Archaeology*. Eds. Kathleen M. S. Allen, Stanton W. Green and Ezra B. W. Zubrow. Pp. 73-79. Taylor and Francis, London.

Dansgaard, Johnson W., S.J. Clausen and C.C. Langway, 1971. Climate Record Revealed by the Camp Century Ice Core. In *The Late Cenozoic Ice Ages*. Ed. K. Turekian. Pp. 37-56. Yale University Press, New Haven.

Dennell, Robin, 1983. *European Economic Prehistory: A New Approach*. Academic Press, New York.

Dennell, Robin, 1985. The Hunter-Gatherer/ Agricultural Frontier in Prehistoric Temperate Europe. In *The Archaeology of Frontiers and Boundaries*. Eds. Stanton W. Green and Stephen M. Perlman. Pp. 117-139. Academic Press, New York.

Dodd, Christine F., 1984. *Ontario Iroquois Tradition Longhouses*. National Museum of Man, Archaeological Survey of Canada, Mercury Series Paper No. 124:181-437.

Dodd, Christine F., Dana R. Poulton, Paul A. Lennox, David G. Smith and Gary A. Warrick, 1990. The Middle Ontario Iroquoian Stage. In *The Archaeology of Southern Ontario to A.D. 1650*, Eds. Chris J. Ellis and Neal Ferris. Pp. 321-359. Occasional Publications No. 5, London Chapter, Ontario Archaeological Society, London, Ontario.

Eder, James E., 1984. The Impact of Subsistence Change on Mobility and Settlement Patterns in a Tropical Forest Foraging Economy: Some Implications for Archaeology. *American Anthropologist* 86:837- 853.

Eley, Betty E. and Peter H. von Bitter, 1989 *Cherts of Southern Ontario*. Royal Ontario Museum, Publications in Archaeology, Toronto.

Emerson, J.N., *1954. The Archaeology of the Ontario Iroquois*. Unpublished Ph.D Dissertation. Department of Anthropology, University of Chicago, Chicago.

Ferris, N., 1988. Southwestern Ontario Radiocarbon Dates V. Kewa 88(6):3-9.

Finlayson, W.D., 1977. *The Saugeen Culture: A Middle Woodland Manifestation in Southwestern Ontario*. National Museum of Man, Archaeological Survey of Canada, Mercury Series Paper No. 61.

Flannery, Kent., 1976. *The Early Mesoamerican Village*. Academic Press, New York.

Fogt, Lisa and Peter Ramsden, 1996. From Timepiece to Time Machine: Scale and Complexity in Iroquoian Archaeology. In *Debating Complexity: Proceedings of the 26th Annual Conference of the Archaeology Association of the University of Calgary*. Eds. D.A. Meyer, P.C. Dawson and D.T. Hanna. Pp. 39-45. University of Calgary Archaeological Association, Calgary.

Foley, Robert, 1981a. A Model of Regional Archaeological Structure. *Proceedings of the Prehistoric Society* 47:1-17.

Foley, Robert, 1981b. Off-site Archaeology: an Alternative Approach for the Short-sited. In *Patterns of the Past: Studies in the Honour of David Clarke*. Eds. Ian Hodder, G. Isaac and N. Hammond. Pp. 157-183. Cambridge University Press, Cambridge.

Fox, William A., 1977. *Southwestern Region Archaeological Survey*. Report on File, Ministry of Citizenship, Culture and Recreation, Toronto.

Fox, William A., 1986. *Annual Archaeological Report for Southwestern Ontario*. Report on File, Ministry of Citizenship, Culture and Recreation, Toronto.

Fox, William A., 1987a. *Annual Archaeological Report for the Ministry of Culture and Communications, Toronto: The 1987 Season*. Report on File, Ministry of Citizenship, Culture and Recreation, Toronto.

Fox, William A., 1987b. Dunk's Bay Archaeology. *Kewa* 89(9):2-8.

Fox, William A., 1988. *The Bruce Peninsula Archaeological Survey*. Report on File, Ministry of Citizenship, Culture and Recreation, Toronto.

Fox, William A., 1989. *The Hunter Site (BdHh-5) A Multi-Component Odawa Fishing Camp on Frenchman Point, Saugeen Reserve*. Report on File, Ministry of Citizenship, Culture and Recreation, Toronto.

Fox, William A., 1990a. The Middle Woodland to Late Woodland Transition. In *The Archaeology of Southern Ontario to A.D. 1650*, Eds. Chris J. Ellis and Neal Ferris Pp. 171-188. Occasional Publications No. 5, London Chapter, Ontario Archaeological Society, London, Ontario.

Fox, William A., 1990b. The Odawa. In *The Archaeology of Southern Ontario to A.D. 1650*. Eds. Chris J. Ellis and Neal Ferris. Pp. 457-474. Occasional Publications No. 5, London Chapter, Ontario Archaeological Society, London, Ontario.

Fried, Morton, 1968. *The Evolution of Political Society*. Random House, New York.

Gilman, P. A., 1987. Architecture as Artifact: Pit Structures and Pueblos in the American Southwest. *American Antiquity* 52:538-564.

Green, Stanton W., 1991. Foragers and Farmers on the Prehistoric Irish Frontier. In *Between Bands and States*. Ed. S.A. Gregg. Pp. 216-242. Center for Archaeological Investigations Occasional Papers No.9, Carbondale.

Gregg, Susan Alling, 1980. A Material Perspective of Tropical Rainforest Hunter-Gatherers: The Semang of Malaysia. In *The Archaeological Correlates of Hunter-Gatherer Societies: Studies from the Ethnographic Record*. Eds. F.E. Smiley, Carla M. Sinopoli, H. Edwin Jackson, W. H. Wills and S.A. Gregg. Pp. 117-135. Michigan Discussions in Anthropology, Volume 5, numbers 1 and 2, Department of Anthropology, University of Michigan, Ann Arbor.

Gregg, Susan Alling, 1988. *Foragers and Farmers: Population Interaction and Agricultural Expansion in Prehistoric Europe*. The University of Chicago Press, Chicago.

Gregg, Susan Alling, 1991. Indirect Food Production: Mutualism and the Archaeological Visibility of Cultivation. In *Between Bands and States*. Eds. S.A. Gregg Pp. 203-215. Centre for Archaeological Investigations Occasional Papers No.9, Carbondale.

Hammond, Frederik W., 1981. The Colonisation of Europe: The Analysis of Settlement Process. In *Pattern of the Past: Studies in Honour of David Clarke*. Eds. Ian Hodder, Glynn Isaac and Norman Hammond. Pp. 211-248. Cambridge University Press, Cambridge.

Hayden, B., 1977. Corporate Groups and the Late Ontario Iroquoian Longhouse. *Ontario Archaeology* 28:3-16.

Hayden, B., 1979. The Draper and White Sites: Preliminary and Theoretical Considerations. In *Settlement Patterns of the Draper and White Sites; 1973 Excavations*. Ed. B. Hayden. Pp. 1-28. Deparment of Archaeology, Simon Fraser University Publication No. 6, Burnaby.

Heidenreich, Conrad E., 1971. *H u r o n i a : A History and Geography of the Huron Indians 1600-1650*. McClelland and Stewart, Toronto.

Hitchcock, R. K., 1987. Sedentism and Site Structure: Organizational Change in Kalahari Basarwa Residential Locations. In *Method and Theory for Activity Area Research*. Ed. Susan Kent. Pp. 374-423. Columbia University Press, New York.

Hodder, Ian, 1990. *The Domestication of Europe: Structure and Contingency in Neolithic Societies*. Basil Blackwell, Oxford.

Hodges, R., 1987. Spatial Models, Anthropology and Archaeology. In *Landscape and C u l t u r e : Geographical and Archaeological Perspectives*. Ed. J. M. Wagstaff. Pp. 118-133. Basil Blackwell, Oxford.

Hoffman, D.W. and N.R. Richards, 1954. *Soil Survey of Bruce County*. Ontario Soil Survey Report No.16, Toronto.

Janusas, Scarlett, Emilie, 1984. *A Petrological Analysis of Kettle Point Chert and its Spatial and Temporal Distribution in Regional Prehistory*. National Museum of Man, Archaeological Survey of Canada, Mercury Series Paper No. 128, Ottawa.

Kapches, Mima, 1981. *The Middleport Pattern In Ontario Iroquoian Prehistory*. Unpublished Ph.D. Dissertation, Department of Anthropology, University of Toronto, Toronto.

Kelly, Robert L., 1992. Mobility/Sedentism: Concepts, Archaeological Measures and Effects. *Annual Review of Anthropology* 21:43-66.

Kensinger, Kenneth M., 1989. Hunting and Male Domination in Cashinahua Society. In *Farmers as Hunters: The Implications of Sedentism*. Ed. Susan Kent. Pp. 18-26. Cambridge University Press, Cambridge.

Kent, Susan, 1989a. New Directions for Old Studies. In *Farmers as Hunters: The Implications of Sedentism*. Ed. Susan Kent. Pp. 131-136. Cambridge University Press, Cambridge.

Kent, Susan, 1989b. Cross-Cultural Perceptions of Farmers as Hunters and the Value of Meat. In *Farmers as Hunters: The Implications of Sedentism*. Ed. Susan Kent. Pp. 1-17. Cambridge University Press, Cambridge.

Kent, Susan (editor), 1989c. *Farmers as Hunters. The Implications for Sedentism*. Cambridge University Press, Cambridge

Kenyon, I.T. and W. Fox., 1983. The Wyoming Rapids Saugeen Component: 1983 Investigation. *Kewa* 83(7):2-10.

Kenyon, Walter, 1958. An Ancient Settlement in Bruce County. *Ontario History* 50(1):45-47.

Kenyon, Walter, 1959. *The Inverhuron Site.* Royal Ontario Museum, Art and Archaeology Division, Occasional Paper No. 1.

Knechtel, Fritz, 1955. *Unpublished Field Notes.* On File, Bruce County Museum and Archives, Southhampton.

Kowalewski, Stephen A., 1989. Introduction. In *Monte Albán's Hinterland, Part III: Prehispanic Settlement Patterns in Tlacolula, Etla, and Ocotlan, The Valley of Oaxaca, Mexico.* Eds. Stephen Kowalewski, Gary M. Feinman, Laura Finsten, Richard E Blanton and Linda M. Nicholas. Pp. 1-30. Memoirs of the Museum of Anthropology No. 23, University of Michigan, Ann Arbour.

Kowalewski, Stephen A., 1990. Merits of Full Coverage Survey: Examples from the Valley of Oaxaca, Mexico. In *The Archaeology of Regions: A Case for Full Coverage Survey.* Eds. Suzanne K. Fish and Stephen A. Kowalewski. Pp. 33-85. Smithsonian Institution Press, Washington D.C.

Lamb, H.H., 1974. *The Changing Climate.* Methuen, London.

Lee, Richard and Irven DeVore, 1968. Problems in the Study of Hunters and Gatherers. In *Man the Hunter.* Eds. Richard B. Lee and Irven DeVore. Pp. 3-12. Aldine Publishing Company, Chicago.

Lee, Thomas E., 1951a. *A Preliminary Report on an Archaeological Survey of Southwestern Ontario for 1950.* National Museum of Canada, Bulletin 126, Ottawa.

Lee, Thomas E., 1951b. *1951 Field Notes.* Manuscript B5F7, on File, Canadian Museum of Civilization, Hull.

Lee, Thomas E., 1960. *Bruce County Materials Catalogue.* Manuscript 1637, on File, Canadian Museum of Civilization, Hull.

Lintz, Christopher, 1991. Texas Panhandle-Pueblo Interactions from the Thirteenth through the Sixteenth Century. In *Farmers, Hunters and Colonists: Interaction Between the Southwest and the Southern Plains.* Ed. Katherine A. Spielmann. Pp. 89-106. University of Arizona Press, Tucson.

MacDonald, E.M. and M.S. Cooper, 1992. The Birch Site (BcGw-29): A Late Iroquoian Special Purpose Site in Simcoe County, Ontario. *Kewa* 92(6):2-15.

MacNeish, R.S., 1952. Iroquois Pottery Types. National Museum of Canada, Bulletin 124, Ottawa.

Matson, R.G., 1991. *The Origins of Southwest Agriculture.* The University of Arizona Press, Tucson.

Molnar, James. 1989. *The Mason Site 1989: The Bruce County Board of Education Excavations,* Report on File, Ministry of Citizenship, Culture and Recreation, Toronto.

Molnar, James. 1991. Excavations at the Hunter's Point Site, Bruce Peninsula, Ontario. *Annual Archaeological Reports of Ontario* 2:104-107.

Molto, J. E., 1979. *Saugeen Osteology: The Evidence of the Second Cemetery at the Donaldson Site.* Museum of Indian Archaeology, Bulletin 14, London.

Murphy, Carl and Neal Ferris, 1990. The Late Woodland Western Basin Tradition of Southwestern Ontario. In *The Archaeology of Southern Ontario to A.D. 1650.* Eds. Chris J. Ellis and Neal Ferris. Pp. 189-278. Occasional Publications No. 5, London Chapter, Ontario Archaeological Society, London, Ontario.

Noble, W.C., 1969. Some Social Implications of the Iroquois "In Situ" Theory. *Ontario Archaeology* 13:16-28.

Noble, W.C., 1975. Corn, and the Development of Village Life in Southern Ontario. *Ontario Archaeology* 25:37-46.

Patterson, Clair C., 1971. Native Copper, Silver, and Gold Accessible to Early Metallurgists. *American Antiquity* 36(3):286-321.

Pearce, R.J., 1984. *Mapping Middleport: A Case Study in Societal Archaeology.* Unpublished Ph.D Dissertation, Department of Anthropology, McGill University, Montreal.

Peterson, Jean Treloggen, 1978. Hunter-Gatherer/Farmer Exchange. *American Anthropologist* 80:335-351.

Potter, Stephen R., 1993. *Commoners, Tribute and Chiefs: The Development of Algonquian Culture Potomac Valley.* University Press of Virginia, Charlottesville.

Prevec, Rosemary, 1987. A Dog From Dunk's Bay. *Kewa.* (9):9-10.

Price, T.D., 1983. The European Mesolithic. *American Antiquity* 48:761-778.

Price, T.D., 1987. The Mesolithic of Western Europe. *Journal of World Archaeology* 1:225-305.

Rafferty, Janet E., 1985. The Archaeological Record on Sedentariness: Recognition, Development and Implications. In *Advances in Archaeological Method and Theory, Volume 8.* Ed. Michael Schiffer. Pp. 113-156. Academic Press, New York.

Ramsden, Peter G., 1988. Palisade Extension, Village Expansion and Immigration in Trent Valley Huron Villages. *Canadian Journal of Archaeology* 12:177-183.

Ramsden, Peter G., n.d. *Call Them Huron: The Indians of Balsam Lake and the Roots of Canadian History.*, unpublished manuscript in possession of author.

Rankin, Lisa K., 1999. *The 1995 Southern Bruce County Survey.* Report on File, Ministry Of Citizenship, Culture, and Recreation, Toronto.

Roseberry, William, 1989. Introduction. In *Anthropologies and Histories: Essays in Culture, History and Political Economy.* Ed. William Roseberry. Pp. 1-14. Rutgers University Press, London.

Rossignol, Jacqueline, 1992. Concepts, Methods and Theory Building: A Landscape Approach. In *Space, Time and Archaeological Landscapes.* Eds. Jacqueline Rossignol and LuAnn Wandsnider. Pp. 3-16. Plenum Press, New York.

Rossignol, Jacqueline and LuAnn Wandsnider (editors), 1992. *Space, Time and Archaeological Landscapes,* Plenum Press, New York.

Sahlins, Marshall, 1972. *Stone Age Economics.* Aldine Publishing Company, Chicago.

Sahlins, Marshall D., and Elman R. Service (editors), 1960. *Evolution and Culture.* The University of Michigan Press, Ann Arbor.

Shutt, D.B., 1944. *1944 Field Notes and Correspondence,* On File, London Museum of Archaeology, London.

Shutt, D.B., 1951. *1951 Field Notes and Correspondence,* Lee Collection B2F14 Manuscripts on File, Canadian Museum of Civilization, Hull.

Shutt, D.B., 1952. *1952 Field Notes and Correspondence,* Lee Collection B2F14 Manuscripts on File, Canadian Museum of Civilization, Hull.

Smiley, F.E., 1980. The Bihor: Material Correlates of Hunter-Gatherer/Farmer Exchange. In *The Archaeological Correlates of Hunter-Gatherer Societies: Studies from the Ethnographic Record.* Eds. F.E. Smiley, Carla M. Sinopoli, H. Edwin Jackson, W.H. Wills and S.A. Gregg. Pp.149-176. Michigan

Discussions in Anthropology, Volume 5, numbers 1 and 2, Department of Anthropology, University of Michigan, Ann Arbor.

Smith, Beverly A., 1985. The Use of Animals At the 17th Century Mission of St. Ignace. *Michigan Archaeologist*. 31(4):97-122.

Smith, David G., 1990. Iroquoian Societies in Southern Ontario: Introduction and Historical Overview. In *The Archaeology of Southern Ontario to A.D. 1650*. Eds. Chris J. Ellis and Neal Ferris. Pp. 279-290. Occasional Publications No. 5, London Chapter, Ontario Archaeological Society, London, Ontario.

Smith, David G. And Gary W. Crawford, 1997. Recent Developments in the Archaeology of the Princess Point Complex in Southern Ontario. *Canadian Journal of Archaeology* 21(1):9-32.

Smith, S.A., 1979. *The Methodist Point Site*. Ontario Ministry of Culture and Recreation, Historical Planning and Research Branch, Research Report No.11, Toronto.

Sokal, Robert R. and F. James Rohlf, 1969. *Biometry: The Principles and Practice of Statistics in Biological Research*. W.H. Freemand and Company, San Francisco.

Spence, Michael W., Robert H. Pihl and J.E. Molto, 1984. Hunter-Gatherer Social Group Identification: A Case Study from Middle Woodland Southern Ontario. In *Exploring the Limits: Frontiers and Boundaries in Prehistory*. Eds. S. DeAtley and F. Findlow. Pp. 117-142. British Archaeological Reports, International Series No. 223.

Spence, Michael W., Robert H. Pihl and Carl R. Murphy, 1990. Cultural Complexes of the Early and Middle Woodland Periods. In *The Archaeology of Southern Ontario to A.D. 1650*. Eds. Chris J. Ellis and Neal Ferris. Pp. 125-169. Occasional Publications No. 5, London Chapter, Ontario Archaeological Society, London, Ontario.

Speth, John D., 1991. Nutrition, Reproduction and Forager-Farmer Interaction: A Comment on the "Revisionist" Debate in Hunter-Gatherer Studies. In *Foragers in Context: Long-term, Regional, and Historical Perspectives in Hunter-Gatherer Studies*. Eds. Preston T. Miracle, Lynn E. Fisher and Jody Brown. Pp.41-46. Michigan Discussions in Anthropology, Volume 10, Ann Arbor.

Spielmann, Katherine A., 1986. Interdependence Among Egalitarian Societies. *Journal of Anthropological Archaeology* 5:279-312.

Spielmann, Katherine A., 1991a. Interaction Among Nonhierarchical Societies. In *Farmers, Hunters and Colonists: Interaction Between the Southwest and Southern Plains*. Ed. Katherine A. Spielmann Pp. 1-17. University of Arizona Press, Tucson.

Spielmann, Katherine A., 1991b. Coercion or Cooperation? Plains-Pueblo Interaction in the Protohistoric Period. In *Farmers, Hunters and Colonists: Interaction Between the Southwest and Southern Plains*. Ed. Katherine A. Spielmann. Pp. 36-50. University of Arizona Press, Tucson.

Sponsel, Leslie E., 1989. Farming and Foraging: A Necessary Complementarity in Amazonia? In *Farmers as Hunters: The Implications of Sedentism*. Ed. Susan Kent. Pp. 37-45. Cambridge University Press, Cambridge.

Stark, Barbara, 1981. The Rise of Sedentary Life. in *Supplement to the Handbook of Middle American Indians, Volume 1, Archaeology*. Eds, Victoria R. Bricker and Jeremy A. Sabloff. Pp. 345-372. University of Texas Press, Austin.

Steward, Julian H., 1955. *The Theory of Culture Change*. University of Illinois Press, Urbana.

Stewart, Francis, 1974. *Faunal Remains from the Nodwell Site (BcHi-3) and from Four Other Sites in Bruce County, Ontario*.

Archaeological Survey of Canada Paper No.16, National Museum of Man Mercury Series, National Museums of Canada, Ottawa.

Stothers, David, 1978. The Western Basin Tradition: Algonquin or Iroquois? *Michigan Archaeologist* 24(1):11-36.

Sutton, Richard E., 1996. *The Middle Iroquoian Colonization of Huronia.* Unpublished Ph.D. Dissertation, Department of Anthropology, McMaster University, Hamilton.

Thomas, Julian, 1988. Neolithic Explanations Revisited: The Mesolithic-Neolithic Transition in Britain and South Scandinavia. *Proceedings of the Prehistoric Society* 54:59-66.

Thomas, Stephen and Roman Zurba, 1973. *The Initial MacGregor Point Archaeological Survey Report.* Report on File, Ministry of Citizenship, Culture and Recreation, Toronto.

Timmins, P.A., 1985. *The Analysis and Interpretation of Radiocarbon Dates in Iroquoian Archaeology.* Museum of Indian Archaeology, Research Report No. 19, London.

Timmins, P.A., 1997. *The Calvert Site: An Interpretive Framework for the Early Iroquoian Village.* Canadian Museum of Civilization, Archaeological Survey of Canada, Mercury Series Paper No. 156, Hull.

Tooker, Elisabeth, 1967. *An Ethnography of the Huron Indians, 1615-1649.* Bureau of American Ethnology, Bulletin 190, Washington D.C.

Trigger, Bruce, 1967. Settlement Archaeology - Its Goal and Promise. *American Antiquity* 32(2):149-159.

Trigger, Bruce, 1968. The Determinants of Settlement Patterns. In *Settlement Archaeology.* Ed. K.C. Chang. Pp. 53-78. National Press Books, Palo Alto.

Trigger, Bruce, 1976. *The Children of Aataentic: A History of the Huron People to 1660.* 2 volumes. McGill-Queen's University Press, Montreal.

Trigger, Bruce, 1981. Prehistoric Social and Political Organization: An Iroquoian Case Study. In *Foundations of Northeast Archaeology.* Ed. D.R. Snow. Pp. 1-50. Academic Press, New York.

Trigger, Bruce, L. Yaffe, M. Diksic, J.L. Galinier, H. Marshall, and J.F. Pendergast, 1980. Trace Element Analysis of Iroquoian Pottery. *Canadian Journal of Archaeology* 4:119-145.

Tringham, Ruth, 1971. *Hunters, Fishers and Farmers of Eastern Europe 6000-3000 B.C..* Huchinson and Co., London.

Turff, Gina M., 1997. *A Synthesis of Middle Woodland Panpipes in Eastern North America.* Unpublished MA thesis, Department of Anthropology, Trent University, Peterborough, Ontario.

Varley, Colin and Aubrey Cannon, 1995. Historical Inconsistencies: Huron Longhouse Length, Hearth Number and Time. *Ontario Archaeology* 58:85-96.

Vencl, Slavomil, 1986. The Role of Hunting-Gathering Populations in the Transition to Farming: A Central European Perspective. In *Hunters in Transition: Mesolithic Societies of Temperate Eurasia and Their Transition to Farming.* Ed. Marek Zvelebil. Pp. 43-51. Cambridge University Press, Cambridge.

Vickers, William T., 1989. Patterns of Foraging and Gardening in a Semi-sedentary Amazonian Community. In *Farmers as Hunters: The Implications of Sedentism.* Ed. Susan Kent. Pp. 46-59. Cambridge University Press, Cambridge.

Warrick, Gary A., 1984. *Reconstructing Ontario Iroquois Village Organization.* National Museum Of Man, Archaeological Survey of Canada, Mercury Series Paper No. 124:1-180, Ottawa.

Warrick, Gary A., 1988. Estimating Ontario Iroquoian Village Duration. *Man in the Northeast* 36:21-55.

Warrick, Gary A., 1990. *A Population History of the Huron-Petun, A.D. 900-1650.* Unpublished Ph.D. Dissertation, Department of Anthropology, McGill University, Montreal.

White, Leslie, 1959. *The Evolution of Culture.* McGraw Hill, New York.

Williamson, Ronald F., 1983. *The Robin Hood Site: A Study of Functional Variability in Iroquoian Settlement Patterns.* Monographs in Ontario Archaeology 1, Ontario Archaeological Society, Toronto.

Williamson, Ronald F., 1990. The Early Iroquoian Period of Southern Ontario. In *The Archaeology of Southern Ontario to A.D. 1650.* Eds. Chris J. Ellis and Neal Ferris. Pp. 291-320. Occasional Publications No. 5, London Chapter, Ontario Archaeological Society, London, Ontario.

Wolf, Eric R., 1982. *Europe and the People Without History.* University of California Press, Berkeley.

Wright, J., n.d. *Numbers: A Message From the Past.* Unpublished manuscript in possession of author.

Wright, J.V., 1953a. *1953 Field Notes.* Manuscript 2398 on File at the Canadian Museum of Civilization, Hull.

Wright, J.V., 1953b. *The Boiled Baby Ossuary in Bruce County, Ontario.* Report on File, Bruce County Museum and Archives, Southampton.

Wright, J.V., 1956. Comments on the Bruce. *Ontario History* 48(4):193-194.

Wright, J.V., 1960. The Middleport Horizon. *Anthropologica* 11:1-8.

Wright, J.V., 1966. *The Ontario Iroquois Tradition.* National Museum of Canada, Bulletin No.210, Ottawa.

Wright, J.V., 1967. *The Pic River Site.* National Museums of Canada, Bulletin No.206: 54-99, Ottawa.

Wright, J.V., 1969. *The Michipicoten Site.* National Museums of Canada, National Museums of Canada, Bulletin No. 224: 1-87, Ottawa.

Wright, J.V., 1972a. *Ontario Prehistory: An Eleven Thousand Year Archaeological Outline.* National Museums of Canada, Ottawa.

Wright, J.V., 1972b. Settlement Pattern at the Steward Site. *Arch Notes* 72(10):6-8.

Wright, J.V., 1974. *The Nodwell Site.* Archaeological Survey of Canada paper No.22, National Museum of Man Mercury Series, National Museums of Canada, Ottawa.

Wright, J.V., 1981. The Glen Site: An Historic Cheveux Releves Campsite on Flowerpot Island, Georgian Bay, Ontario. *Ontario Archaeology* 35:45-59.

Wright, J.V., 1985. The Comparative Radiocarbon Dating of Two Prehistoric Ontario Iroquoian Villages. *Canadian Journal of Archaeology* 9(1):57-68.

Wright, J.V. and J.E. Anderson, 1963. *The Donaldson Site.* National Museum of Canada, Bulletin No. 184, Ottawa.

Wright, M., 1986. *The Uren Site AfHd-3: An Analysis and Reappraisal of the Uren Substage Type Site.* Monographs in Ontario Archaeology 2, Toronto.

Zvelebil, Marek and Peter Rowley-Conwy, 1986. Foragers and Farmers in Atlantic Europe. *In Hunters in Transition: Mesolithic Societies of Temperate Eurasia and Their Transition to Farming.* Ed. Marek Zvelebil. Pp. 67-93. Cambridge University Press, Cambridge.

Zvelebil, Marek, S.Green and M.Macklin, 1992. Archaeological Landscapes, Lithic Scatters and Human Behaviour. In *Time,*

Eds. Jacqueline Rossignol and Luann
Wandsnider. Pp. 193-226. Plenum
Press, New York.

.

www.ingramcontent.com/pod-product-compliance
Lightning Source LLC
Chambersburg PA
CBHW061300270326
41932CB00029B/3418